ETHICS IN PLAIN ENGLISH

ETHICS IN PLAIN ENGLISH

AN ILLUSTRATIVE CASEBOOK FOR PSYCHOLOGISTS

THOMAS F. NAGY

American Psychological Association
Washington, DC

First Printing . . November 2000
Second Printing . . . March 2001

Published by
American Psychological Association
750 First Street, NE
Washington, DC 20002

Copies may be ordered from
APA Order Department
P.O. Box 92984
Washington, DC 20090-2984

In the U.K., Europe, Africa, and the Middle East, copies may be ordered from
American Psychological Association
3 Henrietta Street
Covent Garden, London
WC2E 8LU England

Typeset in Century Schoolbook by EPS Group Inc., Easton, MD

Printer: Sheridan Books, Ann Arbor, MI
Cover designer: Design Concepts, San Diego, CA
Technical/Production Editor: Amy J. Clarke

Library of Congress Cataloging-in-Publication Data
Nagy, Thomas F.
    Ethics in plain English : an illustrative casebook for psychologists / by
    Thomas F. Nagy.—1st ed.
        p.   cm.
    Includes bibliographical references and index.
    ISBN 1-55798-604-5 (pbk. : acid-free paper)
    1. Psychologists—Professional ethics.   2. Psychology—Moral and ethical
    aspects.   I. Title.
    BF76.4.N34   1999
    174′.915—dc21   99-30351
                                                             CIP

British Library Cataloguing-in-Publication Data
A CIP record is available from the British Library.

Printed in the United States of America

To my everlasting sources of inspiration,
my wife Kären and my children Monika and Michael

Contents

Acknowledgments

I would like to thank David Mills and Hugh Baras, who read early stages of the manuscript from cover to cover and offered much constructive criticism about form, content, plausibility, and so forth. Without their diligence, hard work, ruthless criticism, and enduring friendship, this project would still have gone through many iterations, but it would not have evolved to its current state.

I am also indebted to Bill Carroll for his legal and psychological consultation and friendly collaboration for nearly 20 years. Bill can best be described as indefatigable and saintly (there are other adjectives that might apply, but my space is limited). I am also indebted to my other lawyer friends and multidisciplinary colleagues, Lois Weithorn, Alan Scheflin, and George Alexander, for their obsessive attention to details concerning legal matters and the psychology–law interface.

Because it was necessary to familiarize myself with animal research for some of the ethical standards, I am grateful to the staff at Stanford University's Animal Research Facility for allowing me to visit the laboratory. I am also indebted to the Stanford University School of Medicine's Pain Management Clinic and in particular to its director, Raymond Gaeta. I am deeply grateful to Bruce Overmeier and Nancy Ator, whose encouragement and amazing willingness to freely give of their time, energy, and wisdom was immensely helpful in reviewing the vignettes about research with animals. I also wish to thank Steven Maier for his role in adding to my knowledge on the topic.

I would also like to acknowledge José Maldonado, a psychiatric colleague and friend, for his creative energy and consistent willingness to discuss research and clinical concepts from different perspectives and review vignettes.

Many other friends and colleagues were willing to read one or more vignettes and provide detailed feedback about a particular specialty area of theirs; they range from friends and mentors I have known for over 25 years to current colleagues and associates of fairly recent acquaintance. I am grateful for their willingness to participate in this project by putting energy into it and helping shape the final product: James Schuerger, Mary Anne Norfleet, Marguerite McCorkle, Robert Boyd, Thomas Plante, Alex Caldwell, Stephanie Brown, Leonard Goodstein, Karen Schlanger, Barbara Brandt, Allan Berkowitz, Anne Berenberg, Paul Nagy, Ethan Pollack, and Knut Dorn.

I am very grateful to my loving wife, Kären, for her unloving editorial review of the entire text at a time when her work weeks grew to an unconscionably large size. I am also indebted to Ruth Seagraves for not only assiduously typing various versions of the manuscript but for her goodwill and editorial contributions and for continuously facilitating the transfer of late-breaking ideas to the printed page.

Finally, I would like to thank all those who have served to stimulate my thinking about psychological ethics in recent years—the many psychologists, psychiatrists, physicians, social workers, clergy, clients, patients, students, teachers, administrators, researchers, attorneys, plaintiffs, defendants, complainants, complainees, consumers of psychological services, and others who have consulted me and effectively contributed to enriching my knowledge in this interesting and complex area of human interaction.

ETHICS IN PLAIN ENGLISH

"Frivolity at the Edge," by E. Gorey, originally published in *The New Yorker,* March 22, 1993. Reprinted by permission of Donadio & Olson, Inc. Copyright 1993, Edward Gorey.

Introduction

This book represents a rendition, in plain English, of the 102 standards of the American Psychological Association's (APA) Ethics Committee's Ethical Principles of Psychologists and Code of Conduct (hereinafter called the Ethics Code; APA, 1992), with illustrative fictional case vignettes.[1] My intent is to provide a companion piece to the Ethics Code, and this book is meant to be read in conjunction with the original text from which it is derived.

The Ethical Standards, rendered into the vernacular, are not meant to stand alone or to substitute for the Ethics Code. Nor are they intended to characterize the mandatory ethical behavior in a comprehensive or official fashion, although every effort has been made to retain the spirit and requirements represented by the official Ethics Code. Thus, the vernacular version of an ethical standard should never be relied on exclusively in considering matters of professional or ethical conduct of psychologists. Rather the reader is always advised to study the original text for each ethical standard under consideration because its precise language defines that standard with little or no legal ambiguity. For this reason, the original wording of each standard from the Ethics Code is presented in a different typeface, directly before my rendition. This allows the reader to benefit from the rendition and to compare for him- or herself its derivation from the original.

My intention in writing this book was to create a vehicle for conveying the essence of each ethical standard by means of a case vignette illustrating the kind of practical situation represented in the Ethics Code in somewhat dry, conceptual prose. By studying fictional examples of both sound and questionable judgment on the part of psychologists encountering various dilemmas in their everyday work, one can gain an appreciation of the

---

[1]It is important to state clearly and for the record that the opinions about and applications of the ethical principles of APA contained in this book are simply those of the author and do not constitute official policy of any group, board, or body, including APA. The applications cited here are meant to stimulate awareness of ethical issues, not to make policy, define ethical behavior, or define enforceable standards of practice. Neither the vernacular versions of the APA standards nor the vignettes have been reviewed by any APA governance group or the APA Ethics Office or the Ethics Committee. Any citations of this book in the forensic context should always make these caveats known. Psychologists and psychologists in training desiring to obtain official opinions of the APA Ethics Committee should consult statements issued by that body.

ethical standard under consideration as well as how it could be applied. It is my hope that the vicarious experiences gained from reading case vignettes may help the reader to better understand how ethical problems can naturally or suddenly emerge with competent and well-meaning professionals, even under the most ordinary of circumstances.

In reading the vignettes, it is useful to bear in mind that the Ethics Code consists of two parts: General Principles and Ethical Standards. This book focuses exclusively on the Ethical Standards, those 102 standards grouped under the following eight categories (the numbers of standards in each category are in parentheses): general standards (27); evaluation, assessment, or intervention (10); advertising and other public statements (6); therapy (9); privacy and confidentiality (11); teaching, training, supervision, research, and publishing (26); forensic activities (6); and resolving ethical issues (7). These standards essentially require psychologists to do something or to refrain from doing something when carrying out their work. They are enforceable, and the procedures for their enforcement are outlined in the "Rules and Procedures" (APA, 1996a) of the APA Ethics Committee, reprinted in the appendix of this book.

The General Principles, although not the subject of this book, also constitute an important part of the APA Ethics Code. The principles include competence, integrity, professional and scientific responsibility, respect for people's rights and dignity, concern for others' welfare, and social responsibility. These are generically broad philosophical constructs, which do not set specific standards for professional conduct (i.e., behavior to be engaged in or avoided). Rather they are aspirational in nature. Psychologists are encouraged to strive always to exemplify these principles in the course of their professional activities.

Developing Language for an Official Code

An important decision in creating a document such as an ethics code involves the level of linguistic detail or generality that will ultimately convey the philosophical concepts and standards of behavior prescribed. As a participant in the drafting of text for the Ethics Code, I along with the other members of the APA Revision Comments Subcommittee struggled with this very issue: How specific or generic should the language be in setting forth principles and standards of conduct?[2] If the language were too narrow in scope, it would not effectively address the specialty areas of many psychologists, unless of course the number of standards were to be greatly increased. This could result in a long and unwieldy document. However, if the language were broad and generic in scope, the document could be shorter, but many specific and important topics would likely not be included (e.g., specific research and clinical risks, evolving forensic issues,

---

[2]The Revision Comments Subcommittee for the 1992 Ethics Code consisted of Mathilda Canter (Chairperson); Bruce Bennett and Thomas Nagy, who were assisted by APA Ethics Office staff; Stanley Jones and Betsy Ranslow; and legal counsel, Clifford Stromberg.

sexual harassment). The resulting document might also have less practical application for both psychologists and the public because many of the important topics in the science and practice of psychology would be excluded.

A way of resolving the dilemma of establishing a level of language that would be neither too general nor overly specific is to create semantic ways of offering precision to ethical rules that would simultaneously facilitate their application in a broad array of circumstances. The use of such words as *reasonable, feasible*, and *appropriate* are examples of semantic descriptors that do, to some extent, accomplish this end. These words may seem vague, legalistic, or affected, at times. However, their presence in the Ethics Code does serve an important purpose, namely, to accurately broaden its applicability and interpretation.

A Vernacular Rendering of the Ethics Code

By contrast, the very nature of vernacular language involves speaking plainly, in local or regional dialect, and avoiding using words that are literary, scientific, technical, or legalistic. It is clear that a double-edged sword hangs precariously over any attempt to render 102 complex standards of conduct for researchers, teachers, practitioners, and other psychologists into a relatively easily understood series of maxims or rules, without significantly changing their meaning.[3]

My attempt to meet this goal consisted mainly of making strategic cuts in language while being careful never to disembowel, to remove excess verbiage while not transecting a conceptual nerve. At times, my rendition is longer than the original. Additional words were sometimes necessary to make the meaning clear. In creating a plain-English rendition of the ethical standards, I eliminated qualifying words (e.g., *reasonable, appropriate*) from the text and substituted simpler language. As a result, it is possible that there have been some compromises to or losses in meaning.

I have attempted to minimize the potential losses in meaning, such as overly narrowing or otherwise altering the applicability of the ethical standards, while attempting to maintain the heart of the ethical standard under discussion. Although somewhat less precise than the original standards, it is my hope that the vernacular version might be more memorable to and more easily taught or learned by my audience: psychology teachers and students, novice and experienced psychologists, and consumers of a broad array of psychological services.

---

[3]For readers interested in a different kind of interpretive commentary on the Ethics Code, see *Ethics for Psychologists: A Commentary on the APA Ethics Code* (Canter, Bennett, Jones, & Nagy, 1994). This book emerged, in part, from the revision process of the *Ethical Principles of Psychologists* (APA, 1981) as carried out by the Revision Comments Subcommittee. Four of the members of that subcommittee collaborated to produce the book, which includes commentary on each standard and a historical and legal context for the document.

Case Vignettes

The case vignettes that illustrate the standards are drawn, in part, from many years of serving on ethics committees (e.g., APA, various state psychological associations, other professional associations) and consulting with those involved in legal and ethical cases. They are also rooted in my work as a participant in revising APA's (1981) Ethical Principles of Psychologists. This was a 6-year undertaking that involved evaluating thousands of proposals submitted by hundreds of psychologists and by APA divisions, task forces, committees, and other entities. It was my privilege to learn firsthand of problematical areas that were of major concern to psychologists in many specialty areas, and these certainly influenced my decision to include a diversity of vignettes to illustrate the 1992 Ethics Code.

Each vignette depicts an important aspect of the ethical standard under consideration and does so in a plausible setting. Ideally, a casebook might contain several or many vignettes for each standard, representing the various specialties and contexts in which psychologists work, such as teaching, research, forensic or clinical practice, and industrial and organizational consulting. However, this would have resulted in a considerably longer book than would be practical. I attempted to approach this ideal by including, whenever possible, these different areas of psychology based, in part, on the experience of other specialists in these areas with whom I consulted. However, some vignettes may be more reflective of my personal experience as a teacher, psychotherapist, supervisor, and consultant. I offer my apologies to those in specialties or work settings who may not find their work experience equally represented in these pages.

Note that the vignettes in this book are fictitious, and any scenarios or names that may seem to reflect real-life situations or people are purely coincidental and unintended by the author. Any case material that served as inspiration for the development of the fictional vignettes represents composites that are disguised as intended by the Ethics Code in Standard 5.08.

Some of the vignettes manifest exemplary behavior by psychologists, and some illustrate a woeful lack of knowledge about ethics or, even worse, a calculated indifference. Although some vignettes may seem to be exaggerations or even caricatures of professional conduct, they are not as far fetched as might first appear, in my experience. Among individuals who may, at times, behave in an unethical fashion (any one of us), some are capable of extreme deviations from the norm with comparatively little effort. In addition, what may first appear to be extremely anomalous, or even comical at times, is probably well within the range of unprofessional conduct encountered by those bringing ethical complaints and engaged in by those who stand accused. If in perusing the activities of the protagonists in the case vignettes the reader can learn and grow as much as the author did in creating them, then certainly the goals for this book will have been achieved.

1

General Standards

These General Standards are potentially applicable to the professional and scientific activities of all psychologists.

1.01 Applicability of the Ethics Code

The activity of a psychologist subject to the Ethics Code may be reviewed under these Ethical Standards only if the activity is part of his or her work-related functions or the activity is psychological in nature. Personal activities having no connection to or effect on psychological roles are not subject to the Ethics Code.

Obey these rules while acting as a psychologist or in doing any work that is psychological in nature. This includes working in the office, teaching, supervising, doing research or therapy, consulting, writing, talking on the telephone, using the Internet, giving talks to the public, appearing on radio or TV, or performing any professional or volunteer work in this field. Remember, this code is used by your peers, ethics committees, state psychology boards, lawyers, and judges in evaluating your professional conduct. When in doubt, ask someone who knows; do not guess.

Vignette: Dr. Will Helpawl, a psychologist, coached his daughter's soccer team regularly on Saturday mornings. Marsha, a 16-year-old on the team, was extremely dedicated to sports and was an excellent halfback, but she was also anorectic and was becoming dangerously underweight. Dr. Helpawl began to counsel Marsha informally because he felt he was competent to diagnose and treat her eating disorder.

The counseling sessions became a routine part of the week's practice, following every workout, twice a week. This continued for the entire soccer season, with no formal recommendation to her or her parents that she seek psychotherapy or consult a physician for malnutrition. Dr. Helpawl never sought parental consent for offering psychological counseling to their daughter, a minor, because he judged that it was unnecessary due to the informality of their meetings. Because he never charged a fee for these soccer practice counseling sessions, he did not think of them as a psychological service; rather he viewed them as friendly talks to help provide guidance for a troubled adolescent. These regular talks did reflect his theoretical approach to psychotherapy: He had made a diagnosis, decided on a course of treatment, and implemented it, but he neglected to give any consideration to other important elements of psychological services, such as informed consent, confidentiality, and involvement of the parents.

As the weeks went by, Marsha continued losing weight and began to miss practices. Eventually, she dropped off the team, becoming quite ill and needing hospitalization. At this point, Marsha's parents found a competent therapist to treat their daughter and provide needed therapy for the family.

Shortly after therapy began, Marsha began to speak openly of her counseling sessions with Dr. Helpawl. Her parents were shocked to discover that their daughter's soccer coach attempted to offer psychotherapy to her without their consent and in such a casual manner. They confronted Dr. Helpawl with his utter disregard for many ethical standards in his professional counseling with Marsha. They claimed that as a licensed psychologist, he should have known better than to attempt to provide treatment for a serious disorder like anorexia in such an unprofessional and public setting as a soccer field. They further argued that because he had informed Marsha that he was a psychologist and that he would like to offer her counseling, his professional conduct came within the purview of the Ethics Code, even though the setting was informal.

In retrospect, it was clear that Dr. Helpawl's unconventional counseling for this serious eating disorder was not helpful to Marsha in the long run and, in fact, may have delayed her obtaining professional help that might have benefited her sooner. The parents filed an ethics complaint against Dr. Helpawl for his failure to adhere to the Ethical Standards while carrying out work that was clearly psychological in nature.

1.02 Relationship of Ethics and Law

> *If psychologists' ethical responsibilities conflict with law, psychologists make known their commitment to the Ethics Code and take steps to resolve the conflict in a responsible manner.*

If ethics and law conflict, be sure to let others know that you have an obligation to follow this Code of Ethics, and then do the best you can to resolve this difficult situation. Sometimes it may mean coming up with a creative solution, and sometimes, unfortunately, it may mean compromising your ethics to comply with the law.

Vignette: Captain Nathan Black, an Army psychologist, had been providing psychotherapy to an enlisted man for general anxiety disorder and depression for over 2 months. One day, Captain Black was approached by Sergeant Snoopy, his patient's commanding officer, who inquired about the progress of therapy. The psychologist had to address this request because confidentiality rules in a federal installation preempt state laws and permit such a disclosure. However, Captain Black knew he had an ethical duty to make an attempt to protect his patient's confidentiality by informing Sergeant Snoopy of his ethical obligation and the risks of breaching confidentiality in a therapy relationship, even though the law permitted it.

Captain Black carefully explained to the officer that psychotherapy was generally most effective when there was a trusting relationship with the therapist, allowing the client to disclose anything of importance that he might wish to discuss. Captain Black further informed the sergeant that this trust would be undermined if he were to reveal the topics and specific details that were discussed in therapy. Unless the client had some confidence that his discussions with the therapist would remain private, it was likely that he would begin to selectively withhold important information that he would not want his commanding officer to know but might be a contributing factor to his ongoing anxiety and depression. If this were to happen, then it was possible that either the client would eventually drop out of treatment with no substantial benefit or that treatment would become interminable because important issues were not being thoroughly addressed.

Sergeant Snoopy understood the psychologist's resistance to disclosing the details of treatment; however, he persisted in at least discovering if there was progress in therapy. There was some critical training scheduled to take place in 3 months, and the sergeant was curious if the client would be prepared to undertake it.

Captain Black thought that he could address the question of progress in treatment without compromising the trust he had established with his client. But first he thought it was essential to discuss the matter with his client. One whole session was devoted to addressing the sergeant's request for information and how it should be handled. Captain Black and his client discussed what could comfortably be revealed that would satisfy the sergeant's curiosity about progress but would not disclose private information that should remain in the consulting room. They reached a strategy on how to provide a general overview of the therapy progress and an educated guess about the enlisted man's probable readiness to participate in the scheduled special training.

The client appreciated being included in the discussion of such a complicated ethical and clinical issue and was able to be an active participant in its resolution. The sergeant gained an understanding of the dynamics of the therapy relationship and how confidentiality played such a central role in the efficiency of treatment. Captain Black learned from his discussions with both the sergeant and his client about how to process a legitimate request for information that was confidential, placing him in immediate conflict with his professional code of ethics. Thus, all three men understood the issues: (a) the client's concern for his own privacy, (b) limited confidentiality in the military setting, (c) the sergeant's need for information to plan the special training, (d) the psychologist's need to honor his professional ethical standards concerning confidentiality, and (e) the clinical issues that contribute to therapist–patient trust and efficiency in treatment. Each felt that the request for information had been handled in a professional and thorough manner, with due regard for the needs and obligations of all concerned.

1.03 Professional and Scientific Relationship

Psychologists provide diagnostic, therapeutic, teaching, research, super-visory, consultative, or other psychological services only in the context of a defined professional or scientific relationship or role. (See also Standards 2.01, Evaluation, Diagnosis, and Interventions in Professional Context, and 7.02, Forensic Assessments.)

Do your work at work in a defined scientific or professional role. When you're off duty, be off duty. Consider legal, ethical, and professional standards when choosing your work setting.[1]

Vignette: Dr. Babble, a psychology professor at a small rural university, had the habit of indiscriminately offering counseling and psychotherapy to his students and acquaintances in a variety of unprofessional settings. Whenever he was approached by someone experiencing a personal problem, he generally would attempt to offer counseling or some other psychological intervention with little concern for the propriety of the setting. At times, this was entirely appropriate because such a discussion frequently was entirely warranted and appreciated by the other person. Indeed, students frequently sought his opinion about internship sites or even personal matters relevant to their academic work or career path. However at other times, he would have been wiser to refer individuals to someone else for therapy or agree to meet with them in his office rather than to try to accomplish counseling "on the run."

Dr. Babble had little regard for privacy or confidentiality, and he could occasionally be heard discussing intimate details of an individual's life in a public place, such as an elevator. Also as a common practice, he attempted to carry out marriage counseling and even administer a psychological test to individuals and couples who were making social visits to his house, while others were present, observing the process. He sometimes engaged in these activities in other social or recreational settings, such as professional conventions, group bicycle trips, concerts of the local symphony orchestra (during intermission), in the weight-lifting room of the YMCA, and even in the bleachers at his university's sporting events.

He had little understanding of the rationale for restricting his work to a professional setting, maintaining professional boundaries, or employing accepted scientific methods when offering psychological services. He was steadfast in his belief that psychology should be "given away" to people as they appear to need it and not be reserved for the stuffy offices of clinicians and researchers.

---

[1]See also Standard 2.01, Evaluation, Diagnosis, and Interventions in Professional Context.

Unfortunately, Dr. Babble succeeded in harming some of the very individuals he thought he was helping: men and women who had enjoyed his company, trusted him, and followed his often bad advice about such critical issues as chemical dependency, marriage and divorce, chronic pain, and other major life issues. Several individuals eventually brought ethics complaints against him for his unprofessional conduct in undertaking assessment and treatment in an incompetent manner with little concern for professional objectivity. The Ethics Committee raised questions about his casual manner of carrying out therapy in the absence of an established professional relationship as well as his apparent disregard for the scientific method in clinical interventions and the welfare of others that is predicated on it.

1.04 Boundaries of Competence

(a) Psychologists provide services, teach, and conduct research only within the boundaries of their competence, based on their education, training, supervised experience, or appropriate professional experience.

(a) Only do what you are competent to do. Always stay within your depth when providing services, teaching, or carrying out research, even though you may be tempted to go farther at times. Make sure that your professional work reflects your formal education or training in graduate school or continuing education, supervision by someone skilled in this area, or other appropriate professional experience.

Vignette: Dr. Overschoot agreed to do hypnosis with a young woman who requested it for alleviating her long-standing anxiety symptoms. His only exposure to hypnosis had been a half-day workshop, which he took several months previously with no follow-up practice or supervision. Shortly after beginning the hypnotic induction, the woman experienced a panicky flashback with much gasping, weeping, and obvious distress. Dr. Overschoot was ill prepared for such a reaction, and his efforts at calming her with the few hypnotic techniques that he remembered were utterly useless. She eventually opened her eyes, ended her trance, and attempted to orient herself and make sense of what had just occurred. Dr. Overschoot had such little training in hypnosis or dissociation that he was unable to provide significant help in his patient's attempts to comprehend what appeared to be a traumatic flashback because he did not understand it himself. As a result of this experience, Dr. Overschoot resolved to avoid using hypnosis until he acquired substantially more training and supervision.

The experience of working outside his area of competence by using hypnosis, unfortunately, did not deter Dr. Overschoot from overextending himself once again in a different subspecialty area. He agreed to accept a married couple with a long history of alcohol abuse and violence for divorce mediation, in spite of the fact that he had had no specific training in either divorce mediation or working with couples who were violent. The husband appeared mildly intoxicated as the couple's first counseling session began, and he became increasingly belligerent within the first 20 minutes. In response to his wife's taunting and Dr. Overschoot's clumsy confrontations, the husband became physically violent. He assaulted both his wife and Dr. Overschoot, smashing a lamp and an antique table in the process. Dr. Overschoot's untrained style only served to provoke the husband's aggression, and it quickly became obvious that he had few skills to deal with such a crisis.

Finally, as a result of these two events, Dr. Overshoot began to appreciate the potential dangers of practicing outside his areas of competence. By being willing to accept in treatment anyone seeking his services, regardless of the presenting complaint and his level of competence, he not only risked harming consumers but also increased his vulnerability to an ethics complaint or a civil lawsuit by a dissatisfied client. For the first time, he began to admit that he was not competent to provide therapy to anyone who might request it, even though the person's motivation to seek treatment from him might be quite high. He learned a painful lesson from his unskilled attempts at hypnosis and divorce mediation. He now could see the importance of selecting patients with concerns clearly within his areas of competence and the necessity of obtaining more training and consultation before moving into new areas.

> *(b) Psychologists provide services, teach, or conduct research in new areas or involving new techniques only after first undertaking appropriate study, training, supervision, and/or consultation from persons who are competent in those areas or techniques.*

(b) Only render professional services, teach, or research new areas if you have some expertise in these areas. Approach new areas with caution and customary scientific rigor. Remember that a "new area" is either (a) new to you personally or (b) new to the field of psychology in general. In either case, get good training or supervision, or consult with a colleague first. If you think you are on the "cutting edge" of a therapy or intervention, be careful because it may "cut" both ways. You may be harmed, or you could harm someone else in the process.

Vignette: Dr. Thinnice consulted with the CEO of a major pharmaceutical company and was offered a large fee to help assess and predict employee stress and burnout before symptoms that could result in absenteeism developed. He had a strong interest in quantifying human behavior by using statistical methods and developed a regression equation that yielded a "stress status index." The index was based on the age of the employee, number of hours at work each week, history of absences, amount of vacation taken, birth order, number of pounds overweight or underweight, salary, and ethnic origin. He assessed all the employees and then assigned each to a stress management seminar, regardless of the employee's desire to attend.

Dr. Thinnice believed that he had developed a valid means of identifying those workers who were on the verge of burning out with stress and an intervention for reducing potential employee absenteeism before it became a reality. However, he neither empirically validated his technique nor carried out either a pilot study or any research in this area. His assessment procedure appeared to be wholly intuitive, based on the stress management training he had done with employees over the previous 3 years.

Dr. Thinnice collected a large fee from the company for several months, until some employees began to complain about being coerced into the stress management seminar that they felt they did not want or need. Some also complained about the apparent lack of scientific basis to his procedures and his attempt to rely on his title or authority in arbitrarily assigning them to attend the seminar. Because Dr. Thinnice could not support his methods scientifically, he was obliged to stop the program, ultimately conceding that it lacked validity. From this experience, he learned that regardless of the level of confidence he had in his work, he should always attempt to validate a new procedure before putting it into practice.

> *(c) In those emerging areas in which generally recognized standards for preparatory training do not yet exist, psychologists nevertheless take reasonable steps to ensure the competence of their work and to protect patients, clients, students, research participants, and others from harm.*

(c) If you believe that you are so far ahead of the mainstream in your area that there are no guidelines, standards, or rules relevant to your work, take extra care to avoid harming anyone in any way (emotionally, financially, legally, etc.).

Vignette: Dr. Wow was a psychologist practicing in a large midwestern city who viewed his own competence as being on the cutting edge of meditative and trance states. He had much training in different forms of meditation and had most recently developed a radically different form of therapy, which, he thought, incorporated the best of Eastern and Western philosophy. He called this therapy "existential somatic shifting," which he described as a "truly miraculous intervention for resistant clients." In this therapy, he typically touches patients on both shoulders while staring at the center of their forehead for 5 minutes. He then places the patient's "soma" within his own. By noting the patient's skin color, hand temperature, and breathing pattern and synchronizing his own breathing to match, he begins "a psycho-metabolic shift in the patient's soma." With much clever and persuasive advertising in the print and electronic media, Dr. Wow soon convinced many individuals to consult with him for treatment.

Unfortunately, he never attempted to validate his intervention with research; nor did he ever inform patients that it was essentially an experimental technique. He also did not attempt to publish his theories or present them at scientific meetings. He saw no reason to do so because he was convinced that his approach was effective, posed little or no risk to consumers, and was far superior to conventional therapies.

Certainly his approach worked well in a financial sense; Dr. Wow's bank account experienced a "metabolic shift" of major proportions because many patients sought him out for treatment. Some patients reported a "miraculous" improvement in their symptoms and were very pleased with the treatment. These patients became strong advocates of Dr. Wow's work. Other patients, however, experienced poor clinical results in the long run, with either no beneficial changes or an exacerbation of their symptoms over time. Ultimately, several former patients decided to initiate formal ethics complaints against Dr. Wow, claiming that they had been harmed by his fraudulent advertising, incompetence, and unconventional treatment.

1.05 Maintaining Expertise

Psychologists who engage in assessment, therapy, teaching, research, organizational consulting, or other professional activities maintain a reasonable level of awareness of current scientific and professional information in their fields of activity, and undertake ongoing efforts to maintain competence in the skills they use.

Stay on top of new developments in your area, and keep your skills sharp at all times. Read books and journals, go to workshops and conventions, give presentations, join a peer consultation group, and do whatever you need to do to continue growing professionally.

Vignette: Dr. Samantha Green routinely treated adults who had a history of childhood sexual abuse and used hypnosis occasionally as a part of treatment. She was careful to attend workshops and study the latest research on memory and its unwitting contamination with the use of hypnosis. She knew well the caveats and risks concerning the use of implicit suggestion and formal hypnosis in the course of psychotherapy with patients who readily dissociate. Dr. Green was aware of the ongoing controversy on this subject within APA. She also was familiar with the publications by researchers and therapists in APA's Division 30 (Psychological Hypnosis) and studied the medical literature. She also closely followed the research and publications of the American Medical Association, American Society for Clinical Hypnosis, Society for Clinical and Experimental Hypnosis, and other professional associations reporting research on this topic. She knew that hypnosis was not a "truth serum" and was fastidious about informing patients to invest cautiously in hypnotically refreshed memories. She did not discount these memories; nor did she assume they were necessarily wholly accurate in every detail.

   Because of Dr. Green's ongoing interest in and awareness of the clinical, ethical, and legal aspects of the use of hypnosis with this patient population, the efficacy of her work was increased while the welfare of those who consulted her was protected. She had a good appreciation of the concept of competence as an ongoing phenomenon and of the necessity of continually expanding her expertise commensurate with the current research literature in her field.

1.06 Basis for Scientific and Professional Judgments

Psychologists rely on scientifically and professionally derived knowledge when making scientific or professional judgments or when engaging in scholarly or professional endeavors.

Hunches are helpful, but make sure that your opinions and judgments are firmly based on professional training and scientific knowledge. Don't make "factual statements" in your classroom, in the courtroom, on the radio or TV, in print, or on the Internet about research or psychological interventions that go beyond the supporting data, unless you include a disclaimer. Resist the temptation to overgeneralize or oversimplify, regardless of the setting or pressure from others. It's better to be a little dull and accurate than flashy and wrong.

Vignette: For over 6 years, Dr. Daft was a strong advocate of alternative medicine interventions and believed that such remedies had been quite helpful in alleviating her own bouts of depression from time to time. Her primary means of providing therapy to depressed patients was to educate them about the use of certain vitamin and mineral supplements, and she selectively used herbal remedies. She rarely engaged patients in psychotherapy, believing instead in the potency of natural substances to treat mental disorders. Although she knew of no valid empirical support for these theories, she passed them off as factual and "clinically proven" in many trials in this country and abroad. She had many books and articles on herbology and other alternative medicine interventions in her office, and she freely distributed them to patients without any caveats or disclaimers. She also endorsed specific products and brand names and encouraged patients to purchase them at a nearby health food store. If they had difficulty locating a particular product, patients could purchase directly from her because she had a large supply at her office.

Unfortunately, her unscientific approach to the treatment of depression helped few of her patients in the long run, although some reported that they were benefiting from her recommendations. For those whose depression became exacerbated over time, Dr. Daft usually recommended additional herbal remedies and her own special concoction of minerals and teas.

Dr. Daft remained unconcerned about dispensing therapeutic advice that had little or no scientific basis, and she consistently underestimated the danger to clinically depressed individuals who were at risk of suicide. Because she rarely referred patients to other mental health care professionals for psychotherapy or antidepressant medication, she increased the likelihood that their depressive symptoms would become more extreme, possibly resulting in suicide attempts. She was harmful to many who believed in her competence and followed her professional advice. When a young male patient nearly carried out a suicide attempt, the man's wife became quite concerned about Dr. Daft's idiosyncratic treatment methods and decided to formally raise a question of her competence to the state licensing board.

1.07 Describing the Nature and Results of Psychological Services

(a) When psychologists provide assessment, evaluation, treatment, counseling, supervision, teaching, consultation, research, or other psychological services to an individual, a group, or an organization, they provide, using language that is reasonably understandable to the recipient of those services, appropriate information beforehand about the nature of such services and appropriate information later about results and conclusions. (See also Standard 2.09, Explaining Assessment Results.)

(a) Inform those whom you teach, counsel, consult with, or supervise about the nature of your work, and tell them in simple language what they can expect before beginning the work. Patients, organizational clients, students, supervisees, and others should have a clear understanding of the service you are going to render before you render it and should be told about any results and conclusions later on, as warranted. Don't obfuscate; simpler is better.

Vignette: Dr. Tellem routinely informed his patients, clients, students, and supervisees what to expect in their professional interactions with him, and often he used printed handouts that further explained his services. He clearly described both the role he would play and the expectations he had of others. In discussing psychological testing, he did not exaggerate a test's usefulness or imply that it could yield information for which it had no validation. He gave feedback to patients about the Minnesota Multiphasic Personality Inventory–2 (MMPI-2), Beck Depression Inventory–II, and other instruments of assessment in a simple, nontechnical way.

When discussing psychotherapy, Dr. Tellem avoided giving guarantees to patients, but he did give them information about the process of therapy. He discussed what therapy consisted of; what might be expected of them; the possible risks (e.g., the stressful aspects of treatment); and who could, with their permission, become involved in the treatment (e.g., specialists, physicians, spouses).

In carrying out clinical supervision, he was careful to inform his trainees about the frequency and duration of the supervisory meetings. He also told them what to expect from him and gave specifics about the format and content of the supervisory sessions, how these would be assessed, and other relevant details.

Whenever Dr. Tellem instructed recipients of his services about what to expect in their work with him, he was always careful to invite their questions and gladly discussed any aspect of his work that they wished.

Also he generally solicited their feedback to be certain they comprehended what he was presenting to them.

> *(b) If psychologists will be precluded by law or by organizational roles from providing such information to particular individuals or groups, they so inform those individuals or groups at the outset of the service.*

(b) If you will not be permitted to inform those whom you counsel, assess, or consult with about the nature of your work or its results due to your employment setting or the formal role you play, be sure to inform them of this at the outset of the interaction.

Vignette: Dr. Hirem worked in the human resources department of a large oil company assessing candidates for employment. Due to company policy, he was not permitted to give individual feedback to applicants about their interview or testing results. However, he always informed applicants of this policy in advance, making it clear that he considered his client to be the company, not the applicant.

By scrupulously informing candidates about these restrictions inherent in his professional role, he was generally successful in preventing candidates from developing unrealistic expectations about receiving assessment results. Nevertheless, there were always some applicants who, when they failed to be hired by the company, expressed curiosity about the factors that contributed to the decision. This sometimes resulted in telephone calls or letters to the human resources department requesting such information from Dr. Hirem. A policy of clear information at the outset not only helped candidates understand the limits of his involvement with them, it also reduced the likelihood that a complaint would be raised by disappointed applicants for his failure to provide assessment results.

His colleague, Dr. Noetell, devoted much of her time to forensic assessments in civil and criminal cases, using formal testing, clinical interviews, collateral interviews, and other means. She was frequently called on to assess families for litigation concerning child custody, perform mental competency examinations for defendants and death row inmates awaiting execution, and perform other psychological assessments in a broad range of cases.

Most of the time, Dr. Noetell was expected to write a psychological report describing the results of her assessments and then submit it directly either to the attorney who had retained her or to the court. On other occasions, her results would be communicated less formally to the attorney of the individual whom she had assessed. However, it was generally true that in her role as psychological evaluator she rarely had the opportunity to provide those she examined with direct feedback about the results of any specific test or the general assessment itself. The adversarial nature of litigation and the rules of discovery and procedure in her state precluded, in most situations, any opportunity to disclose information directly to the defendant during ongoing litigation. Therefore, she considered it important to inform individuals clearly about this fact prior to assessing them. The individuals would generally learn of the results of the assessment from their attorney or from the report that would be presented in open court.

On some occasions, however, she would carry out an assessment when the results might never be reported during the course of the litigation; hence, the individual being assessed might not learn of her findings, either directly or indirectly. This might occur if she carried out a psychological assessment pursuant to a motion of a party that was averse to the individual being evaluated and who, under local court rules, enjoyed the option of using the findings in support of his or her case. Should the party moving for the evaluation decide not to raise the issue of the assessed individual's mental status or psychological fitness (perhaps because the evaluation findings were not helpful for that strategy), he or she might be relieved of a legal duty to share the unused assessment with the person evaluated. The results of the psychological assessment would then be permitted to silently "disappear," almost as though it had never occurred. Whenever Dr. Noetell knew in advance that the results of the assessment might not become available to the person she was evaluating, for whatever reason, she so advised that person, in accordance with this ethical standard, even though she was not required to do so by law.

1.08 Human Differences

> *Where differences of age, gender, race, ethnicity, national origin, religion, sexual orientation, disability, language, or socioeconomic status significantly affect psychologists' work concerning particular individuals or groups, psychologists obtain the training, experience, consultation, or supervision necessary to ensure the competence of their services, or they make appropriate referrals.*

When working with someone who differs from you in culture, values, or some other important way (e.g., ethnicity, sexual orientation, religion), make sure that you have an adequate understanding of these differences to provide competent intervention. If you are uncertain, either refer the person to someone who is more competent (i.e., someone who shares their values) or obtain consultation or supervision (see APA's *Guidelines for Providers of Psychological Services to Ethnic, Linguistic, and Culturally Diverse Populations,* 1993b).

Vignette: Mrs. Lopez, a 60-year-old Puerto Rican woman who had been visiting relatives in Manhattan, was brought to the emergency room of a hospital following a relatively minor automobile accident. The taxicab she was riding in made a turn onto a one-way street near Times Square and collided with another car. The cabby blamed her for the accident and belligerently cursed at her for distracting him. When Mrs. Lopez was examined by the physician, she appeared to be inconsolably irrational and overexcited. The physician detected no evidence of a head injury or any other significant injury and no evidence of drug or alcohol use. She found Mrs. Lopez's apparent cognitive impairment, anxiety, and emotionalness to be excessive and triaged her to the psychologist on call, Dr. Andrew Caucashe.

Although she was highly anxious, appearing to be delusional at times, and was struggling to speak English intelligibly, Mrs. Lopez was able to provide a sketchy history in response to questions from the psychologist, Dr. Caucashe. The White psychologist learned that she was visiting her two sons and their families. Unfortunately, her oldest son had been diagnosed only the day before with a rare neurological disorder, and his prognosis was uncertain. She also had lost her husband, to whom she had been married for 40 years, to a heart attack 2 months before.

Dr. Caucashe noted many of the symptoms that were consistent with a panic attack, such as trembling, shortness of breath, lightheadedness, dizziness, and a feeling of warmth in her chest along with a cold sweat. However, he also found her speech to be incoherent at times and observed that she persisted in talking about her deceased family members. Their "presence" in her life appeared to be consistent with delusional thinking. He diagnosed her as having a brief psychotic disorder and recommended that she be admitted to the hospital and assessed by the attending psychiatrist, who would likely treat her with appropriate psychopharmacological agents.

As he was about to implement his recommendation, he was joined by his colleague, Dr. Carlos Mendoza, a Hispanic psychologist, who fortuitously was just beginning his shift at the hospital. After hearing Dr. Caucashe briefly review Mrs. Lopez's case, Dr. Mendoza was intrigued by her symptoms and asked if he might interview her. After doing so, he concluded quickly that Ms. Lopez suffered from no psychotic disorder at all but that she had the familiar signs he had witnessed many times before among Hispanic women who had recently experienced a major loss in life. This is called *ataque de nervios* and is characterized by many symptoms similar to anxiety and psychotic disorders. The death of her husband and the illness of her son had all caused mounting levels of stress in her life, and the automobile accident was the final stressor that triggered this reaction. The treatment of choice, as many Hispanic families knew, was decidedly not hospitalization. That would isolate her from her social support network and likely worsen her symptoms. The administration of neuroleptic medication, which would only cause side effects and not substantially affect her mental health, was not the answer either. Instead, Mrs. Lopez needed the solace, love, and support of family members who would virtually surround her with a functional therapeutic milieu. This could readily be accomplished because Mrs. Lopez had many extended family members living in New York. After making the diagnosis and recommending the family's supportive involvement as the only treatment needed, Dr. Mendoza then contacted her sons to help facilitate its implementation.

Dr. Caucashe learned a valuable lesson about taking cultural variables into account when diagnosing and treating mental disorders. Had it not been for his colleague's intervention, he would have made a formal recommendation for treatment that would have been entirely inappropriate and likely would have exacerbated an existing condition.

1.09 Respecting Others

In their work-related activities, psychologists respect the rights of others to hold values, attitudes, and opinions that differ from their own.

When working, teaching, or collaborating with people who hold values, attitudes, or opinions that vary from your own, respect their right to be different from you. Live and let live.

Vignette: As an instructor for a master's degree program in a university located in a large metropolitan area, Dr. Riteway regularly encountered a great diversity of students and faculty members. This represented a personal challenge to him because he held some long-standing prejudices that, at times, affected the quality of his teaching and mentoring of students.

He had a broad religious bias against everyone who was not committed to a Christian viewpoint. For example, he found himself avoiding students from other cultures who discussed or endorsed Buddhism or had other spiritual beliefs that were not based on his narrow conception of Christianity. At times, he would use language or concepts while lecturing that reflected his Christian bias. In discussing a particular theory of psychotherapy, he made subtle allusions to New Testament stories, from time to time, but would never refer to other religious sources, such as the Torah or the discourses of Buddha.

Dr. Riteway's prejudice against obese men and women also created conflict for him and those with whom he worked. He was noticeably less friendly and nurturing to these students and sometimes assumed an openly disapproving or even mildly chastising stance toward them and their physical condition. Occasionally, he discussed the merits of physical exercise or other health-oriented topics inappropriately and out of context, with the specific intent of educating those whom he thought needed such instruction. Students and colleagues invariably found these comments to be offensive, and more outspoken individuals were occasionally able to confront him with his outlandish behavior.

Furthermore, if a student dressed in an unusual fashion, wore unusual jewelry, sported a tattoo or body piercing, that student found that Dr. Riteway behaved in a disapproving manner and sometimes made hostile and demeaning comments. Indeed, there was little room for diversity in his classroom, and this appeared to become more pronounced as the years went by.

With increasing discomfort and a growing sense of being in the minority, Dr. Riteway slowly became more receptive to the feedback and advice from several close friends on the faculty. These individuals had known him for many years. Although they disagreed with his narrow-mindedness and rejected his prejudices, they knew he was a skilled teacher and was capable of rendering good supervision and fulfilling the necessary administrative duties in the department with much dedication and competence. These colleagues finally prevailed on him to consider seriously the long-term risks to his career as well as the potential harm to those with whom he interacted if he continued to reject everyone who held different values from his own. They also pointed out this ethical mandate to respect the rights of others and warned him of the real risk he ran of encountering an ethics complaint from an angry student or colleague some day if he did not change his ways.

Dr. Riteway was eventually persuaded by their persistence. He decided to seek consultation with a therapist to examine the sources of his strong prejudices and explore what steps he might take to free himself from their intensity.

1.10 Nondiscrimination

In their work-related activities, psychologists do not engage in unfair discrimination based on age, gender, race, ethnicity, national origin, religion, sexual orientation, disability, socioeconomic status, or any basis prescribed by law.

In your work, do not treat people unfairly or provide them with less care just because they happen to be different from you. Whether someone is "straight" or gay, male or female, of a high or low socioeconomic background, physically disabled or not, or of any age, race, ethnicity, or religion unlike your own, remember that state and federal discrimination laws may apply to your work. Treat others impartially.

Vignette: Dr. Hetter, a heterosexual faculty member in a professional school of psychology, never felt comfortable with gay men and lesbians, believing them essentially to be "abnormal" and in need of treatment to change their sexual orientation, regardless of their personal desire to do so. The school was small, and Dr. Hetter rarely had any contact with students that he knew were gay.

One year, however, two openly gay men, Richard and Sal, were admitted to the program. Both were highly competent and experienced in clinical settings. It was not very long before Dr. Hetter found himself in the position of supervising Richard in an individual psychotherapy practicum course. Dr. Hetter began to notice his feelings of personal conflict increasing as the supervisory relationship got under way. He could feel his fear and hostile feelings beginning to emerge as the weeks went by, raising some questions in his own mind about his ability to remain objective and provide good training for Richard. At first, he thought that these reactions would pass; he hoped that he could overcome his resistance to accepting a student whose sexual orientation conflicted so fundamentally with his views. However, he continued to feel apprehension before each supervisory session and found himself looking for excuses to cancel a meeting or end it early. Although Richard perceived no blatant discriminatory behavior on the part of his supervisor, he became aware of Dr. Hetter's general avoidance of him and began to wonder how or if he should raise the question of his sexual orientation as a contributing factor.

Dr. Hetter decided that he should consult a trusted senior psychologist about the advisability of continuing in his role as Richard's clinical supervisor. Also for the first time in his life he began to formally explore his philosophy and feelings about homosexuality as a mental disorder. He was willing to consider, in light of the emerging research, that his concepts might be overly rigid and outmoded. As a result, he decided to try to desensitize himself to gay men and lesbians because it was increasingly likely that he would have more exposure to openly gay students and faculty in the future. As a part of this effort, his senior consultant referred Dr. Hetter to a gay colleague, also a psychologist, who was willing to further explore these issues with him. With this help and support, Dr. Hetter was able to continue working as Richard's supervisor, and eventually he overcame his anxious and avoidant reactions.

1.11 Sexual Harassment

(a) Psychologists do not engage in sexual harassment. Sexual harassment is sexual solicitation, physical advances, or verbal or nonverbal conduct that is sexual in nature, that occurs in connection with the psychologist's activities or roles as a psychologist, and that either: (1) is unwelcome, is offensive, or creates a hostile workplace environment, and the psychologist knows or is told this; or (2) is sufficiently severe or intense to be abusive to a reasonable person in the context. Sexual harassment can consist of a single intense or severe act or of multiple persistent or pervasive acts.

(a) When at your workplace, don't continue to engage in the following behaviors after you've been told they are offensive or if they are so extreme that most people would consider them undesirable:

1. Don't continue to flirt with others when told this is unwelcome.
2. Don't continue to physically touch, hug, or kiss others.
3. Don't continue to engage others in titillating conversations, such as telling sexual jokes, making allusions to or suggesting sexual activity, commenting on others' sexual and physical attributes, and so on.
4. Don't behave in nonverbal ways that are overtly sexual, such as staring, making inappropriate gestures, displaying sexual photos or materials, and so on.

Also don't assume that others will necessarily appreciate your concept of sexual humor or conduct in the workplace, particularly when there is a difference in ascribed or real power or authority. Be aware of the distinction between showing your romantic interest in another and harassing him or her by such behavior as exposing him or her to sexually embarrassing humor, violating his or her personal space, or initiating unwanted touching, to name a few.

Vignette: Dr. Testos was a new psychology instructor on the faculty and had little awareness of the concept of sexual harassment. He occasionally told his female supervisees sexual jokes that were offensive and inappropriate, both during supervisory hours and in social settings. Once in a while, he brought pornographic videotapes to the office to swap with his male colleagues, most of whom were oblivious to the effect their conduct might have on both female and male students. Furthermore, it was a regular habit for some of the male faculty to spend part of each workday connected to the Internet, exploring pornographic web pages and trading their latest discoveries with each other, sometimes carelessly within the earshot of students and other colleagues.

One of Dr. Testos's colleagues, Dr. Libidish, often sat too close to his female trainees, touched them, or even put his arm around them while observing group therapy sessions through a one-way mirror in the darkened observation room. Students reacted differentially to these touches: Some felt quite flattered that a faculty member would behave so affectionately, but others felt quite repelled and distracted from what was supposed to be a didactic experience. Dr. Libidish also attempted to pat his supervisees inappropriately or hug them at the end of many sessions. He sometimes referred to them as "darling" or in some other unacceptably familiar or affectionate manner and implied that the professional relationship could readily progress into a romantic one if the student were interested.

Occasionally, students would complain to the offending faculty members or to the administration, but they were usually met with denials and rationalizations for the sexualized behavior. The pattern of sexual harassment was extensive in the male-dominated department and had deep roots, a long history, and tradition that was consistent with the "good old boy network." There was seemingly no way to bring a successful in-house grievance because sexual harassment was endemic to the institution and was considered to be an acceptable part of campus life, even within the graduate departments and the upper administrative levels. This ultimately led to significant disappointment among many female and some male students and caused many of them to drop out of the program. The predominantly male students remaining behind were comfortable with the climate of female sexual harassment. Unfortunately, they received much social validation in their graduate school experience for any culturally sanctioned sexist views that they brought with them to the psychology program.

(b) Psychologists accord sexual-harassment complainants and respondents dignity and respect. Psychologists do not participate in denying a person academic admittance or advancement, employment, tenure, or promotion, based solely upon their having made, or their being the subject of, sexual harassment charges. This does not preclude taking action based upon the outcome of such proceedings or consideration of other appropriate information.

(b) If someone complains that they are being sexually harassed, take her or him seriously and listen respectfully. It is a difficult subject to handle, especially if you may share some of the values of the harasser. Don't "punish" someone who complains of sexual harassment by denying employment, promotion, tenure, and so on. However, remember that a charge of sexual harassment is only that—a charge. It is not a fact.

Therefore, you must also avoid discriminating against someone who has only been complained about, such as by denying employment, promotion, tenure, and so on.

Vignette: Dr. Mentor was complained against for sexually harassing a female colleague on an inpatient unit at a county psychiatric hospital, although he had an excellent professional record working there for over 12 years. His clinical supervision and services had been exemplary, he was well liked and admired by his peers, and he had even served on the hospital ethics committee for several terms. Recently, he had been awarded the medical center's distinguished psychologist award, and he was currently being considered for the directorship of the psychology service inpatient unit.

Dr. Mentor's supervisor carefully reviewed the sexual harassment complaint and waited for the hospital's human relations office to investigate it thoroughly, even though it appeared unlikely to have any validity. Despite social pressure from certain individuals in the hospital administration to disregard the complaint, Dr. Mentor's supervisor did not discount it; neither did he attempt to coerce the woman to withdraw her complaint, as some would have preferred. Dr. Mentor's consistently high level of achievement in the hospital was not permitted to be a rationale for trivializing the complaint or short circuiting the investigative process. Ultimately, the complaint was found to be without merit, and Dr. Mentor's promotion to director of the inpatient unit became a reality.

1.12 Other Harassment

> *Psychologists do not knowingly engage in behavior that is harassing or demeaning to persons with whom they interact in their work based on factors such as those persons' age, gender, race, ethnicity, national origin, religion, sexual orientation, disability, language, or socioeconomic status.*

Do not deride, belittle, make fun of, or otherwise harass your colleagues, clients, students, or others with whom you work based on factors such as their age, sex, race, ethnicity, country of origin, sexual orientation, disability, or native language.

Vignette: Dr. Merth was an administrator and part-time psychology faculty member in a small university. He was hypomanic in his interpersonal style and had a reputation for a sardonic sense of humor. He thought that teaching was maximally effective when it was entertaining both for the student and the professor. He also believed that a good administrator should be able to engage others on various levels and that humor should be the social lubricant facilitating most administrative interactions.

At his best, he was somewhat reminiscent of the comedian Don Rickles, whom he admired: He was able to comment spontaneously, creatively, and humorously on the behavior of others and sometimes got them to laugh at themselves. At his worst, however, he was simply offensive and crudely insulting, arousing feelings of hurt, anger, and even shame in those who were the butt of his humor. At these times, it seemed that his intention was to humiliate others or simply to vent his own hostility, and he often would tell his jokes or imitate the style of his intended target to their faces or well within their earshot.

Part of his repertoire included sarcastic comments and jokes about women, African Americans, Jews, gays, older people, immigrants from Asia and Eastern Europe, and various other members of groups to which he did not belong. When teaching his statistics classes, he made a point of telling jokes or weaving a humorous story into his lecture that was based on the minority-group distribution present in the class. If there were Mormons or African Americans in a particular class, for instance, then his humor would focus on the values and behavior of Mormons and African Americans. As an administrator, he frequently participated in meetings with the same mix of individuals he had derided, hence, his humor and harassment would tend to be repetitive and not funny.

At times, Dr. Merth was endearing to others and succeeded in charming them or lightening their mood. Indeed, his behavior seemed to be rooted in attempts at gaining their approval and validation. However, Dr. Merth was generally less successful in entertaining, and more often he simply inflicted humiliation and insults on students and colleagues. His deeply held prejudicial views and harassing behavior were not successfully balanced by his wit or humor, resulting in a pervasive negative effect on those who were the targets of his hostility. By his consistent pattern of harassment in the workplace, he made himself vulnerable to valid ethics complaints from those whom he estranged.

1.13 Personal Problems and Conflicts

(a) Psychologists recognize that their personal problems and conflicts may interfere with their effectiveness. Accordingly, they refrain from undertaking an activity when they know or should know that their personal problems are likely to lead to harm to a patient, client, colleague, student, research participant, or other person to whom they may owe a professional or scientific obligation.

(a) Periodically throughout their lives, psychologists, as do most people, suffer the consequences of stress, personal losses, and resulting changes in mood and productivity. You would do well to know when your distress has the potential for affecting your work and possibly harming others. You should also be aware of your personal weaknesses and "blind spots" and attempt to compensate for them.

Vignette: Dr. Ire was an excellent researcher and highly respected professor at a large, prestigious university. For the past 6 months, however, he was experiencing increasing stress from his difficult marital situation because his wife had recently sued for divorce and was demanding that he move out of the house. The situation was becoming more painful as the months went by because his wife's attorney was aggressively pursuing his client's goals of obtaining custody of their two young daughters and a large financial settlement.

It was clear that the ongoing stress of Dr. Ire's personal life was beginning to intrude on his research and teaching responsibilities, impairing his concentration and competence. He had been concluding the data collection and analysis for the final year of a 3-year research project of an examination of the communication style of couples engaged in marital therapy. Unfortunately, he found that he could no longer be impartial in evaluating the subjective oral and written comments by the wives participating in the study. His personal feelings of anger and loss from the ending of his own marriage were ever present, causing him to generalize his negative feelings for his wife to other women. His negative mood also was beginning to contaminate his work, which was resulting in a consistent antifemale bias in analyzing the data from his protocol. He wondered if he should seek a colleague's assistance in completing the final phase of his research.

Of more immediate concern, he also noticed that he expressed stronger feelings of irritation toward female colleagues in response to relatively minor provocation or disappointments. Several friends and colleagues called attention to his reactions and offered to assist him in some way if he wished. Dr. Ire was beginning to appreciate the deep impact of the stressful divorce on his mood, his professional competence, and his professional relationships and considered discussing his situation with a therapist.

> *(b) In addition, psychologists have an obligation to be alert to signs of, and to obtain assistance for, their personal problems at an early stage, in order to prevent significantly impaired performance.*

(b) Be on guard for early signs of impaired performance (e.g., short temper, depression, drinking more alcohol, physical pain, stress-related illness). If you know you are experiencing a major life transition, such as divorce, financial stress, death of someone close, or any other major stress, be sure to get help for yourself. It is a kindness to yourself and good protection for those you work with also.

Vignette: One day, Dr. Ire received a letter from his wife's attorney demanding physical and legal custody of his children and containing a long rationale implying that he had been repeatedly abusive of them, had endangered their safety on several vacation trips, and generally was not a competent father. The possibility was raised that that he might only be permitted to have supervised visits with his children to protect them from his negligence.

This letter evoked intense feelings in Dr. Ire and led to several angry outbursts at work that culminated in his physically pushing a female colleague who happened to disagree with his interpretation of the research data. He immediately realized that his hostility and intensity were related to the ongoing divorce proceedings because the female colleague bore a striking physical similarity to his estranged wife. This insight provided little relief, however, and his hostile mood continued to strongly affect his interactions at work.

One of Dr. Ire's younger female research assistants, Dawn, was quite sympathetic to his obvious distress. Although she was his student, she felt a special affinity for him in this time of transition and loss. Dr. Ire responded to her gentleness and compassion and experienced feelings of affection and sexual attraction to her that grew with each passing day. With little concern for his professional role or the possibility of harming one of his students, he began to yield to the intense romantic pull in his relationship with Dawn.

His close friend and colleague, John, was able see that an affair between Dr. Ire and Dawn was imminent and, perceiving his friend's suffering, prevailed on him to consider a course of action that would best meet his own long-term needs. Dr. Ire decided to consult a psychotherapist, a step that he had been delaying, believing that, as a psychologist, he should be able to manage his own problems.

> *(c) When psychologists become aware of personal problems that may interfere with their performing work-related duties adequately, they take appropriate measures, such as obtaining professional consultation or assistance, and determine whether they should limit, suspend, or terminate their work-related duties.*

(c) Take whatever steps are necessary to help restore your own good functioning, and protect those with whom you work. This might include consulting with a respected colleague, limiting your work activities temporarily, or obtaining psychotherapy or any other necessary help or rehabilitative experience essential for your recovery.

Vignette: Dr. Ire's conversation with his friend John helped him to see the extent to which his deteriorating marital situation was affecting his professional life in a variety of ways. He now could accept the extent to which his mood affected his work in the final phase of his research project. He noted that sometimes during the final face-to-face interview, he had been argumentative with the participants in his research project, particularly the wives. He also realized that he sometimes made systematic distortions in his interpretations of the data from the transcripts and ratings of the therapy sessions, ascribing ulterior motives to the women that were clearly unwarranted by the data.

With John's help, Dr. Ire concluded that it was essential to distance himself from the interviewing and data analysis at this particular time because he clearly was not competent to continue doing the work. Fortunately, he was able to engage several senior research assistants to help carry out his responsibilities. Although the project was slowed down considerably, taking 6 more months to complete than originally planned, at least the research team no longer ran the risk of significant threats to the study's validity due to the work of an impaired and biased researcher.

As for the budding relationship with Dawn, his research assistant, Dr. Ire found that he was grateful for her friendship but did not pursue the romantic aspect anymore. As he processed his own stressful reactions about his own divorce in therapy, his intense feelings for Dawn began to subside, with no further need to act on his initial sexual attraction to her.

Although he had entered the most emotionally demanding transition of his adult life, Dr. Ire appreciated the fact that friends and colleagues came to his support, guiding his judgment and encouraging him to obtain the psychological treatment that so benefited him. Because of their help, he was able to acknowledge the immediate need to limit his work responsibilities and make sound decisions about his personal life.

1.14 Avoiding Harm

Psychologists take reasonable steps to avoid harming their patients or clients, research participants, students, and others with whom they work, and to minimize harm where it is foreseeable and unavoidable.

Never harm patients, clients, research participants, students, or anyone else with whom you work. In those cases where you think that someone might *feel* harmed by what you do or neglect to do and you can't avoid it, be sure to minimize the harm as much as possible.[2]

Vignette: Dr. Lastlap thought he would help his patient, an unemployed auto mechanic diagnosed with bipolar mood disorder, to ease the financial burden of psychotherapy. The doctor raced cars as a hobby, and one of his older race cars needed a new transmission. Because his patient had the skills to replace it and had offered his skills in auto repair on more than one occasion in exchange for psychotherapy, Dr. Lastlap agreed to the bartering arrangement. The risk seemed minimal, and Dr. Lastlap thought that he could keep the professional boundaries clear.

His patient was highly enthusiastic about the idea and was much relieved that he could now afford additional sessions of psychotherapy in this fashion. He worked on the car after hours in his friend's shop, successfully installed the new transmission, and returned the car to his therapist several days later.

The next weekend, while driving on the highway on the way to the race track, the transmission overheated and suddenly failed, causing Dr. Lastlap to swerve off the road into a ditch. On inspection, it appeared that the new problem was due to an oversight on the part of the patient.

Dr. Lastlap suffered head and neck injuries, which required medical treatment and physical therapy over a period of several months. He was in constant pain and began harboring such negative feelings toward his patient that he could no longer effectively treat him. Dr. Lastlap finally

---

[2]*Author's Note:* Standard 1.14 is a very broad principle, which states, generically, the most important rule of all. There are at least 102 ways that psychologists could visit harm on someone, that is, by violating any one of the 102 standards in the Ethics Code. It is wise to consider the various professional roles that you play in carrying out your work and the ways that each of those roles could result in harming somebody, personally, emotionally, cognitively, physically, sexually, professionally, financially, or legally, to name a few.

terminated therapy at the very time his patient wished to process his emotional reactions to the role he felt he played in the accident, primarily feelings of guilt and apprehension that he would lose his therapist.

After therapy ended, the patient felt abandoned by Dr. Lastlap and was somewhat fearful of entering therapy again with someone else. Originally, he thought that his idea of bartering automotive skills in exchange for therapy was a good one, and he was very pleased that his therapist had agreed with him. He had never engaged in such an exchange of services before with a health care professional, and the possibility of any negative consequences never occurred to him. It was clearly Dr. Lastlap's responsibility, however, to have considered the risks of bartering for services with his patient and the possibility of long-term harm by participating in such an agreement. He failed to do so, thinking that he was helping his financially needy patient, and ultimately placed the professional relationship at risk by agreeing to such an arrangement.

1.15 Misuse of Psychologists' Influence

Because psychologists' scientific and professional judgments and actions may affect the lives of others, they are alert to and guard against personal, financial, social, organizational, or political factors that might lead to misuse of their influence.

What you say and do as a psychologist has the strong potential of affecting people or groups in important ways, so be cautious. Your influence could be felt in ways that you never would have anticipated and be harmful or damaging to others. Always consider how your actions could affect others (a) personally, (b) financially, (c) socially, (d) organizationally, and (e) politically.

Vignette: A media psychologist, Dr. Johanna Swifter, had a daily radio show and participated in an Internet advice chat room that addressed a broad array of psychological topics. Her producer thought that psychological information should be dispensed in a simple manner and that answers to callers' questions should be short and to the point, without qualification or complicated disclaimers. He also thought that psychology should provide an "upbeat" message to the radio audience and be more positive and happy and less focused on pathological or analytical content.

Dr. Swifter concurred with this philosophy of broadcast journalism, and her lucrative contract of $225,000 per annum helped sustain that belief. To her, this justified an almost total abandonment of a scientific approach in her regular broadcasts, with little or no reliance on psychological research in responding to queries from callers. As a result, her answers to callers' questions were generally authoritarian and dogmatic, rather short and simple, sometimes humorous, and frequently laced with generalities passed off as facts, regardless of their scientific validity.

The callers speaking with her on the air as well as the millions of silent listeners invested her comments with significant authority because she was identified as "a licensed psychologist with many years of counseling experience." The fact that she held a psychology license helped validate her comments in the minds of many, even though such validation might have been unwarranted because of her consistent failure to rely on psychologically sound concepts. The long-term potential damage she did by giving such advice to a listening population that might include individuals suffering from significant emotional distress and mental disorders may well have constituted a misuse of her influence in her radio broadcasts.

Dr. Swifter's printed remarks in the Internet chat room yielded feedback from many web users, and she was often corrected by other psychologists who participated in the dialogue. Even in this environment, she usually took little care in tempering her comments with a scientific basis. She continued to give ill-founded advice and misinformation like she did in her radio show, regardless of the challenges she received from others. It was only a matter of time before several psychologists and consumers initiated formal ethics complaints against her for misusing her influence in a public forum and violating several different ethical standards.

1.16 Misuse of Psychologists' Work

(a) Psychologists do not participate in activities in which it appears likely that their skills or data will be misused by others, unless corrective mechanisms are available. (See also Standard 7.04, Truthfulness and Candor.)

(a) Do not engage in professional activities where your skills or data will knowingly be misused (e.g., misstated, exaggerated, improperly suppressed).

Vignette: In the early 1970s, a major tobacco company offered to employ Dr. Spinnit to carry out research on the possible addictive potential of tobacco. The research was intended by the company to "prove" that the only people who become addicted to nicotine had preexisting mental problems, such as significant depression or anxiety. Dr. Spinnit was encouraged to develop and use his own instruments of assessment in arriving at this conclusion. But it was made clear to him that the outcome of the research was preordained.

It was obvious to Dr. Spinnit that the research hypothesis had to be supported for the research to be published. Funding for the project was virtually unlimited, and Dr. Spinnit's personal compensation for the work was over twice his university income for a comparable time period. He could certainly make use of the extra income because he currently had three children attending college. Dr. Spinnit was a moderate smoker and thus was favorably inclined to do the research because he had a personal interest in the outcome. Furthermore, he owned stock in the tobacco company.

During the very week he was pondering his decision about accepting the offer, a close friend and mentor, also a smoker, was diagnosed with lung cancer. The friend's oncologist was firm in his belief, based on the most current research data, that 40 years of smoking cigarettes played a direct role in the malignancy. Dr. Spinnit was stunned by this bad news and pessimistic about his friend's survival based on the doctor's report. This caused him to reevaluate his philosophy about tobacco use and participating in research that was geared to promote it. He ultimately had a change of heart and decided to decline the offer, despite its lucrative potential. Instead, he decided he would devote his energies to a very different kind of research project at his university—one that could help determine factors related to the addictive potential of nicotine in young adults.

> (b) If psychologists learn of misuse or misrepresentation of their work, they take reasonable steps to correct or minimize the misuse or misrepresentation.

(b) If you discover that someone has misused or misrepresented your work, be sure to make corrections, or at least make the attempt to do so.

Vignette: Dr. Herald, a school psychologist, was misquoted by the River City High School principal concerning the extent of drug and alcohol use of students. The principal, Ms. Dee Nile, essentially ignored most of the recent survey data gathered by Dr. Herald over the previous 4 months and relied instead on a study he conducted 3 years ago, which reported a much lower rate of alcohol and drug use. This deliberate misquote not only appeared in the local newspaper but was carried by the local radio and television stations as an important story that "proudly conveyed a picture of healthy adjustment for the River City teenagers, with use of drugs and alcohol at significantly lower levels than the national average."

In spite of pressure from some teachers to let the false story continue to be aired, Dr. Herald was troubled by the deliberate misrepresentations and wished to take some formal action to correct the situation. This was not the first time the psychologist and principal had opposed each other; they had a long history of philosophical differences concerning school policy, administrative matters, and involvement with the media. He discussed the matter with Ms. Nile, emphasizing the importance of presenting a corrected update, based on his current survey data. She was resistant to his challenges however, fearing that the most current survey data would reflect poorly on the school, its administration, and herself. She felt that little good would come from releasing the results of his recent research, regardless of its high validity.

The psychologist then discussed this issue with the pupil services administrator and the head of the school system's research committee. Both these individuals fully supported him and suggested that he might contact the district superintendent's office if Ms. Nile continued to pursue her course of misrepresenting Dr. Herald's report.

The research committee chair offered to speak with the principal herself, as she had on other occasions, about the importance of presenting the public with accurate information derived from in-house research. Dr. Herald welcomed this suggestion. A collegial resolution to the stalemate was certainly preferable to a confrontative one in the eyes of the staff members involved. Fortunately, Ms. Nile was receptive to the words of her research committee's chair and reluctantly agreed to report the corrections to the media. An accurate version of the survey results finally appeared in print, and Dr. Herald was pleased that he had persevered in correcting the erroneous report.

1.17 Multiple Relationships

(a) In many communities and situations, it may not be feasible or reasonable for psychologists to avoid social or other nonprofessional contacts with persons such as patients, clients, students, supervisees, or research participants. Psychologists must always be sensitive to the potential harmful effects of other contacts on their work and on those persons with whom they deal. A psychologist refrains from entering into or promising another personal, scientific, professional, financial, or other relationship with such persons if it appears likely that such a relationship reasonably might impair the psychologist's objectivity or otherwise interfere with the psychologist's effectively performing his or her functions as a psychologist, or might harm or exploit the other party.

(a) Keep your professional and scientific relationships (e.g., with patients, clients, students, supervisees, research participants) clear, simple, and straightforward. Don't begin or promise to begin a second relationship with anyone if it could (a) interfere with your objectivity, (b) impair your competence, or (c) in some way harm or exploit them.

Vignette: Dr. Beeawl felt that he could be a resource to doctoral students in many different ways, and he regularly entered into several concurrent professional roles with them. In spite of the fact that his various roles sometimes were confusing to his students, it was his normal practice to offer psychotherapy to his graduate student advisees.

One of his patients, Lillian, revealed in therapy that she had guilty feelings over plagiarizing parts of her doctoral dissertation and altering some of her data. Dr. Beeawl found himself in great personal conflict in his attempts to fulfill his role as both a university professor, who models and enforces ethical conduct among students, and a psychotherapist, who accepts virtually all patient disclosures in confidence and processes this material in treatment.

The situation became further complicated when Lillian decided to take a course from him. Her therapy was not yet complete, and Dr. Beeawl found himself in the uncomfortable position of teaching and evaluating the same individual for whom he was providing therapy. He wondered if this gave his patient an unfair advantage because it was difficult for him to maintain objectivity in evaluating her classroom performance and, eventually, assessing her overall performance and giving her a final grade.

He also noticed that he felt inhibited by having Lillian in class because his classroom presentation normally included more humor and self-disclosure than his interactions with his patients.

Dr. Beeawl wished he had never allowed so many professional roles to develop with Lillian, and it became progressively more uncomfortable for him to function competently in all of them simultaneously. He attempted to resolve this complex situation by giving Lillian the option of dropping the class that he was teaching without any penalty or selecting a different therapist. Regardless of which of these options she chose, Lillian also would be required to rewrite the sections of her dissertation that were plagiarized and to report only her original data, again, without any penalty. Lillian initially felt coerced and frustrated by her mentor's "resolution." However, as time went on, she eventually appreciated the wisdom of it. Dr. Beeawl learned the importance of being more aware of boundaries in his professional conduct and generally avoided engaging students in multiple roles from then on.

> *(b) Likewise, whenever feasible, a psychologist refrains from taking on professional or scientific obligations when pre-existing relationships would create a risk of such harm.*

(b) Don't accept someone as a patient or in some other professional or scientific role whom you already know in another setting, such as your dentist or your wife's best friend. The original relationship will suffer, your psychological work will be compromised, or both, and things could permanently change between the two of you.

Vignette 1—Impaired Objectivity: The relationship boundaries in Dr. Goodboy's extended family became somewhat complicated when Blanche, his mother-in-law who was clinically depressed, sought him out "to talk over some important matters about the family." She insisted on meeting him in his office and actually paid him a small fee because she valued his opinion and wanted to make it clear that she was consulting him "as a professional, not as a son-in-law." She was obviously depressed, refused to seek professional help with anyone else, and highly valued his professional opinion, and so Dr. Goodboy agreed to talk with her in his office. He also honored her request to keep the meetings a secret from his wife. But this was a somewhat uncomfortable accommodation to make because honesty very much was valued in his marriage.

After three meetings in 2 weeks, it slowly emerged that the cause of Blanche's depression was her daughter's marriage to Dr. Goodboy himself 2 years before. Evidently, Dr. Goodboy had some personality traits that were similar to Blanche's older brother, with whom she had been in conflict for much of her life. As she became aware of the similarity, she became openly angry and blaming toward her son-in-law, demanding that he change his ways.

Dr. Goodboy wished dearly that he had never agreed to provide counseling to his mother-in-law. Certainly, his objectivity was impaired in dealing with this depressive, now-hostile woman. He had only been trying to provide much-needed help to her, and he found himself trapped in a complex family web, which seemed to become tighter with every movement. He finally informed his mother-in-law that for obvious reasons, he could no longer continue to discuss these matters with her, unless they consulted a third party, such as another therapist, or unless she began counseling with a separate therapist.

Vignette 2—Impaired Competence: Dr. Kindly was carrying out research in chronic pain management using biofeedback training, hypnosis, and other interventions. As an inducement for research participants, she offered to provide some limited psychotherapeutic treatment at the conclusion of their involvement in the protocol. Although she generally did not accept colleagues as research participants, she made an exception for Dr. Spinnit, a colleague with chronic back pain and chronic bronchitis. Dr. Kindly thought this was a benevolent act on her part, offering this opportunity to her friend and colleague who was in such chronic pain. But the situation became complicated when she learned that Dr. Spinnit's pain probably had a psychosomatic component, exacerbated by his having a major conflict with the psychology department chair, who happened to be the regular tennis partner of Dr. Kindly.

One day, Dr. Spinnit saw Dr. Kindly on the tennis court engaged in a lively match with the psychology chair and was quite dismayed that she was playing tennis with the very man he considered his nemesis. From that moment on, he felt such conflict that it was impossible for him to be involved in the research any further, and he certainly did not feel that he could freely discuss the problems with the department chair, even though the stress contributed significantly to his back pain.

Dr. Spinnit also felt somewhat betrayed by Dr. Kindly because she had promised to be a therapeutic resource for him. But now, he felt that she could not fulfill that role. Dr. Kindly felt incompetent to manage the situation, in either the research setting or by following up on delivering the therapy that she had promised. She now understood that accepting a friend as a research participant could be harmful to the friendship as well as to the research and the promised therapy.

Vignette 3—Differences in Real or Ascribed Social Power[3,4]:   Dr. Stone had been providing clinical supervision to Harmony, a 2nd-year student, for 3 months. One day, he asked Harmony to assist him with several research projects that he had started. Specifically, he needed about 6 months worth of clerical assistance coding responses and entering them into the computer and carrying out many telephone interviews. Although Dr. Stone

---

[3]*Author's Note:* Harming or exploiting another in a less powerful position can occur almost before you realize that it has happened.

[4]The social power ascribed to individuals is sometimes important to consider in multiple-role relationships. The formal authority of one's rank or position within an institution may invoke premature compliance in another. The following scenario is an example of a power differential between two people in an academic setting resulting in coercion of the one with less authority.

could offer no financial compensation for this work, he reassured Harmony that it would be a useful learning experience in acquiring research methodology skills, even though it had no relevance to her own clinical work or supervision and was not a part of the original supervisory agreement.

Harmony reluctantly complied with his request, even though her time was already in short supply because of two research projects that she was already working on with another professor. She could ill afford to devote the extra hours that these new projects required. However, being somewhat deferential by nature, she thought that she had little choice but to accept her clinical supervisor's request. He appeared to be quite needy. She spent a large amount of time assisting him, to the detriment of progress on her own work. Harmony did not feel that she could even discuss the possibility of refusing to cooperate with him. She felt that it would impact negatively on the clinical supervisory relationship, so she simply deferred to his authority and agreed to work the long hours required.

Several months went by before Harmony was able to bring herself to discuss her objections to working such long hours for Dr. Stone. At that time, they came to a satisfactory agreement, but not before she had experienced significant distress as a result of overcommitting herself to his projects.

> *(c) If a psychologist finds that, due to unforeseen factors, a potentially harmful multiple relationship has arisen, the psychologist attempts to resolve it with due regard for the best interests of the affected person and maximal compliance with the Ethics Code.*

(c) If you discover that you are caught up in a potentially harmful dual relationship, do what you can to get out of it, keeping in mind the best interests of the other person and obeying the Ethics Code.

Vignette: Dr. Yna Fix had been consulting with her new accountant for 5 months about the business aspects of her practice, including problems she had been encountering with the managed health care system. She had been considering closing her 35-year practice in a rural New England community and was exploring various retirement options, but she had not yet told any of her patients.

One day, the accountant informed her that he had just learned that his wife's brother Joe was Dr. Fix's patient. Joe was a middle-aged man who was suicidally depressed and had been alcohol dependent for most of his life. He had begun therapy with Dr. Fix over 6 months ago and had a productive therapeutic relationship with her. Dr. Fix wondered if her accountant would agree to keep their discussions confidential and refrain from revealing to Joe, just yet, her plans to retire. She feared that such a disclosure might increase the likelihood of Joe's binge drinking and attempts at suicide, given his current fragile state.

Certainly, Dr. Fix was aware that social coincidences frequently occur, particularly in small communities and that one must be prepared for them. But this particular scenario was something that she had never encountered before, and it called for a creative solution. In the interest of preserving the continuity of Joe's treatment, she considered changing accountants, despite having paid his fees in advance and having a good business relationship with him. She also considered the possibility of referring the patient to a colleague, although starting therapy all over would often constitute a hardship for a patient.

She consulted with a senior colleague ultimately to help resolve this dilemma and arrived at a decision that attended to her patient's best interests. She requested that the accountant avoid disclosing to Joe anything about her retirement plans for a period of several weeks. The accountant agreed to keep her plans confidential for that period of time. At the end of 3 weeks, she planned to discuss her long-range retirement plans with Joe, while offering to remain his therapist until a time when they both felt that he could transfer to another therapist in the community.

1.18 Barter (With Patients or Clients)

Psychologists ordinarily refrain from accepting goods, services, or other nonmonetary remuneration from patients or clients in return for psychological services because such arrangements create inherent potential for conflicts, exploitation, and distortion of the professional relationship. A psychologist may participate in bartering only if (1) it is not clinically contraindicated, and (2) the relationship is not exploitative. (See also Standards 1.17, Multiple Relationships, and 1.25, Fees and Financial Arrangements.)

Ordinarily, don't accept goods or services in exchange for your services because doing so creates the potential for conflicts, exploitation, and tension within the professional relationship. However, if patients have no other way to pay, then you may engage in barter. But do so only if the barter (a) is not clinically contraindicated or (b) doesn't exploit the patient.

Vignette: Dr. Rex Changer practiced in a small midwestern town and was accustomed to routinely engaging in bartering in exchange for his psychological services. He was scrupulous about reporting this as income at a fair-market value. At the end of each year, he filed his taxes using IRS Form 1099-B.[5] He knew that bartering was the only way for poorer patients to obtain his services, particularly farming families who were frequently in financial distress. He accepted chickens, sides of beef, cords of wood, and even machinery in some cases in exchange for psychotherapy.

On the rare occasions when he bartered for a patient's services, such as gardening, he agreed to a reduction in the fee schedule. He knew that failure to reduce his fee would raise the likelihood that the gardener, who normally charged $15 per hour, would accumulate a huge debt over time while attempting to repay Dr. Changer at his customary rate of $95 per

---

[5]The IRS form for the barter of services or goods.

hour. This would effectively result in the gardener becoming an "indentured servant" long after the therapy ended.

One day, a young man with bipolar mood disorder called Dr. Changer for treatment. He was a roofer by trade but had little money and wished to exchange his roofing skills for treatment. Dr. Changer had needed a new roof for months and thought this would be opportune and beneficial for both doctor and patient. Unfortunately, however, while working on the roof the patient entered a floridly manic state and worked far into the night by moonlight and took risks with his own safety. He slipped and fell, plunging into the doctor's flower garden, and broke his collar bone. Dr. Changer drove him to the hospital, many miles away, and saw that he was adequately cared for in the emergency room.

This incident had strong negative repercussions for the therapist–patient relationship, resulting in much conflict and disappointment on both sides. The patient who was now in a cast, had negative feelings about Dr. Changer and his clinical judgment, and ended treatment abruptly. Ultimately, he held Dr. Changer responsible for allowing him to put himself in a dangerous situation as a direct result of the bartering arrangement, particularly when he was in a manic state. Dr. Changer agreed that he had possibly used poor judgment in allowing someone diagnosed with bipolar disorder to work on his roof in exchange for treatment. Parenthetically but also of importance, Dr. Changer noticed that the roofing work that his patient had accomplished before falling off the roof was of poor quality; he eventually had to hire another roofer to undo the shoddy work already done before completing the job.

The roofer was unaware of the ethical responsibility of his therapist, so no formal ethics complaint or civil suit resulted from his disappointment with his therapist. But the community developed a great deal of ill will toward Dr. Changer after this incident.

1.19 Exploitative Relationships

> *(a) Psychologists do not exploit persons over whom they have supervisory, evaluative, or other authority such as students, supervisees, employees, research participants, and clients or patients. (See also Standards 4.05–4.07 regarding involvement with clients or patients.)*

(a) Don't use your power or authority over someone else to your advantage, namely, employee, patient, student, supervisee, and so on. You function as a psychologist to fulfill your professional role and provide a service for which you get reimbursed. You are not entitled to anything else from the other person, even though he or she may be very willing to provide it.[6]

Vignette: For over 25 years, Dr. Robert Guile had been teaching and chairing dissertation committees at a professional school. He prided him-

---

[6]Also see Standards 4.05–4.07 regarding sexual involvement with clients or patients.

self on the good relationships he had with students; he was genuinely willing to befriend them and their families. He frequently invited them to dinner or included them in family outings and sometimes had them babysit and perform other domestic chores such as grocery shopping.

At his office, he assigned tasks to his teaching assistants, such as bringing him coffee, buying flowers or the morning paper, and even washing the windows of his office when they needed it. He also required that his students routinely peruse journals for articles of interest to him, regardless of their needs or interest, for no remuneration.

Occasionally, he engaged in more serious exploitation, such as using data from his students' dissertations in his own publications, without citing his sources or asking the students for permission. On one occasion, he plagiarized part of a chapter from a student's master's thesis without citing it. When the student encountered his article in print and discovered the plagiarism, she brought the matter to him. He informed her coldly that if she wanted to ever receive her doctoral degree, she'd better not publicize this matter. Besides, he reassured her, she could take it as a compliment that his actions represented a tribute to the high quality of her work.

Finally, Dr. Guile disregarded all professional boundaries by using the expertise of the few patients he saw to his own advantage if they had skills that might benefit him. When a lawyer consulted him for depression, Dr. Guile frequently would use part of the hour to seek legal advice about some matter or other. When a stock broker consulted him for panic attacks, the doctor sought inside advice about investments and acted on the tips that his patient gave him.

Dr. Guile had little understanding of the concept of personal exploitation of students or clients. He continued to use others to his own advantage, feeling entitled to do so, until several students brought formal complaints against him after they no longer had any affiliation with the school.

> *(b) Psychologists do not engage in sexual relationships with students or supervisees in training over whom the psychologist has evaluative or direct authority, because such relationships are so likely to impair judgment or be exploitative.*

(b) Do not become sexual with your current students, supervisees, interns, psychological assistants, or anybody else whom you evaluate directly or over whom you hold direct or legal authority.

Vignette: Dr. I. Needer, who was recently widowed, found himself strongly attracted to a new supervisee, Susan. She was more mature than the rest, had (in his opinion) a seductive manner, and had more life experience than the other students. He obsessed about her almost continuously, and during clinical supervision he found himself inquiring about the sexual aspects of her patients' treatment much more than was necessary. Susan made it clear that she too would like to see Dr. Needer "after hours." Soon, pleasantries, sexual innuendoes, and friendly touches opened the door to an intense and intimate relationship.

Dr. Needer was unable to competently maintain his role as her mentor, although he was unaware of his loss of objectivity. With his strong personal feelings for Susan, he could no longer provide an adequate supervisory experience. He was consumed by his own emotional needs, however, and mistakenly believed that he could continue the romantic relationship while remaining objective and rendering competent supervision.

It was many months before the romantic relationship came to an end. With the ending of the academic year, Dr. Needer no longer was interested in continuing the relationship with Susan. Susan felt rejected and depressed by this turn of events, having invested much of herself in this passionate love affair with a man whom she admired so much as an authority figure and who indeed held real power over her at the university. As the months passed and she lost hope of ever regaining his affections, she came to view the entire episode as an abuse of power and to see herself as a victim of a needy man's emotional and sexual exploitation.

1.20 Consultations and Referrals

(a) Psychologists arrange for appropriate consultations and referrals based principally on the best interests of their patients or clients, with appropriate consent, and subject to other relevant considerations, including applicable law and contractual obligations. (See also Standards 5.01, Discussing the Limits of Confidentiality, and 5.06, Consultations.)

(a) Seek professional consultation if the client exceeds your competence or presents issues that are outside your training and experience. Make sure the client knows about this and gives consent if you intend to reveal names or identifying information to the person you are consulting. Also refer individuals and ongoing patients according to their needs and best interests; don't automatically refer everyone to your friends or those in your group practice, unless they possess the required competence. Always remember your formal agreements, your professional role, and state and federal laws when consulting or referring.

Vignette 1:   In the middle of one session, a teenage patient suddenly told Dr. Limmit that she could not remember what had transpired in the office 10 minutes ago. The patient appeared to be confused and troubled by this. She reported that she'd had these lapses for quite a while and said that usually they did not pose a problem. But when it became obvious in the session that she could not follow what Dr. Limmit was discussing, she was compelled to address it. The therapist suspected correctly that this might be symptomatic of a dissociative disorder; but having had little experience in this area, Dr. Limmit decided that it was essential to learn more to be a good resource for this patient. She began supervisory consultations with a senior colleague in town who was experienced in dissociative disorders and began to read about and attend workshops on the topic.

Vignette 2:   Occasionally, a psychologist will encounter a situation in his or her place of employment that may create a conflict with the requirements of this particular standard. This occurred in the case of a human resources psychologist, Dr. Norefer, whose work primarily consisted of assessing new candidates for employment in a large Silicon Valley computer company. Although this ethical standard requires psychologists to make appropriate referrals for clients and patients, it appeared to be countermanded by the professional role the psychologist played at work.

Dr. Norefer was discouraged from referring job applicants he was assessing to a psychotherapist for therapy if, during the course of his assessment, he formed the opinion that the candidate was in need of treatment. This company policy was in effect for three reasons: (a) by serving as a resource person to the candidate in need of treatment, he showed that his objectivity as an evaluator for employment could become diminished; (b) a candidate considering it the company's duty to make a good referral could be dissatisfied with the referred therapist, thereby increasing the company's chances of being targeted for an ethics complaint or lawsuit; and (c) by referring a candidate to a psychologist and attempting to make a good patient–therapist match, the company psychologist would be using time and energy more properly spent on his assessment work.

Dr. Norefer honored this company policy and refrained from making referrals. At times, he encountered job applicants, such as individuals who were alcohol or drug dependent or suffered from other mental disorders, who could have benefited from referrals. However, he was always certain to inform candidates at the outset of the interview that he was unable to make such referrals.

> *(b) When indicated and professionally appropriate, psychologists cooperate with other professionals in order to serve their patients or clients effectively and appropriately.*

(b) Cooperate with other therapists or health care professionals when treating or referring patients.

Vignette: Dr. Connie Sultant, a psychologist working in a behavioral medicine clinic, frequently treated patients who had both psychological symptoms and somatic complaints, such as chronic pain, irritable bowel syndrome, and migraine headaches. She was fastidious about collaborating with referring physicians, such as general practitioners, pain management specialists, neurologists, and other specialists. When Dr. Sultant thought that assessment for psychotropic medication would be helpful, she referred the patient to a psychiatrist, psychopharmacologist, or other qualified health care provider who was knowledgeable about psychopharmacology.

If a patient complained of a new pain or physical symptom, she always referred him or her for a medical assessment rather than making the assumption that the symptom was functional in nature and treatable with psychological interventions. When a patient threatened suicide or behaved in a way that might increase his or her risk of serious harm, she was quick to consider hospitalization as an appropriate intervention.

Dr. Sultant also was scrupulous in responding to phone calls and correspondences from other health care professionals who were providing care for her patients. In keeping within the requirements of this standard, she always attempted to provide timely and effective collaboration when requested by others.

(c) Psychologists' referral practices are consistent with law.

(c) Refer patients and clients and accept referrals from others in a manner that is consistent with law.

Vignette: Dr. Strokem developed a motivational strategy designed to increase colleague referrals. He would send a letter acknowledging the referral along with a gift certificate to a local restaurant for dinner for two to each health care professional who sent him a patient. The gift certificates were worth $80. When the referring doctor lived some distance away, he would simply send the acknowledgment letter along with a $50 bill. He did not know about this ethical standard; neither did he know that his state had a law prohibiting giving or receiving money for patient referrals.

Dr. Strokem was opposed to collaborating with the managed health care system because it had significantly reduced his income. As part of his private way of protesting against managed care, he raised patients' co-payments over and above the contract limit whenever he could get away with it, charging them more than the agreed-on fee. He justified this practice by informing patients that he was providing longer sessions than the usual 50-minute ones (an extra 10 minutes), hence the copayments would be slightly higher. This practice was not legal, however, and was certainly outside the limits of the contractual agreement with the managed care company because extended sessions were coded with the same current procedural terminology (CPT) code as regular 50-minute sessions.

It was only a matter of time until people complained about his unethical and fraudulent business practices, namely for both reimbursing those who referred patients to him and raising the copayment fee for managed care patients. He eventually was required to face the serious consequences of his flagrant disregard for ethical and legal standards pertaining to the business aspects of his practice.

1.21 Third-Party Requests for Services

(a) When a psychologist agrees to provide services to a person or entity at the request of a third party, the psychologist clarifies to the extent feasible, at the outset of the service, the nature of the relationship with each party. This clarification includes the role of the psychologist (such as therapist, organizational consultant, diagnostician, or expert witness), the probable uses of the services provided or the information obtained, and the fact that there may be limits to confidentiality.

(a) If you are asked to perform therapy, assessment, or some other psychological service by a third party (e.g., a parent, teacher, referring physician, human resources office, court, commanding officer), make sure that each party understands at the outset (a) what your role will be, (b) how the services or information you provide will be used, and (c) any limitations to confidentiality or privacy. Although not required by this standard, it may be wise to make use of printed handouts or correspondence and record all this information in your patient records.

Vignette: Dr. Tiu Yung was contacted by a recently divorced father of an 11-year-old girl who was depressed. The father did not share physical or legal custody of his daughter, but he wanted Dr. Yung to assess her and provide therapy if needed. Unfortunately, however, Dr. Yung could not meet with the daughter because of a state law requiring that consent for psychological services must be obtained from the legal guardian of a minor. Because the girl's mother had sole legal custody, she alone could authorize treatment. Dr. Yung informed the father that the girl's mother would have to either initiate the request or at least document her agreement with it.

Even though she would not necessarily be providing services to the daughter, Dr. Yung decided to address some of the broader issues facing the father because he had many questions about how treatment might proceed. She informed the father about her policy of confidentiality with minors and about phone calls or other inquiries from the father or mother about ongoing treatment, if it were to take place. She also gave a balanced presentation about the advisability of joint sessions with one parent or the other and the pros and cons of collaboration with the father's therapist if he were willing to permit it.

Dr. Yung had several printed handouts on these topics, which she agreed to send the father after speaking with him on the telephone. She began the process of providing good informed consent, with an appreciation for the complexity of the family's needs. She attempted to clarify many important issues in her conversation with the father concerning ethical, legal, professional, and clinical matters, but she was careful to avoid offering professional advice or opinions about the family or any of its members.

> *(b) If there is a foreseeable risk of the psychologist's being called upon to perform conflicting roles because of the involvement of a third party, the psychologist clarifies the nature and direction of his or her responsibilities, keeps all parties appropriately informed as matters develop, and resolves the situation in accordance with this Ethics Code.*

(b) If you anticipate being in a conflicting role because of a third party, be sure to clarify the nature and direction of your responsibilities and do so on a continuing basis as the need may arise, in accordance with this code.

Vignette: Dr. Yung also worked part time as the consulting psychologist for the staff of a small electronics company, providing a range of psychological services (e.g., communication skills training, group relaxation training). One day, the CEO, Mr. Frankly, called Dr. Yung into his large office and asked her to give her opinion about the mental health and competence of a particular employee she was treating. Several employees had complained to the CEO about the abusive manner of this departmental manager and the constant smell of alcohol on his breath.

Dr. Yung carefully considered her role within the corporate structure. She served as the only psychologist on staff and as an individual psychotherapist for some of the employees. She weighed her duty to her patient and the departmental manager against her duty to her employer, Mr. Frankly, and took into account the safety risks posed by an alcohol dependent manager.

Dr. Yung had never formally discussed with Mr. Frankly her role as a therapist within the organization or the potential for conflicts in attempting to carry out her clinical responsibilities. She took this opportunity to inform him about various aspects of her professional role and obligations and her duties as she saw them, namely, to provide individual treatment to employees as needed and to refer chemically dependent clients to a 12-step program or alcohol treatment rehabilitation program. She also informed him about the concept of privileged communication and the protection offered by legal statutes governing the communications between psychologists and their patients. She reminded him that under the law, she was prohibited from disclosing any information about a patient, unless that patient signed a consent form authorizing such disclosures. Furthermore, she explained there were many good reasons to protect patient disclosures, not the least of which was that she might lose her effectiveness if patients could not trust her to keep their confidences.

Ultimately, of course, she refused to disclose information that Mr. Frankly had requested about the employee in question. Although disappointed that he was unable to obtain the information from Dr. Yung, Mr. Frankly did understand her rationale and ultimately agreed with it despite his initial opinion to the contrary.

1.22 Delegation to and Supervision of Subordinates

> *(a) Psychologists delegate to their employees, supervisees, and research assistants only those responsibilities that such persons can reasonably be expected to perform competently, on the basis of their education, training, or experience, either independently or with the level of supervision being provided.*

(a) Whenever you delegate professional responsibilities to others or supervise their professional activities, make sure that they are competent according to their education, training, or experience. Know the skill level of your supervisees, research assistants, or employees because both you and they could be vulnerable to a complaint from a dissatisfied person. In addition to possibly harming others, there could be grave legal, scientific, and professional consequences for you in any psychological role you play, such as researcher (e.g., threats to the validity of your data, future funding), clinician (e.g., civil lawsuits, malpractice insurance), or academician (e.g., formal grievance, academic standing), to name a few.

Vignette: As the owner of a large, interdisciplinary group practice, Dr. Cagey, an aggressive entrepreneur, paid his employees for their professional services. However, he was only minimally aware of their skills and training and did little to monitor them. As referrals decreased over the years, the income of the business also declined, leaving some staff members with a very small caseload. More concerned about the financial success of his personal friends on staff than the company as a whole, Dr. Cagey frequently carried out the task of in-house patient referrals based on the welfare of his associates rather than that of the patients. For example, he referred patients in need of psychological testing to his closest friend on the staff, a clinical social worker, who actually had little formal training in assessment. He also routinely referred patients for bio-feedback training to one of his psychological assistants, an unlicensed practitioner accruing supervisory hours toward licensure, whose entire biofeedback training consisted of a 2-hour seminar at a convention and no follow-up supervision or training in carrying out biofeedback with patients.

By consistently referring individuals to his personal friends, who often happened to be less than minimally competent at providing needed services, Dr. Cagey was placing patients at risk of receiving a poor quality of service or being harmed. He thought that his obligations to carry out the administrative work of the group practice and to vigorously promote their psychological services within the community took precedence over consultative or supervisory duties or any obligation to make careful in-house referrals. Unfortunately, several patients were significantly damaged by Dr. Cagey's lax referral policies and eventually brought formal complaints against the unlicensed practitioner and Dr. Cagey himself.

One case involved a child custody dispute. Both parents were formally assessed by one of Dr. Cagey's employees, resulting in a report submitted to the court. However, the psychologist doing the assessment had used improper and biased methods while evaluating the family and wrote a report that was not objective or comprehensive. The litigation was prolonged due to the problematical psychological report, nearly resulting in a decision by the court to award sole custody to the less competent parent.

Another case involved a clinically depressed cancer patient with pain and nausea from chemotherapy. The patient was referred by a social worker on the oncology team for biofeedback training to help manage her physical discomfort and anticipatory anxiety about further treatment. Dr. Cagey referred the patient to his psychological assistant and subsequently took little interest in her treatment. Unfortunately, the psychological assistant's theoretical approach in the application of biofeedback was unsophisticated and rather mechanistic. He overlooked her significant depressive and anxious symptomology and proceeded directly with electro-myographic and thermal training on the biofeedback equipment. The patient did poorly with biofeedback, failed to practice at home on her own, became increasingly despondent, and eventually dropped out of treatment after 3 weeks.

Dr. Cagey's irresponsible practices not only resulted in harm to many individuals consulting his employees but also contributed to the further decline in the financial health of his group practice. He learned too late that an extensive working knowledge of his employees' competence and ongoing monitoring of unlicensed employees is essential whenever professional duties are delegated to subordinates.

> *(b) Psychologists provide proper training and supervision to their employees or supervisees and take reasonable steps to see that such persons perform services responsibly, competently, and ethically.*

(b) Always take the time and effort to carry out supervision adequately, with regularly scheduled meetings, to ensure competence and responsibility in your employees and supervisees.

Vignette: Dr. Lenore Wiser was the clinical supervisor of several psychological assistants in a large, county hospital outpatient clinic. She was consistent in scheduling weekly 1-hour supervisory sessions with each one, in spite of her many administrative and clinical duties, and she screened and monitored their patient loads meticulously. She also kept comprehensive notes about every supervisory session and carefully tracked each patient the assistants saw in therapy.

Dr. Wiser was alert to the personal issues, conflicts, and countertransference reactions of her supervisees that would surface periodically when they worked with particularly challenging patients. She was available for telephone consultations during the week, if needed, or emergency consultations on evenings or weekends should they occur. When she was out of town or otherwise unavailable, she was fastidious about letting her supervisees know in advance and obtaining someone to provide coverage for her if needed.

Dr. Wiser considered it important to provide trainees with a diversity of learning experiences, including suggested attendance at psychiatry grand round presentations and clinical staff meetings, referring them to relevant journal articles and books, and exposing them to other learning experiences. She took her mentoring responsibilities seriously and felt that she too grew professionally in the process.

> *(c) If institutional policies, procedures, or practices prevent fulfillment of this obligation, psychologists attempt to modify their role or to correct the situation to the extent feasible.*

(c) If you find that the policy, structure, or functioning of your institution prohibits the proper supervision of employees and others for whom you are responsible, make an attempt to correct the situation. After all, patients or others could be harmed and you could be held responsible.

Vignette: One of Dr. Cagey's employees, Dr. Amelia Lesser, was a young, unlicensed postdoctoral intern who was accumulating supervisory hours so that she would be eligible for the licensing exam. She was expected to work with virtually all patients assigned to her, according to the contract she had signed. Frequently, she saw over 35 patients per week, many of them on evenings and weekends, and was beginning to feel the stress of such a demanding schedule. She had little time to pursue her friendships, social engagements, or other activities, which would bring some balance into her life.

One of Dr. Lesser's patients, Mr. Clinger—a 46-year-old man who was dependent and narcissistic—was in the final stages of ending his marriage of 15 years when he began to develop romantic feelings for her. This evoked some countertransference reactions in her because she had also experienced some recent losses. Her father had died unexpectedly just 2 months before, and her fiancé had broken a long and ambivalent engagement 1 month before her father's death.

When Dr. Lesser sought additional supervisory time with Dr. Cagey to discuss these developments, he refused, suggesting that she study the APA Ethics Code if she wanted guidance on the issue of professional boundaries. He claimed that he was too busy with the administrative duties of running the practice to allocate additional time for her supervision. He also pointedly reminded her of her contractual obligations and rejected her request that she be permitted to refer the patient to another therapist, possibly a man, who was outside the group practice. Such a blatant disregard of her professional needs was unsettling to Dr. Lesser, and she began to have grave misgivings about her supervisor's competence and ethical integrity.

Late one evening, following a particularly difficult therapy session with Mr. Clinger, the patient asked Dr. Lesser if she would like to join him for a quick cup of coffee in the all-night coffee shop on the lobby level of the building. Dr. Lesser was feeling the stress of a very long work day, and she was physically and emotionally exhausted. In a moment of poor judgment, she agreed, yielding to the need to have some relaxation and companionship. She sat with Mr. Clinger for 35 minutes in the coffee shop, sharing some of her recent stresses, namely, the death of her father, the loss of her fiancé, and, to some extent, her resulting depression. She found Mr. Clinger to be quite understanding and comforting as she stepped out of her therapist's role and spoke with him as she might with a friend.

During the next few days, Dr. Lesser began to develop an awareness of the complications inherent in the changing relationship with her patient. She was beginning to rely on him to meet some of her emotional needs, and she began to view him more as a potential friend than a consumer of her services. This resulted in an increasing degree of personal conflict in her therapeutic work with him, and she felt compelled to discuss the situation with her own therapist because Dr. Cagey was essentially unavailable.

During the following week, Dr. Lesser came to the decision that she could no longer continue to work with Mr. Clinger in treatment; the social roles of friend and therapist had become hopelessly intertwined, with frequent phone calls and email messages between office visits. She also realized that she did not wish to remain in a work setting where her supervision was negligent and she was expected to shoulder responsibilities for which she felt unprepared. This was a sound, although extremely difficult decision for Dr. Lesser from a professional, financial, and emotional standpoint. She had made every reasonable attempt to change the situation and obtain adequate supervision but clearly was unable to have an impact on Dr. Cagey's unethical practices.

Several months after leaving the practice and establishing herself with another supervisor, Dr. Lesser initiated a formal ethics complaint against her former employer for his blatant disregard of his professional obligations concerning supervision.

1.23 Documentation of Professional and Scientific Work

> (a) Psychologists appropriately document their professional and scientific work in order to facilitate provision of services later by them or by other professionals, to ensure accountability, and to meet other requirements of institutions or the law.

(a) Maintain a written record of your professional work to help with the continuity of services by yourself or others at a later time and to have a record of your activities if ever questioned. Keep all consent forms, history sheets, raw test data, inducements to cooperate in research, and any other documents that could have a bearing on your work. Also bear in mind that documenting your work may be required by law or by your institution (hospital, university, mental health center, etc.).[7]

Vignette: Dr. Michael Wings worked in the human resources department of a commercial airline company. He routinely interviewed and assessed managers and staff and had records for over 850 employees.

Occasionally, a dispute arose regarding the quality of an employee's work, the competence of a supervisor, or a delay in promotion. Dr. Wings would be called on to facilitate the situation at times; on other occasions, he would be expected to know facts about the employees involved and the facts being disputed. Because he kept good records of his formal assessments of employees, he could readily rely on them to help in resolving the conflict. Employees whom he had evaluated were routinely provided informed consent at the time of assessment about the limits of confidentiality and the likely use of assessment results within the organization.

Dr. Wings had discovered long ago that thorough documentation was indispensable to the careful tracking of so many employees over long periods of time. On those occasions when he was asked to testify in civil proceedings, his records proved to be an invaluable resource.

> (b) When psychologists have reason to believe that records of their professional services will be used in legal proceedings involving recipients of or participants in their work, they have a responsibility to create and maintain documentation in the kind of detail and quality that would be consistent with reasonable scrutiny in an adjudicative forum. (See also Standard 7.01, Professionalism, under Forensic Activities.)

---

[7]See also Standard 5.09, Preserving Records and Data, and Standard 1.26, Accuracy in Reports to Payors and Funding Sources.

(b) If your records are likely to be used in legal proceedings or you are expected to testify in court (e.g., child custody, mental competency assessments), be certain that they are sufficient in detail and scope to be useful for the purpose at hand.

Vignette: Dr. Sterling Reddy was consulted by a depressed, angry executive secretary who complained of ongoing sexual harassment by her boss, who was also the owner of the company. She was considering contacting an attorney to initiate a civil suit, claiming that she had suffered much anguish over the previous year from his crude jokes, inappropriate staring, and touching, regardless of her requests that he stop.

Dr. Reddy knew that it was likely that he might ultimately be asked to testify as to the probable harm that his patient may have suffered as a result of continuing to work in such a stressful setting. Therefore, he was scrupulously thorough and comprehensive in creating case notes, knowing that he would likely be referring to them during the course of litigation at a future time.

One day 16 months later, he received a valid subpoena from the secretary's attorney. He was expected to appear with all his psychological records for a deposition. After contacting the secretary, now his former patient, he asked that she sign a consent form, formally allowing him to release his records and discuss her history in open court. She gladly complied, hoping that her therapist's testimony would help substantiate her claims of suffering reactive depression from enduring her boss's harassment, which required treatment by a psychologist.

In the course of responding to direct and cross examination, Dr. Reddy was able to faithfully reconstruct his client's presenting complaints, diagnosis, and course of treatment and describe his impressions of the stress the secretary reported in her workplace, even though much time had elapsed since treating her. He could also recount specific instances of alleged abuse, which she had described to him during treatment. He was pleased about the extra care he had taken in documenting her therapy because it increased his credibility as a witness, allowing him to provide accurate information in a well-ordered fashion.

1.24 Records and Data

Psychologists create, maintain, disseminate, store, retain, and dispose of records and data relating to their research, practice, and other work in accordance with law and in a manner that permits compliance with the requirements of this Ethics Code. (See also Standard 5.04, Maintenance of Records.)

You must obey state and federal laws and this Ethics Code in documenting your work. It is essential to create a written record of your professional activities, keeping it safely stored, releasing it appropriately to others, and ultimately destroying it. This is for the benefit of your patients, clients, research participants, and also for you (e.g., in the case of an ethics complaint, litigation, a board of psychology investigation). Remember, secretaries and other clerical support staff are not bound by this Ethics Code; however, you are responsible for training them to comply.

Vignette: A neuropsychologist who was very careful about creating and maintaining her records for the number of years required by state law kept them locked in file cabinets in her office. She filed them by termination date so that she could easily access them when the time was right for their destruction. However, she was very conscious of preserving natural resources, so when it came to actually disposing of the records, she would dump them into a huge bin at the city's recycling center. Her rationale was that "such a mountain of paper would never be of interest to anyone," and that disposing of them in this fashion was as good as shredding them.

Unfortunately, several teenagers who worked at the recycling center were quite interested in these regular deposits and would paw through her obsolete records with great interest whenever they had the chance. Occasionally, they came across an old assessment of someone they knew. On one occasion, they uncovered the records belonging to the daughter of one of their teachers at the high school.

Needless to say, this was a high-risk practice and a foolish way to dispose of confidential psychological records. Although the psychologist was probably correct that in the majority of cases nobody cared to dig through this mass of paper and read these private assessments, the worst-case scenario did come true, as it sometimes can. The neuropsychologist would have been wise to invest in a shredder, burn her records, or otherwise permanently dispose of them.

1.25 Fees and Financial Arrangements

> *(a) As early as is feasible in a professional or scientific relationship, the psychologist and the patient, client, or other appropriate recipient of psychological services reach an agreement specifying the compensation and the billing arrangements.*

(a) Inform clients and patients about your fees and payment policies early in the professional relationship. It also may be wise, although not required, to use printed handouts or signed consent forms to reduce any uncertainty about financial obligations.

Vignette: Before meeting with a new patient or client for the first time, Dr. Gold routinely sent out an informational brochure that clearly described his psychological services and his policies about fees and financial arrangements. In this brochure, he attempted to anticipate consumers' questions and clarify potential uncertainties or misunderstandings about the business aspects of his practice well before they could become problematic. He had learned from experience that inadequate disclosure about fees and payment policies or simply inaccurate assumptions by him or his patients could lead to significant disappointment or disruptions in the treatment at a future point in time.

The information he presented in his brochure included the following:

1. fee structure for each psychological service (e.g., clinical services, assessment, consultation)
2. requirement that fees and copayments are due when the service is rendered, unless other provisions are made
3. policy of sending out monthly itemized statements
4. review of managed health care issues and obligations
5. telephone and email availability and fees for these services
6. policies regarding canceling of appointments and the time frame required to avoid being charged
7. handling of missed appointments
8. fees for providing written reports and consultations to third parties.

When a patient arrives for his or her first session, Dr. Gold would commonly review the above information in the office and explore any questions or misunderstandings that may have arisen. In many cases, some of the information, such as adjustments in fee or changes in the payment schedule, would already have been discussed on the phone. At other times, it was necessary to devote office time to negotiating these matters to reach an agreement that was acceptable to both parties. As a result of this policy of thorough informed consent about fees and financial arrangements, Dr. Gold rarely encountered a client who was surprised or dissatisfied with the business aspects of his practice.

> *(b) Psychologists do not exploit recipients of services or payors with respect to fees.*

(b) Don't exploit your patients or others who are responsible for funding your clinical, consulting, or research activities.

Vignette: Dr. Will Billem had a standard fee for all new patients, with some flexibility for those who were on a tighter budget. However, whenever he received patients referred by the chronic pain center of a nearby hospital, he characteristically charged a higher fee because he was well aware of these patients' intense physical suffering, accompanying depression, and high motivation to achieve psychological relief. His justification for such a practice was that these patients required additional time and energy on his part because their psychological and physiological problems were frequently intertwined, resulting in additional diagnostic and treatment considerations. He also knew that their medical and psychological care was generally financed by third-party payors, so that paying a higher fee often would not constitute a problem for them.

Also when treating wealthy patients who were not relying on a third-party payor, Dr. Billem still attempted to charge a higher fee. The only justification he made in these instances was that the wealthy could afford to pay a fee reflective of the true worth of the services that he rendered; he felt that he "deserved" such remuneration in light of the high quality of his care.

Dr. Billem's fee schedule clearly was exploitative of wealthy individuals, those suffering chronic pain, and third-party payors in that he allowed his rates to be determined privately by the amount of available resources. Lowering his rates below a standard fee in response to a patient's financial need was discretionary and legal. However, raising his rates above a standard fee for a wealthy patient or third-party payor with ample resources was considered to be exploitative and illegal (i.e., insurance fraud). His unethical practices were finally exposed when two of his patients who happened to be good friends, one with average financial resources and one who was wealthy, discovered that they were being charged markedly different fees for the same service and same expenditure of time. They decided to bring a formal complaint against him by contacting the state board of psychology with this information.

(c) Psychologists' fee practices are consistent with law.

(c) Obey the law, managed care contracts, and hospital or group practice agreements concerning fees and copayments, or else you may be guilty of insurance fraud, breach of contract, or some other illegality.

Vignette: When the state board of psychology investigated Dr. Billem's business practices, it discovered that he had been engaging in many illegal activities over a considerable period of time. For instance, he routinely billed third-party payors, such as Medicare and various managed health care companies, for psychotherapy sessions that never occurred. For example, if a patient cancelled late or failed to show up for an appointment, which insurance would not reimburse, Dr. Billem would simply indicate on the health claim insurance form that a session took place, with the proper date and corresponding CPT code number for a therapy session. He felt entitled to take such a measure because he informed his patients of his policy requiring a 24-hour notice to cancel appointments without being charged. In this way, Dr. Billem would receive his fee for the missed session and the patient would not have to pay for it. A complaint was unlikely (if indeed a patient was even aware of the fraudulent billing) because the patient had been spared having to pay for the missed session.

Dr. Billem engaged in additional fraudulent billing by claiming that a telephone consultation with a patient in crisis was really an office visit. Again, telephone consultations are not covered by most managed care policies, but they were a significant part of Dr. Billem's work. He knew that patients would use this medium less often if they were required to pay for the calls.

The psychology board's investigation also revealed Dr. Billem's practice of claiming that couple sessions or family sessions were really individual consultations whenever these were not reimbursable under managed care contracts. Again, this necessitated writing inaccurate CPT codes on the billing statements and violated both the Ethics Code and state law. Finally, Dr. Billem frequently misidentified certain procedures to guarantee payment under a particular managed care contract. If an intervention such as hypnosis for pain management or smoking cessation was not a service reimbursable under the terms of the contract, he relabeled it *psychotherapy*. Conversely, if biofeedback training was not covered but hypnotherapy was, he identified the treatment as *hypnotherapy*.

Dr. Billem had engaged in systematic fraudulent business practices consisting of the erroneous reporting of diagnostic codes and procedural codes to increase his income from managed care companies. Although he may have felt entitled to do so and knew that he was sparing his patients additional expense even when they had the resources to pay, he continuously violated the law, his contract with the managed care companies, and the Ethics Code in the process.

(d) Psychologists do not misrepresent their fees.

(d) Describe your fee structure accurately.

Vignette: Dr. Gold, in contrast to Dr. Billem, always described his fee scale for patients orally and sent a printed form to them before the initial session. Patients knew approximately what would be required of them financially before beginning their consultations. He generally reviewed his expectations about payment at the first session and discussed any exceptions to his policies with those in financial need.

With students, lower income patients, or those on disability, he frequently lowered his fee when his personal finances could accommodate such a measure. He also made attempts to find other creative but ethical ways of managing the financial aspects of his practice when patients could not afford his regular fee. This might include such departures from his customary procedures as offering extended sessions for the same fee as his regular 50-minute sessions, shorter sessions for a commensurably lower fee, less frequent meetings than his usual weekly therapy sessions, or cautiously considered barter for goods (see Standard 1.18). He might also suggest that a patient try supplementing less frequent individual sessions by participating in a lower cost or free group intervention (e.g., 12-step program, men's or women's support group).

He also informed patients at the outset about his policy of an annual fee increase that roughly paralleled the rate of inflation, unless, of course, such an increase constituted a hardship for the patient. Dr. Gold went well beyond the mandates of this standard in attending to patient welfare concerning fees and financial matters by carefully providing clear information and discussing any concerns about payment at the time of first contact, regardless of the patient's initiative.

(e) If limitations to services can be anticipated because of limitations in financing, this is discussed with the patient, client, or other appropriate

recipient of services as early as is feasible. (See also Standard 4.08, Interruption of Services.)

(e) If you must limit your services because of a client's or patient's inability to pay or other restrictions (e.g., managed health care, available funding), discuss this and the implications of these restrictions at the outset.

Vignette: A young woman experiencing paranoid thoughts and much anxiety began therapy with Dr. Plannow for relief of her distress and for relaxation training for her stressful symptoms of irritable bowel syndrome. The case manager of her managed health care system had only preauthorized five sessions, although there was a possibility that additional sessions could be authorized when the woman completed these.

Dr. Plannow carefully discussed with his patient the problems of attempting to begin treatment of such complexity, consisting of anxiety disorder, paranoid thoughts, and a diagnosed medical disorder, when only five sessions were currently allocated. He attempted to help the patient prioritize her goals for treatment and to examine the possible relationship, if any, among her presenting complaints. They discussed the overall goals of their sessions and reasonable expectations of what could be accomplished in the time allotted.

Together, they also reviewed the process of collaborating with the case manager, including the necessity of filing outpatient treatment progress reports at regular intervals and the losses in confidentiality entailed by such a practice. Dr. Plannow also informed his patient about the process of formally seeking additional sessions and the possibility that none would be forthcoming. They then discussed some alternate possibilities if, in fact, therapy was not funded beyond the initial five sessions.

Dr. Plannow was very familiar with the constraints of being on a managed care panel of providers, often experiencing resistance to allocating additional sessions when asked and truncating the therapy at the end of the authorized number of sessions. He also was quite familiar with the formal process of seeking additional sessions. He knew well the importance of at least making an attempt to formally appeal such a decision, even when the case manager was resistant to any further consideration of extending treatment.

When considering a treatment plan for his patient, Dr. Plannow took into account the risk of failing to make such an appeal, when the time might come, and the patient's dynamics. Certainly, if it was in the patient's best interest, it was always wise to formally seek additional sessions and appeal a case manager's denial. If a patient felt that the therapist was not sufficiently proactive in seeking additional sessions and was prone to be litigious later on, then it was crucial to communicate to him or her that every reasonable step had been taken in the appeal process. Dr. Plannow met his patient's expectations by discussing the implications of the likelihood that sufficient sessions would not be allocated to meet all of her goals. As therapy progressed, they occasionally referred back to this conversation and reevaluated their objectives, keeping in mind the extent of therapy authorized by the case manager.

> *(f) If the patient, client, or other recipient of services does not pay for services as agreed, and if the psychologist wishes to use collection agencies or legal measures to collect the fees, the psychologist first informs the person that such measures will be taken and provides that person an opportunity to make prompt payment. (See also Standard 5.11, Withholding Records for Nonpayment.)*

(f) If a former patient refuses to pay your bill and you are thinking of using a collection agency, attorney, or small claims court to obtain payment, make sure that you notify him or her in writing well in advance of taking additional action to collect the debt. Give such patients a final chance to pay before they are contacted by a third party.

Vignette: Dr. Thunder rarely gave or sent billing or receipt statements to his patients because he wished to minimize his clerical work. He made this clear at the beginning of treatment, as he did with his policy that patients must pay in full at the time of the session or do so at the last session of each month.

On one occasion, Lester, a patient of Dr. Thunder's for 3 months, who generally was scrupulous about paying by the end the month, ended treatment on the last day of the month without paying. Because of recent unexpected expenses for automobile repairs, he wished to stop treatment for several months and begin again when he was more financially solvent. His balance due at that time was $360.

At first, Dr. Thunder accepted this plan and agreed that the reasonable course of action was to allow payment to be deferred until Lester could again afford therapy. After 5 weeks went by and there was no communication from Lester, Dr. Thunder became concerned that his patient might simply be attempting to avoid paying his balance altogether. Because he was quite busy with other projects at work and did not wish to take the time to personally contact Lester, Dr. Thunder delegated that task to his attorney, Mr. Will Gogettum.

Mr. Gogettum sent a strongly worded letter with a menacing tone 6 weeks after Lester terminated with Dr. Thunder. This letter threatened civil action in small claims court if full payment was not made in 3 weeks.

Lester was out of town when the letter arrived, having traveled a great distance to his home state to assist his older father who was recovering from recent surgery. After returning and discovering the attorney's letter, he became extremely upset and felt somewhat betrayed by his therapist, who had been a good resource to him in the past. He intended to pay his overdue bill in its entirety but was currently facing other more urgent, unexpected expenses in addition to his automobile repair bills. He dutifully telephoned Dr. Thunder, explained the situation, and requested another extension. Dr. Thunder apologized for the letter from the attorney and quickly granted the extension. Unfortunately, however, Lester already had lost faith in his therapist, thinking that he was more concerned about money than providing a service. Lester never returned for treatment.

Such an outcome could have been avoided had Dr. Thunder simply attempted to contact Lester himself, instead of delegating the task to his attorney, and inquired about his welfare and financial circumstances. Certainly, consistent with the spirit of this ethical standard, he bore an obligation to at least inform Lester that his policy was to use the services of a collection agency or an attorney if payment was not made in a timely fashion. Thus, he would be providing his patient the opportunity to make a payment or propose a payment plan before engaging the services of a third party for collection.

1.26 Accuracy in Reports to Payors and Funding Sources

> *In their reports to payors for services or sources of research funding, psychologists accurately state the nature of the research or service provided, the fees or charges, and where applicable, the identity of the provider, the findings, and the diagnosis. (See also Standard 5.05, Disclosures.)*

Don't lie or distort information you provide to third-party payors and funding sources. State honestly your fees, expenses, and the nature of the research or service provided, and furnish other accurate information as requested.

Vignette: Because she had been participating in managed health care panels for over 8 years, Dr. Truesdale had noticed a more restrictive trend in operating policies, which resulted in adverse consequences for her and her patients. This included a lower number of allocated sessions per year, a tendency to restrict sessions for Axis II disorders, and reduced reimbursement or none for certain services, such as marital and family therapy and hypnosis. She also noticed more invasiveness in the required treatment progress reports and negative responses on the part of case managers. In particular, there was a tendency by some case managers to suggest interventions or approaches that would supposedly expedite treatment, despite the lack of research data to support such approaches. However, Dr. Truesdale considered the welfare of her patients had paramount importance and resisted pressure from case managers to promote supposedly expeditious forms of treatment that were lacking in validation.

She was scrupulous about her billing practices and was quick to adopt the most current technological advances in this regard; she had been using electronic billing to communicate with insurance companies almost since its inception and rarely made errors in her statements. On those occasions when a session was missed without formal cancellation or when she conducted a telephone session, she always identified them as such in her billing statements, even though she knew that no reimbursement would be forthcoming from the managed care company.

There were times, however, when Dr. Truesdale struggled with the temptation to file inaccurate reports to benefit her patients, such as exaggerating the suicide potential or dangerousness of an individual. She also wondered about reporting only a partial diagnosis, such as panic disorder or alcohol dependence, and omitting diagnoses for personality disorders, for which there would be less likelihood of allocating a sufficient number of sessions. Furthermore, she considered omitting the diagnosis of chronic pain (for which psychotherapy or hypnosis would not have been reimbursed under *psychological services* but would have been covered as a *medical service* if performed by a physician or psychiatrist). She weighed the benefits and risks of substituting a diagnosis that reflected an adjustment or mood disorder instead of chronic pain. In this way, her patient would have been able to afford treatment for chronic pain.

Ultimately, Dr. Truesdale decided to accurately report all diagnoses and treatment codes and to press for additional sessions, when needed, by using the formal procedures available to panel providers. She regularly discussed with case managers the ethical and clinical issues concerning disallowing treatment for certain clients and, when appropriate, would put her thoughts in writing and encourage patients to do likewise by way of formally appealing a decision.

Although carrying out these activities was time consuming, Dr. Truesdale considered it essential to adhere to a policy of accuracy and honesty in disclosures in conformance with this standard, thereby maintaining her professional integrity. She also thought that it was important to promote interest among colleagues about challenging and changing a system that seemed to fail so frequently at meeting patient needs.

On the other side of town, a distant colleague of Dr. Truesdale, Dr. I. Pocket, was developing an outreach program for preteens who belonged to a socioeconomic group at high risk for drug abuse. He was the director of a small nonprofit organization (IRS Category 501C3) and would routinely create grants to be submitted to large corporations and government agencies. Over the years, his efforts resulted in funds for many projects, and he generally was regarded as quite successful at grantsmanship. Others did not know, however, that his tendency was to take occasional risks by engaging in fraudulent practices involving grants. Because he was well aware that funding sources are more likely to award money requested when matching funds are also available, Dr. Pocket indicated on grant applications that such was the case, even though it was untrue. By so doing, he hoped to increase the odds that his project would be funded.

More egregiously, he attempted to acquire large sums of money for his personal use by covertly submitting the identical grant proposal for the same project to various corporations simultaneously, without indicating the existence of other possible funding sources on the proposals. Such "double dipping" into the resource pool required that he engage in elaborately fraudulent accounting procedures in case he had to respond to grant contract compliance requests at the conclusion of the funded project. By doing so, he was putting himself and the organization at grave risk.

Such unethical and illegal activities carry severe penalties, and with increased vigilance among funding sources to such abuses, the odds of getting caught are greater. However, Dr. Pocket enjoyed the risk and the remuneration that accompanied it. His grossly fraudulent practices in grantsmanship were discovered, and they resulted in civil and criminal penalties that significantly effected him and his institution.

1.27 Referrals and Fees

When a psychologist pays, receives payment from, or divides fees with another professional other than in an employer–employee relationship, the payment to each is based on the services (clinical, consultative, administrative, or other) provided and is not based on the referral itself.

Never pay anyone or accept payment from another for a referral for psychological services.[8]

Vignette: Dr. Bribermann had a multifaceted practice providing consultation to various electronic firms in the Boston suburbs and providing clinical services at his downtown office. He was eager to expand his clinical practice and thought that this goal would be well served by reimbursing each individual in his client firms who referred therapy patients to him from outside sources (i.e., friends or associates that were not connected to the firm). His practice was to send $100 to anyone who successfully referred patients to him for treatment; this included individuals such as the CEO, CFO, managers, or anyone else in the firm who had consulted him and was aware of his clinical expertise and interest.

Most of the referrals made in this fashion were limited to affluent individuals able to pay for psychological services directly without relying on managed health care. Dr. Bribermann thought that his "rebate" policy was a small price to pay "up front" for rapidly generating a referral base that would allow him to avoid completely the managed health care system and its limitations and reduced fees.

He was unaware of the ethical rule that flatly prohibited the practice of providing payment to individuals making referrals for his professional services. This had been an ethical proscription for many years within APA, but Dr. Bribermann never knew about the rule or considered its implications for protecting consumers from potential harm. He also was unaware of the Massachusetts state law that similarly prohibited either giving or receiving commissions or rebates in exchange for referrals for psychological services.

Selecting a therapist may be a difficult task at best for most individuals, fraught with pitfalls of misinformation, persuasive advertising, and biased or bad advice. The process is made even more complex by those covertly reinforcing referral sources through monetary compensation to encourage a patient to seek treatment with a certain individual, regardless of that individual's competence. By asking those who consulted him at the electronics firms to refer patients and then offering them a "kickback," Dr. Bribermann was engaging in a practice that encouraged consumers to seek his services without informing them of the incentive system that strongly encouraged the referral. It is likely that there were psychotherapists in the area who might have been better choices for certain consumers; they may have been more competent to treat certain disorders than Dr. Bri-

---

[8]See also Standard 1.20, Consultations and Referrals.

bermann. But potential consumers were unlikely to seek out other therapists because they were, in effect, being referred to "the highest (and only) bidder" while remaining unaware that any "bidding" was going on in the first place. This lack of informed consent for the referral process placed some patients at a distinct disadvantage. These patients required the services of a psychologist who was more competent that Dr. Bribermann but were told, instead, that Dr. Bribermann was skilled at treating all psychological disorders.

Dr. Bribermann's referral incentive resulted in substandard therapy for the patient who might actually be harmed by his interventions or simply waste his or her money on fees for useless consultations. This serious breach of ethics was remedied one day when a potential patient discovered that a payment was made for his referral from an offhand remark made by his friend who gave him Dr. Bribermann's name. That potential patient telephoned the Massachusetts Psychological Association to inquire about this practice and was informed of its unethicality. From this inquiry, a formal complaint ensued against Bribermann, triggering an investigation and ultimately resulting in a sanction from the committee and the requirement that he end this harmful business practice.

2

Evaluation, Assessment, or Intervention

2.01 Evaluation, Diagnosis, and Interventions in Professional Context

(a) Psychologists perform evaluations, diagnostic services, or interventions only within the context of a defined professional relationship. (See also Standards 1.03, Professional and Scientific Relationship.)

(a) Carry out psychological assessments, diagnoses, and interventions only in a defined professional relationship.

Vignette: Dr. Balm was the human resources director for an office furniture company. It was his custom to administer objective and projective tests "in a natural, comfortable setting," as he put it, and he frequently could be found giving a structured clinical interview in a local, quiet restaurant, outside in a park, or even in the employee lounge area during the afternoon. He had little regard for formality. He felt that it interfered with the psychologist–employee relationship and created an artificial barrier in the communication.

Occasionally, he would perform covert evaluations of employees and managers while they were eating lunch in the cafeteria. In this way, he reasoned, he "could observe minimal cues and social interactions that otherwise would be unavailable." When providing counseling to employees or evaluating them for possible reassignments to other positions or plants, he did not believe in providing structure to the session at the outset because, he thought, it tended to increase defensiveness in the employee and yield less useful information. Therefore, an employee was never quite sure if a conversation with Dr. Balm was purely social or if it was intended to have a specific purpose or goal.

Although lacking empirical support for his opinions that assessment and counseling are more effective outside of his office than inside, Dr. Balm continued these practices. Some employees were quite comfortable with his casual approach, and they enjoyed his willingness to be flexible and meet them in a nonprofessional setting. Many others, however, felt that the lack of concern for confidentiality, privacy, and formal structure or informed consent made it difficult to trust Dr. Balm. They tended to feel suspicious and thought that he was constantly gathering information about them and analyzing their behavior, which created a stressful work environment.

These employees felt distinctly disadvantaged by Dr. Balm's assessment practices. One employee was denied a promotion to a district managerial position, partly as a result of Dr. Balm's evaluation. This employee was quite dissatisfied with the evaluation process. He felt that being interviewed in the lounge area with employees wandering in and out was distracting and that he did not present his "best side" to Dr. Balm, which resulted in a negative evaluation. Furthermore, this employee did not even know at the outset that his conversation with Dr. Balm was to be an evaluative interview; he had come to the lounge for a cup of coffee and left 1 hour later, after answering many probing personal questions by Dr. Balm. He brought a complaint to his supervisor about the casual assessment process.

Regardless of the accuracy or validity of his judgments and recommendations, Dr. Balm did a disservice to the employees by carrying out evaluations casually and spontaneously and showed little regard for providing informed consent or structuring the relationship first, which are in violation of this principle and Standard 1.07. His informality gave the appearance of a lack of objectivity and professionalism, was not conducive to good relations with employees, and increased the likelihood of employee complaints.

> *(b) Psychologists' assessments, recommendations, reports, and psychological diagnostic or evaluative statements are based on information and techniques (including personal interviews of the individual when appropriate) sufficient to provide appropriate substantiation for their findings. (See also Standard 7.02, Forensic Assessments.)*

(b) When you carry out assessments, don't assume anything to be factual, unless you have a solid basis for doing so. Never rely on unverified reports from third parties, idle talk, or gossip. Base all your statements, reports, and recommendations on verifiable information (e.g., personal interviews, test results, relevant documents and other materials, research literature).

Vignette: A psychologist with a general practice in a rural area was nearing retirement. He had little formal training in child custody assessments, but with the rising divorce rate, he was being asked to perform an increasing number of them over the years. He had never read "Guidelines for Child Custody Evaluations in Divorce Proceedings" (APA, 1994a) and was generally unfamiliar with conventional standards for such assessments.

Unfortunately, his methodology was flawed because he often failed to perform a comprehensive assessment of all parties. If he was unable to evaluate both parents, he relied on secondhand information concerning the parent he did not see. He also failed to provide disclaimers to the court about the limitations of such data. Instead, he presented information or allegations that one parent might state about the other as objectively valid. He would buttress this information with interviews and comments from young children, neighbors, and friends but never discussed the possible decreased validity of this information because of its source. As an example, he might refer to a husband's "known history of occasional alcohol abuse" instead of carrying out a face-to-face evaluation or using appropriate assessment instruments to supplement his opinions about the husband.

Such practices resulted in psychological reports of flawed validity that were of minimal use to the court and the parents and failed to protect the best interests of the child. These one-sided evaluations effectively harmed the parents who had never been personally assessed by depriving them of participation in joint custody or reducing the visitation agreement. Sometimes his methods were successfully challenged by opposing counsel, but unfortunately, there were few attorneys, fewer psychologists, and little sophistication in matters of custody assessment in his jurisdiction.

2.02 Competence and Appropriate Use of Assessments and Interventions

(a) Psychologists who develop, administer, score, interpret, or use psychological assessment techniques, interviews, tests, or instruments do so in a manner and for purposes that are appropriate in light of the research on or evidence of the usefulness and proper application of the techniques.

(a) Base and select your assessment activities on relevant research, proper techniques, and validity for the task at hand. This includes creating, administering, scoring, interpreting, and using tests and other assessment techniques. Don't take shortcuts. Do things "by the book."

Vignette: Dr. Lovalid, a young therapist with minimal grounding in test construction, developed a marital distress syndrome inventory (MDSI). This instrument was used to assess and treat married couples who had repeatedly sought counseling or crisis management over the course of their marriage.

The items she created were drawn primarily from her own clinical experience, which consisted of providing counseling to approximately 10 couples over a period of 1 year. She had not yet attempted to do a pilot study to establish the instrument's reliability or validity, but she had already begun to use it routinely as a basis for making formal assessments about the long-term viability of the couple's relationship. In presenting the instrument to new couples, she failed to inform them of its experimental nature—its utter lack of established validity. She thought this was unnecessary because she had much faith in the instrument, based on her clinical experience, so she used it routinely as an important guide in treating couples. At times, she would recommend to the husband and wife that they experiment with a trial separation, based primarily on their scores on the MDSI.

When a colleague inquired about her application of this instrument, he sought reliability and validity data because he was considering using it in his own practice. But Dr. Lovalid could supply no information other than her clinical intuition and experience. The colleague then discussed the problems of her continuing to use an unvalidated instrument and the possibility of harm to clients by her failure to provide informed consent in advance concerning the experimental nature of the assessment.

As a result of her colleague's friendly confrontation, Dr. Lovalid began to consider the actual risks of continuing to use the MDSI and the possibility of harming others. She reviewed her therapy records for the couples she had worked with over the previous 8 months and discovered that a majority of them had scored in such a way as to warrant a formal recommendation of trial separation. As it turned out, only one out of five couples took Dr. Lovalid's advice to separate, at great financial expense and with a great deal of emotional upheaval. The other couples strongly considered her advice but ultimately rejected it, some losing faith in the therapist and dropping out of treatment.

Dr. Lovalid began to understand that her unscientific application of assessment principles had the potential for serious negative effects on the lives of her clients, causing unnecessary hardship at times when there was already great stress. She decided to stop using the MDSI as a diagnostic tool and began to use it as a concise means of gathering data for the marital therapy itself. She also began to formally instruct every couple about its experimental nature and told them that the results of this assessment would not necessarily be predictive of compatibility or outcome of the therapy. Dr. Lovalid finally gained an appreciation for the necessity of adhering to scientific principles in constructing and using instruments of assessment.

> *(b) Psychologists refrain from misuse of assessment techniques, interventions, results, and interpretations and take reasonable steps to prevent others from misusing the information these techniques provide. This includes refraining from releasing raw test results or raw data to persons, other than to patients or clients as appropriate, who are not qualified to use such information. (See also Standards 1.02, Relationship of Ethics and Law, and 1.04, Boundaries of Competence.)*

(b)   Don't misuse or allow others to misuse your assessment techniques, interventions, results, and interpretations. Your patient and the test's usefulness to others in the future can be harmed. Also never release copies of tests, completed answer sheets, results, raw data, interpretations, or information about your interventions to those unqualified to use them, such as lawyers, journalists, school teachers, managers and supervisors, family members, or anyone else who may ask for them. A subpoena for such items calls for a special response.

Vignette: Dr. Thomas Grimm received a *subpoena duces tecum* ordering him to appear for a deposition and bring all psychological records in his possession concerning one of his clients, a defendant in a criminal case. He first attempted to determine if the subpoena was valid. He noted that the court issuing the subpoena was located in the same state and county as his office and, therefore, the issue of jurisdiction was adequately addressed. However, he decided to contact his insurance carrier and request subpoena counsel, just to help rule out any possibility that the subpoena may not have been valid.

Although the subpoena was determined to be valid, Dr. Grimm was still reluctant to reveal the psychological records; they not only contained all of his consultation notes but also raw test scores of all the assessments he had performed to date, including his patient's MMPI-2, Beck Depression Inventory–2, Millon Clinical Multiaxial Inventory–III, and Symptom Checklist 90–R. Dr. Grimm, in consultation with his attorney, decided to raise an objection to releasing the entire record, arguing that patient confidentiality was at stake and that Ethics Code Standard 2.02b prohibited the release of raw test scores to those who are not qualified to interpret them. If Dr. Grimm were to release his patient's assessment records to the attorney as ordered by the subpoena, he would be in direct conflict with a provision of his own professional code of ethics.

The court, however, did not yield to this argument and held that the subpoena would prevail. Dr. Grimm and his attorney then entered into dialogue with the plaintiff's attorney, offering a possible compromise that would allow for the release but also honor this ethical standard. They requested the option of releasing the testing materials to another licensed psychologist, agreeable to both parties, to interpret the patient's information to the court, rather than giving the file to the attorney, citing compliance with this and other ethical standards as the supporting rationale. The plaintiff's attorney saw the merit of this request and was willing to agree to such an arrangement.

2.03 Test Construction

Psychologists who develop and conduct research with tests and other assessment techniques use scientific procedures and current professional knowledge for test design, standardization, validation, reduction or elimination of bias, and recommendations for use.

When developing assessment techniques or conducting research with them, be sure to use current scientific procedures and professional knowledge of test design, standardization, validation, reduction of bias, recommendations for use, and so on.

Vignette: Dr. Goodvale and several colleagues had worked for many years at a university clinic in a large city in the midwest. They were currently engaged in developing a paper-and-pencil test that would measure an individual's hypnotic capability. With such an instrument, a new client wishing to be hypnotized could be rapidly assessed and then confidently referred for treatment to the proper therapist on the staff. In some cases, the use of hypnosis would likely increase the efficiency of the therapy—

an important consideration with the restrictions on treatment imposed by the managed care system.

In carrying out each phase of the work, the research team adhered to well-established scientific standards of test construction. They reviewed carefully the *Standards for Educational and Psychological Testing* (APA, 1985) before beginning their work. Each psychologist was experienced in both the applications of hypnosis and various hypnotizability measures. The team members began by reviewing many of the hypnosis assessment instruments that had been developed over the years, such as the Harvard Group Scale of Hypnotic Susceptibility (Shor & Orne, 1962), the Stanford Hypnotic Susceptibility Scales (Weitzenhoffer & Hilgard, 1962), the Dissociative Experiences Scale (Bernstein & Putnam, 1986), and the Tellegen Absorption Scale (Tellegen & Atkinson, 1974), to name a few. This valuable step, reviewing the subject areas and items from other scales, was helpful in generating a content grid with rows and columns representing different areas to be filled in the course of developing the new instrument.

As the work continued, groups of items periodically were pilot tested with small samples of individuals. The researchers attempted to determine whether those taking the test understood the language of the test items and what the item response characteristics were. High numbers of people answering a particular item in the same way would detract from that item's discriminatory value and make it less useful for inclusion on the test.

Establishing validity, reliability, and carrying out the necessary administrations for standardizing the instrument with those of different gender, age, ethnic, and other groups required many months of testing, data gathering, and careful analysis. The final version of the instrument was validated by using criterion-related validity. This was accomplished by establishing correlations between an individual's performance on the instrument and his or her hypnotic capability as measured by both an individual induction procedure and performance on several other measures of hypnotic susceptibility, including the Hypnotic Induction Profile (Spiegel & Spiegel, 1978).

Retest reliability measures for the instrument were obtained by readministering the test to the same individuals after a lapse of several months and computing correlation coefficients between the first and second testing. The team members also decided to compute homogeneity reliability, or interitem correlations, because they considered hypnotic capability to be a construct (though there were different opinions on this subject held by other researchers). Dr. Goodvale and her team were highly diligent and painstaking in their work and successfully met their goal of creating a paper-and-pencil instrument that was useful in assessing hypnotic capability.

2.04 Use of Assessment in General and With Special Populations

(a) Psychologists who perform interventions or administer, score, interpret, or use assessment techniques are familiar with the reliability, val-

idation, and related standardization or outcome studies of, and proper applications and uses of, the techniques they use.

(a) Be well informed about tests or other assessment instruments you plan to administer, score, and interpret. Know their uses and applications, standardization, limitations, reliability, and validity, and make sure you use them properly.

Vignette: Dr. Nouveau was a White psychologist who has just joined the staff of an outpatient clinic in a large, understaffed county hospital with many African American patients. The psychologist who hired him provided very little guidance, structure, or consultation about his specific duties. But it was clear that a major part of his responsibilities would include carrying out the initial screening of new patients and diagnosing and treating individuals with a broad range of Axis I and Axis II disorders.

Dr. Nouveau used several instruments that he was most familiar with to fulfill his assessment responsibilities. He used, among others, a nearly obsolete objective instrument that had been standardized many years before on young White men and women. He had used this aging instrument in his doctoral dissertation 4 years ago, and he thought that he could rely on it to assess depression, anxiety, personality disorders, organicity, and many other mental disorders. It was a poor choice for use with a predominantly African American population, however, and had little validity or established diagnostic use in this clinical setting.

A particularly complicated case involved a 39-year-old man who was currently divorcing his wife. He had been suffering chronic back pain for 3 years and was diagnosed as having a significant amount of psychopathology based on Dr. Nouveau's test results. Dr. Nouveau relied on this test even though it had never been standardized for African American clinical populations and no norms were available for individuals suffering chronic pain. The results of this assessment eventually found their way into open court 1 year later when the divorced couple was attempting to negotiate custody of their three children. The man's mental health was raised as a consideration in his parenting abilities and Dr. Nouveau, who was subpoenaed to testify as the man's former therapist, was placed in the position of having to defend and interpret the results of testing that were essentially invalid. It was clear that Dr. Nouveau's incompetence in selecting appropriate instruments at times resulted in biased and invalid test results, which had the potential for adversely affecting patients, sometimes with serious and long-term consequences.

(b) Psychologists recognize limits to the certainty with which diagnoses, judgments, or predictions can be made about individuals.

(b) Know the limits of the instrument that you are using for accurately assessing or diagnosing your patients or predicting their behavior. Test results have limitations. They may not reveal as much as you might expect.

Vignette: Dr. Judgem was a consultant to several midsized businesses that employed many Latino men and women, some of whom spoke no

English. His professional role was to assess the performance of employees, supervisors, and managers and to make formal recommendations about workers' competence to accept new responsibilities and their readiness for a promotion.

He was assessing social skills, the ability to engage in problem solving, and the ability to tolerate ambiguous and unresolved situations, among other traits, and he decided to use a paper-and-pencil instrument for evaluating these as a part of his total assessment. Although quite useful for assessing the European and North American workers, the test had never been standardized on a Latino population and could, therefore, only be used with great caution and some means of compensating for the lack of norms. It consistently provided biased results for Latino employees, who constituted over 50% of the workforce.

Dr. Judgem felt justified in using the instrument, however, because he was quite familiar with it, had been using it extensively for several years, and thought he knew how to make appropriate inferences from the test results to compensate for its lack of norms with various ethnic groups. Unfortunately, he also had a long-standing personal prejudice against Mexican Americans, which combined with biased test results created erroneous evaluations and recommendations. Over time, many employees were deprived of promotions within the company because of poor scores on the test that required English-writing skills, even though these employees would have been perfectly competent to accept a broader range of responsibilities. When competing for advancement with European American employees—all of whom, at this company, were native English speakers—their test performance and overall assessment would generally be deficient, thus supplying Dr. Judgem with a rationale to support his formal recommendations that they not be promoted.

Eventually, it became obvious to the Latino employees that they were being systematically discriminated against by means of such an inappropriate assessment procedure. They approached upper level management with a formal complaint about Dr. Judgem's use of the test and his systematic ethnic prejudice. Ultimately they were successful in having him replaced with a more objective and knowledgeable psychological consultant.

> *(c) Psychologists attempt to identify situations in which particular interventions or assessment techniques or norms may not be applicable or may require adjustment in administration or interpretation because of factors such as individuals' gender, age, race, ethnicity, national origin, religion, sexual orientation, disability, language, or socioeconomic status.*

(c) Be alert to characteristics of others (e.g., foreign language, gender, culture, race, disability) that would require that you change how you would normally (a) carry out an assessment, (b) make an intervention, or (c) interpret results.

Vignette: A young man who recently immigrated from Vietnam to Los Angeles sought out a psychologist for his addiction to heroin. Unfortunately, he spoke very little English, so it was difficult to make a formal assessment of his needs. Wanting to capitalize on the man's strong interest in obtaining treatment, the psychologist dispensed with the usual paper-and-pencil intake forms and questionnaires and asked the man, as best as he could, if he would agree to use an interpreter.

By coincidence, one of the secretaries in the outer office spoke fluent Vietnamese and English. The man agreed to discuss his problems in the presence of the secretary, at least in a preliminary way, and she was invited in for the remainder of the interview. The first order of business was to create a short consent form, which, in effect, allowed the interview to take place with a third-party present for the purposes of a brief assessment and referral. Once the interview got under way, with the secretary's help as a translator, the psychologist was able to determine where the patient lived, the nature of his addiction, the fact that his wife had just left him, and that he had significant anxiety, but he did not currently constitute a significant danger to himself or others. Armed with his information, she was able to make a good referral to an Asian American mental health center that could immediately accept him as a patient.

The psychologist had considered the risk to confidentiality in inviting an interpreter (the secretary), who was not a mental health provider, to assist her with the interview. She decided that it was more important, however, to serve as an immediate resource to this patient and make an appropriate referral rather than to turn him away when he was actively seeking help and might be at risk of harming himself or another. Her professional decisions were consistent with this ethical principle, allowing a significant and creative departure from her standard way of assessing patients' needs when it was essential to do so.

2.05 Interpreting Assessment Results

When interpreting assessment results, including automated interpretations, psychologists take into account the various test factors and characteristics of the person being assessed that might affect psychologists' judgments or reduce the accuracy of their interpretations. They indicate any significant reservations they have about the accuracy or limitations of their interpretations.

In assessing others, always remember to consider both (a) the characteristics of the person and (b) the test factors themselves that might affect your judgment or reduce the usefulness of the results. Also be sure to disclose any reservations you may have, out loud or in writing, when giving your results or creating a report.

Vignette: Dr. Offset had contracted with the research and development section of a large manufacturing company of office supplies and computer accessories. He was expected to select employees to participate in focus groups that would help determine new products and services to be offered by the company. Toward this end, he used an experimental assessment instrument to measure employees' social aptitude, intellectual fluency, and collaborative and competitive traits.

However, the test only had norms for White participants and had never been standardized on participants mirroring the the cultural diversity of the company's employees, which included a number of Asian Americans and African Americans. Thus, Dr. Offset was reluctant to rely exclusively on the results of the test for the selection process. He appropriately informed management of his reservations, although he recommended that the test might be able to make a partial contribution to the selection process.

He decided to offer each employee who tested below a cutoff score an opportunity to have a structured interview with him, if he or she desired, that would be useful in assessing his or her eligibility for the focus groups. Even this compromise might have been flawed because some low-scoring employees might have felt undeserving to participate or others may not have been assertive enough to request an opportunity for the structured interview. At least providing such an interview opportunity clearly communicated the message that instruments of assessment would not be relied on exclusively when they had never been normed on the populations for which they were being used.

Dr. Offset also informed employees that he intended to use the data from the test to help accumulate standardization norms for Asian Americans and African Americans, so that the test could be more validly used in the future with these populations. In general, he was clear about informing employees and management of the somewhat experimental nature of his selection process. Likewise, he took every reasonable step to encourage employees from the various ethnic and racial groups to help compensate for the biased testing by requesting an individual interview. At the end of this selection process, he carefully reviewed the overall results by soliciting employee's input with a questionnaire and by reviewing all results with several Asian American and African American psychologist colleagues.

2.06 Unqualified Persons

Psychologists do not promote the use of psychological assessment techniques by unqualified persons. (See also Standard 1.22, Delegation to and Supervision of Subordinates.)

Don't teach or allow unqualified people to use tests or assessment techniques.[1]

Vignette: Dr. Watcher was the clinical supervisor of Dr. Saul Lidd, a new PhD who was not yet licensed to practice independently. Dr. Watcher expected his supervisee to carry out and score all the diagnostic testing for him, including the MMPI-2, various anxiety and depression inventories,

---

[1]See also Standard 6.04, Limitation on Teaching.

and the Wechsler Adult Intelligence Scale–III when appropriate and tests to assess individuals with chronic pain, attention deficit disorder, and other psychological disorders. He also expected Dr. Lidd to carry out structured clinical interviews for patients presenting symptoms of eating disorders and some Axis II disorders. Some of these activities were audiotaped or videotaped with patients' awareness and consent.

Dr. Lidd was also to write and sign most psychological reports resulting from these assessments and then take them to his supervisor to be signed. Dr. Watcher was knowledgeable about his supervisee's strengths and weaknesses and was well informed about his background and training. He viewed the videotapes of Dr. Lidd administering structured clinical interviews and scrupulously reviewed the psychological reports and other work that Dr. Lidd completed.

When necessary, Dr. Watcher encouraged additional training, such as workshops and seminars, and took the time to nurture his supervisee's professional growth and development in many ways. It was clear that he took a responsible interest in his mentoring role and spent much time and energy providing a good learning environment that was well paced to the needs of his supervisee. Above all, he was careful to limit Dr. Lidd's duties to his areas of expertise and provide close supervision in new areas, as needed.

2.07 Obsolete Tests and Outdated Test Results

(a) Psychologists do not base their assessment or intervention decisions or recommendations on data or test results that are outdated for the current purpose.

(a) Don't use outdated data or test results as a basis for your assessments, interventions, or recommendations.

Vignette: Dr. Yawn, a busy school psychologist, was asked to assess a 14-year-old boy who was having problems in school. The boy, Steven, had great difficulty with reading over the last 6 months, had recently gotten in a fight with two other students, and was being defiant with teachers. As a part of her assessment, Dr. Yawn relied on teachers' comments from the previous 2 years. She also reviewed test data on reading aptitude and personal problems that were several years old and thought it was unnecessary to carry out any additional testing or formal assessment.

She remembered Steven from an interview she had with him 7 months ago and did not think that she required any additional information about his current status. Besides, she was quite involved working with boys and girls who had "more serious behavior problems" involving drug use or extremely violent and aggressive behavior. She failed to interview Steven again or refer him for counseling. Instead, she referred him to a remedial reading group and agreed to review his case again in 6 months.

Her recommendations, which were based on obsolete data and outmoded information, were inappropriate. By failing to interview Steven again, she never learned that his mother had recently been diagnosed with cancer, which was having a strong impact on the entire family. By refusing to update her knowledge of Steven by using appropriate and current instruments of assessment or having a face-to-face evaluation with him, she made a formal recommendation that failed to address the cause of his suffering and misbehavior and was unlikely to be very helpful to him.

> *(b) Similarly, psychologists do not base such decisions or recommendations on tests and measures that are obsolete and not useful for the current purpose.*

(b) Don't use obsolete tests. Be sure you have the latest available edition of a given assessment instrument, unless there is a good reason why you should use an older version.

Vignette: A school psychologist had been providing services to the same two secondary schools in an ethnically diverse, rural school system for 27 years, and much of her time was spent doing psychological assessments of students who had special needs. Over the years, she had accumulated quite a library of individual tests.

In recent times, she had become less fastidious about obtaining current editions of recently revised tests, and she refused to purchase revisions of intelligence, reading, and personality tests, even though she knew of their existence. She justified the use of obsolete tests in relation to her impending retirement; because she was planning on leaving the district in 4 years, she thought that she should not be expected to purchase and become familiar with the newer instruments. Tests were costly, and the "learning curve" required for some of the revisions appeared to be too steep for her. Even though she knew the school district would have readily purchased new versions of certain tests, she refused to requisition them because she did not wish to spend time and energy learning the new procedures. She rationalized that she was saving the school money that could be better spent elsewhere.

Her refusal to use current versions of tests over an extended period of time proved to be harmful to certain students. Those particularly effected were boys and girls for whom English was a second language, and there were many first- and second-generation Asian and Latino families in this school district. These students would have been more accurately assessed with the revised editions of tests that were more culturally sensitive, or at least somewhat more fair to test takers of various cultures, than the older editions. Although Dr. Yawn was used to compensating for these deficiencies in the older instruments and had a wealth of personal "data" and a "feel" about students' characteristic performance on them that helped in her judgments and recommendations, she placed her students at a disadvantage by relying on them exclusively. By systematically using obsolete instruments of assessment, the psychologist occasionally made incorrect decisions about the educational and mental health needs of her students, resulting in inappropriate intervention recommendations with significant negative long-term consequences.

2.08 Test Scoring and Interpretation Services

(a) Psychologists who offer assessment or scoring procedures to other professionals accurately describe the purpose, norms, validity, reliability, and applications of the procedures and any special qualifications applicable to their use.

(a) Be truthful in advertising your assessment or scoring services. Don't make exaggerated claims about the purpose, norms, validity, reliability, or applications.

Vignette: Dr. Van Slykk was a shrewd businessman who was somewhat less concerned with professional business ethics than with building a strong assessment and test-scoring company. He was ill informed about a psychologist's ethical duty to restrict access to psychological instruments to those who were not competently trained and experienced in using them. In his promotional materials and ordering forms, he never requested a state license number from the individual wishing to make the purchase, nor did he seek any other credentials or evidence of a customer's competence in the area of formal assessment. He also had a policy of accepting completed answer sheets from anyone, regardless of their professional discipline or training in assessment.

A major part of Dr. Van Slykk's business plan included developing instruments that could be of use in various forensic settings. One such instrument was the Slykk Parenting Competence Assessment System, a short instrument with very little empirical validation and few safeguards against motivational distortion but wide promotion in legal journals. It was his hope to encourage attorneys representing litigants in divorce proceedings to use his instrument, which was advertised to be suitable for a broad range of individuals, regardless of gender, age, socioeconomic status, religion, or ethnic origin.

To facilitate administration and scoring, Dr. Van Slykk allowed individuals to take his test over the Internet. Users needed only to access his web page to take the test on-line. It was scored almost immediately, and an automated narrative report was then generated by computer for the psychologist's use. Unfortunately, because his assessment system was available to anyone who wished to access it on-line with no protective measures, it could be easily downloaded and analyzed by anyone who wanted it. This may have further detracted from its already questionable validity because a potential user would have the opportunity to review the test items and prepare responses that would place her or him in a more favorable light than the opposing parent, who might have been entirely naive to the test when it was administered in a psychologist's office.

With such lax administration procedures, there was no way to verify the true identity of the test taker or to control for lapses in confidentiality at various stages of the process. Furthermore, advertisements placed in psychological journals and newspapers were filled with exaggerations about the instrument's usefulness, applicability, and validity.

Van Slykk also promoted his quick turn-around time for scoring other tests, claiming a 24-hour maximum, through the extensive use of fax machines and email correspondence. However, these promises fell flat because his clerical staff members varied in their competence level. They were not especially efficient or well trained in the use of the technology or customer relations. They occasionally mixed up answer sheets and computer printouts, thus sending the wrong client's test results to a particular psychologist.

Dr. Van Slykk demonstrated his incompetence in many ways: not only by promoting his scoring services unfairly and inaccurately but also by constructing assessment instruments in an idiosyncratic fashion and lacking proper statistical and standardization procedures. He failed to honor ethical principles that have evolved over many years to safeguard both the public and the science of psychology. Many formal complaints from colleagues and consumers materialized, but not before he had contributed substantially to the litigation process of many divorces, resulting at times in poor child custody decisions and additional stress for families who were already suffering difficult transitions.

> *(b) Psychologists select scoring and interpretation services (including automated services) on the basis of evidence of the validity of the program and procedures as well as on other appropriate considerations.*

(b) Choose test scoring services wisely. Read the fine print about validity, turn-around time, and other factors that might affect your decision to use a particular service.

Vignette: Dr. Askem was the owner of an employee assistance program providing a full range of psychological services to several large corporations. Dr. Askem's many responsibilities included decisions regarding using scoring services for results of various instruments of assessment, including the MMPI-2, Millon Clinical Multiaxial Inventory–III (MCMI-III), the 16-Personality Factor Questionnaire, and the Symptom Checklist–90–R, to name a few. For some of these instruments he had the option of purchasing software that would score answer sheets and produce narrative reports. For others, he would select scoring services that processed mailed answer sheets and were most cost effective for his needs and those of his corporate clients.

Because most of the tests his employees used were produced by different publishers, Dr. Askem was faced with the task of comparing different services on a variety of criteria. In some cases, there was only one scoring service available. However, where there was a choice, he sought documentation about the validity of computer-generated narratives and the bases for any extra scales or interpretations provided. He carefully reviewed the sample narrative reports, when available. He noted that in some cases, the reports contained confusing or contradictory language. In others, the statements were overly strong, lacking qualifiers or disclaimers, and seemed to present an exaggerated trait or profile of an individual. When he observed these problems, he sought information from the test-scoring service about the additional scales or accompanying narratives, such as software algorithms or configurable rules for creating computerized text, even though the services were not always cooperative in fulfilling his requests.

He considered other factors in selecting a service: the availability of telephone consultation support; the use of fax machines for sending answer sheets and receiving results; cost; and the service company's willingness to provide references, bibliographies, or research information about specialized assessment needs. Although Dr. Askem's comprehensive approach to evaluating and selecting test-scoring services was time consuming, it proved invaluable and yielded final selections that provided competent and scientifically sound services addressing the specific needs of his clients.

> *(c) Psychologists retain appropriate responsibility for the appropriate application, interpretation, and use of assessment instruments, whether they score and interpret such tests themselves or use automated or other services.*

(c) The "buck" stops with you when doing psychological testing, no matter who does the scoring. You must have a sound rationale for your choice of a test with a particular client or patient and be able to support all evaluative statements that you make about a person.

Vignette: Dr. Newelby, a recently licensed psychologist, worked in the human relations department at city hall. When performing psychological assessments for job candidates, she frequently used verbatim paragraphs from the computer-generated report from a well-known scoring service when writing her psychological report. However, she usually deleted all qualifying phrases and disclaimers so that her report read more definitively, without the tentative language that was deliberately included by the test-scoring service. Lacking these qualifiers, the report seemed to make diagnostic and predictive statements that went far beyond the established validity of the assessment instrument and provided a distorted or exaggerated picture of the candidate examined. Not only did this result in an inaccurate psychological report, it also adversely affected the employment opportunities for certain candidates who were being depicted in a far more negative way than was necessarily true.

On one occasion, Dr. Newelby noticed some significant differences between the computer-generated report from the scoring service and her own clinical assessment of a particular candidate. There were major diagnostic discrepancies between her clinical assessment of the individual and the test report, with strong implications about the candidate's potential for employment. However, she decided to rely on the computerized report without question because she was relatively naive about using and integrating narrative reports from scoring services. Little did she know that a new employee at the scoring service had made a serious error, interchanging the printout of Dr. Newelby's client with that of a young man indicted for check forgery. By an unfortunate coincidence, the code numbers used on both reports were almost identical, and each was mailed to the wrong party. The employee at the scoring service never detected the mistake; neither did Dr. Newelby. It was never corrected, and her psychological report reflected the error, eventually contributing to a poor endorsement of the candidate and his failure to be hired for the managerial position for which he had applied.

Dr. Newelby should have been alert to the ever present possibility of a scoring or clerical error. She should have taken appropriate measures when her clinical judgment yielded such a radically different assessment of the candidate than the one from the computer-generated report received from the scoring service. Also she should have refrained from altering the language of the text so significantly because the tentative language and disclaimers reflect the inherent uncertainty of the assessment process and should always be retained.

2.09 Explaining Assessment Results

> *Unless the nature of the relationship is clearly explained to the person being assessed in advance and precludes provision of an explanation of results (such as in some organizational consulting, pre-employment or security screenings, and forensic evaluations), psychologists ensure that an explanation of the results is provided using language that is reasonably understandable to the person assessed or to another legally authorized person on behalf of the client. Regardless of whether the scoring and interpretation are done by the psychologist, by assistants, or by automated or other outside services, psychologists take reasonable steps to ensure that appropriate explanations of results are given.*

Explain the results of your formal assessments in simple English—not "psychologese"—to the person you are evaluating unless, of course, you are prohibited from discussing test results by virtue of your role or the setting (e.g., personnel screening, mental competency examinations). In those cases, be sure to tell test takers in advance that you will not be giving them any results or interpretations.

Vignette: Lester, a 26-year-old man who had been addicted to heroin for 3 years was brought to a chemical dependency center by Tina, his exasperated girlfriend. He had been raised in the inner city and did not graduate from high school, never held a full-time job, and showed little interest in making constructive changes, other than continuing his relationship with Tina. The psychologist who interviewed him, Dr. Sharper, was familiar with the type of problems Lester was experiencing because he had been born and raised in a similar environment and had struggled with drug addiction many years earlier.

Over the next few weeks, Dr. Sharper administered several objective tests, which helped determine Lester's diagnosis and treatment. When the assessment phase was finished, he explained the results of the diagnostic testing in everyday language and gave the young man some printed handouts that helped him understand the test interpretations. Given Lester's level of education, it was important for Dr. Sharper to interpret the results for Lester in accessible language and clear concepts, lest they be misunderstood. With such good communication at the outset, Dr. Sharper established a good working alliance with Lester and created a solid foundation on which to build a course of treatment.

2.10 Maintaining Test Security

Psychologists make reasonable efforts to maintain the integrity and security of tests and other assessment techniques consistent with law, contractual obligations, and in a manner that permits compliance with the requirements of this Ethics Code. (See also Standard 1.02, Relationship of Ethics and Law.)

Maintain the integrity and security of tests and assessment techniques by keeping them away from the eyes of those who are not trained to use them. You are obliged to comply with the law and your contractual obligations, but you must attempt to do so in a way that complies with this Ethics Code as well.

Vignette: Dr. Eve Madison was being interviewed for a television talk show on the subject of mental competency assessments for prisoners on death row. Before she went on the air, she requested a chance to speak with the host of the show, Mr. Gladmouth, to educate him briefly about the testing materials she routinely used in carrying out assessments with prisoners. She also showed Mr. Gladmouth a copy of the MMPI-2 and the other instruments she used to enhance his understanding of the complex process of assessment and help him frame his questions on the air more intelligently.

Unfortunately, Dr. Madison did not realize the risk she was taking in giving him a copy of the tests; neither did she give much thought to the ethics or judgment of talk show hosts. In the interest of "public awareness," Mr. Gladmouth had his engineer display many of the test items on the screen while he interviewed Dr. Madison. He was planning to place all the test batteries, including several Rorschach cards, on his talk show's web site so that viewers could download them and use email to send their opinions back to him.

Dr. Madison was outraged by Mr. Gladmouth's opportunistic style and flagrant disregard for protecting test security, and she strongly verbalized her opposition to his intention of placing the protocols on the web site when she found out about it from one of the show's producers. She confronted him about the ethical and legal aspects of protecting these materials, which were to be used by licensed practitioners only. She described the potential for harm to numerous individuals (potential future patients and clients) by compromising their naiveté concerning the test items and the threat to future diagnostic testing if test items were revealed in such a manner that the public had an opportunity to study them.

Fortunately, she was successful in prevailing on him to refrain from placing the tests on the Internet. She also succeeded in having him delete the test items shown on the screen from subsequent rebroadcasts of the interview. Mr. Gladmouth then became intrigued with the topic of test security, the public's "right to know," and psychologists who were "obsessed with secrecy" about these materials. He decided to invite Dr. Madison back for an interview on this topic the following week. She discussed the conditions under which she would be willing to return for another interview and scheduled a second interview when he agreed to her terms in writing. Wisely, however, she left all copies of tests at her office this time.

3

Advertising and Other Public Statements

3.01 Definition of Public Statements

Psychologists comply with this Ethics Code in public statements relating to their professional services, products, or publications or to the field of psychology. Public statements include but are not limited to paid or unpaid advertising, brochures, printed matter, directory listings, personal resumés or curriculum vitae, interviews or comments for use in media, statements in legal proceedings, lectures and public oral presentations, and published materials.

Keep in mind every section of this code whenever you make a statement in your professional role, that is, everything pertinent to your work that you say, write, publish, broadcast, or send over the Internet. This includes advertisements for services or products, resumés, lectures, interviews with journalists, legal testimony, reports, and books and journal articles, to name a few arenas.

Vignette: One evening each month, Dr. Fluff gave a presentation at the Springfield Public Library on stress management for couples who were expecting their first child. As a part of the process of learning how to identify stress in their lives, the attendees filled out a short inventory he had created that culled items from the Beck Depression Inventory–2 and the Symptom Checklist–90–R into one brief questionnaire, the Winnetka Pregnancy Stress Inventory.

Although lacking research to support his claims, Dr. Fluff routinely began each new lecture with the assertion that potential mothers or fathers endorsing seven or more items in the inventory were "definitely at risk for developing a stress-related disorder, which would likely affect the development of the baby in utero, with lifelong untoward consequences for his or her physical and mental health." He would make this utterance in as grave and authoritative a tone as he could muster. Dr. Fluff would go on to assure his audience that there was a remedy, which was "guaranteed" to reduce stress and enhance the quality of life during these difficult months. He would then announce that his psychoeducational seminar would address both the stressors of concern to those present and the general topic of pregnancy stress prophylaxis. For those still interested, the series of six 45-minute lectures would begin the following week for a total fee of $199.95.

By coincidence, Dr. Watcher, a psychologist, and his pregnant wife, Betta Watcher-Out, who happened to be an attorney, were attending the lecture. Dr. Watcher was well aware of the many ethical infractions in Dr. Fluff's tendency to overpromote himself as well as those in his questionnaire, his services, and his tendency to misstate the research. His wife noted the copyright violation of plagiarizing test items from others' published materials without citation or permission. Dr. Fluff's public statements seemed to be in violation of Ethics Code Standards 1.06 (Basis for Scientific and Professional Judgments), 1.07 (Describing the Nature and Results of Psychological Services), 1.14 (Avoiding Harm), 1.15 (Misuse of Psychologists' Influence), 2.02 (Competence and Appropriate Use of Assessments and Interventions), 2.03 (Test Construction), 2.10 (Maintaining Test Security), and 6.03 (Accuracy and Objectivity in Teaching), to name a few.

In his zeal to be enterprising and expand his practice, Dr. Fluff disregarded many fundamental ethical standards and legal statutes. He also used scare tactics in making statements to highly receptive individuals— pregnant mothers and their husbands—which could not be substantiated and were intended to be manipulative. Dr. Watcher and his wife confronted Dr. Fluff with his apparent oversights and urged him to consider these matters seriously in promoting his seminars and using instruments of assessment that were essentially plagiarized.

3.02 Statements by Others

(a) Psychologists who engage others to create or place public statements that promote their professional practice, products, or activities retain professional responsibility for such statements.

(a) The "buck" stops with you for the accuracy of any public statements you authorize about yourself, your products, or your services. You could be held ultimately responsible for how an advertising agency, public relations department, or anyone else portrays or promotes your work.

Vignette: Dr. Emilia Rate routinely assessed chronic pain patients treated at a pain management center of a large and financially troubled hospital. Recently, the hospital census had been dropping because in part of the impact of the managed health care system. In response to this financial crisis, the hospital administration began placing advertisements in local newspapers and on television stations extolling the virtues of various departments within the hospital. Statements made about the pain management clinic included the following voice over to a picture of a back pain patient undergoing diagnostic assessment and treatment in the hospital:

> All pain has a psychological component, and with help from our pain specialists, you will access your inner pain thermostat and learn how

to *turn it off*. Research into pain management shows conclusively that all physical pain can virtually be eliminated with the proper combination of medical and psychological interventions. Assessment and treatment by our medical and psychological staff, including a 3-day hospital stay, will unlock the powers of your mind to overcome all major pain. Call now for an appointment!

Dr. Rate believed that this advertising message made unwarranted promises and required hospital stays for all new patients when, in fact, there was no evidence to indicate that such a policy would increase the efficiency of treatment. She brought her concerns to the hospital administrators and made them aware of her obligation to abide by her professional code of ethics. She requested that they only release public statements about her work that were accurate, and she informed them that they were jeopardizing her good standing with APA by running this advertisement.

The hospital's director of marketing and public relations listened sympathetically to her complaint and agreed to some minor changes in the wording. These changes resulted in an improved and more accurate promotional message. Although the advertisement still contained too much suggestion and too little science, according to Dr. Rate, at least it no longer used such sensational language or offered guaranteed results. Dr. Rate successfully discharged her ethical responsibility to voice her disagreement with the content of the advertisements when there was an apparent ethical conflict. Fortunately, her objections were considered seriously and the advertisement was modified, although the 3-day required hospital stay for virtually all new patients, regardless of their treatment history, was not so easily addressed by the hospital administration. But the matter was brought up for review because of Dr. Rate's voiced opposition to the policy.

> *(b) In addition, psychologists make reasonable efforts to prevent others whom they do not control (such as employers, publishers, sponsors, organizational clients, and representatives of the print or broadcast media) from making deceptive statements concerning psychologists' practice or professional or scientific activities.*

(b) When you hire others to promote your products, services, or professional activities (e.g., advertising agency), make sure that you review the final product before it reaches the public. Remember, you are personally accountable, not those you retain to create your publicity.

Vignette: Dr. Littler's clientele had been diminishing over the years, and he decided to employ the services of a small advertising agency in town, which had a good reputation for fast results. The agency designed a ⅛-page ad to run in the local newspaper for 2 weeks. They published it before Dr. Littler viewed it because he was away attending a convention at the time. The ad displayed his picture and included the following text:

> Do you drink a little too much just a little too often? Have you been noticing your weight inching upward, year by year? Does the boss get

on your nerves a little more often than ever before? Do little things seem to affect you much more than in previous years? You could be suffering from "invisible depression," a clinically proven syndrome that improves with treatment. I will show you a simple technique for making your life happier. My results are guaranteed to improve your daily functioning.

A colleague pointed out to Dr. Littler that he was not in a position to "guarantee" anything about outcomes in psychotherapy, and he wondered about the phrase *clinically proven syndrome* as a diagnostic entity. Dr. Littler considered the advice of his colleague and, reading the ad for the first time on his return, agreed that the language was somewhat inappropriate: It was not scientifically based, and it made promises that could not necessarily be kept. He immediately stopped the ad, although he was obligated to pay for the remainder of the days for which he had contracted.

Dr. Littler decided that significant revision of the wording of his advertisement was in order. He knew that he was accountable for the content of his ad and that the inaccuracies appearing in the newspaper were his responsibility to correct. Dr. Littler significantly revised the text and even invited his colleague to review the final version before it went to press. He also realized that he should have specified in his agreement with the ad agency that he wished to receive a final proof of the ad to review and approve before it was released to the public.

> *(c) If psychologists learn of deceptive statements about their work made by others, psychologists make reasonable efforts to correct such statements.*

(c)   When you discover that someone has made inaccurate statements about you or your services in promotional messages, media interviews, and the like, always make an effort to correct the false statements. You don't necessarily have to be completely successful in your attempts, but you do have to try.

Vignette: Late on a busy Friday afternoon, Dr. Willa Mendit was interviewed between appointments by a local journalist on the subject of panic disorder. In the paper's Sunday edition, the reporter incorrectly identified Dr. Mendit as a psychiatrist and reported that she claimed that panic disorder was always successfully treatable in 5 to 10 sessions of cognitive–behavioral psychotherapy. Dr. Mendit carefully read the article and found the errors, much to her dismay. The reporter had said he would fax her a preview copy of the story before it went to press but, as is common, neglected to do so in the rush to meet his editor's deadline.

Dr. Mendit telephoned the reporter with her corrections on Monday morning. She made it clear that (a) she was a psychologist, not a psychiatrist, and (b) panic disorder *can* be treated in under 10 sessions but frequently requires additional individual or group sessions. The reporter acknowledged his errors and printed the corrections on the following day.

Dr. Mendit learned an important lesson about the necessity of actually reading prepress copy to check for accuracy after granting media interviews. She also had firsthand experience of vulnerability as an interviewee and essentially being at the mercy of a reporter's computer keyboard after the interview is over. She resolved to emphasize accuracy and comprehensiveness in future interviews, regardless of time pressure on the journalist or herself, even though she knew that she could never completely control journalistic distortions or exaggerations.

> *(d) Psychologists do not compensate employees of press, ratio, television, or other communication media in return for publicity in a news item.*

(d)   Never pay a newspaper reporter or any other journalist in the print or electronic media for an interview in return for publicity in a news story.

Vignette: A social psychologist, Dr. Seemee, completed a small research project that he thought had great significance, and he wished very much for it to be disseminated to the professional and lay public. It involved analyzing violent behavior in adolescent boys at school and suggested ways of predicting and possibly forestalling it before it erupted. He decided to turn to the popular press because every professional journal to which he submitted his research rejected it because of its poor statistical design, small sample size, and unwarranted conclusions. However, believing in its validity and wishing to get his message to the public, he telephoned the science editor from a local newspaper and offered them $300 in exchange for an interview about his research.

By coincidence, the science editor, Dr. Halt, happened to be well educated in psychology and knew more about the APA Ethics Code than Dr. Seemee did. She declined the offer to interview him and reminded him that he would be violating his professional ethics if he ever paid a journalist for such a "news item." Dr. Seemee then described the problems he was encountering in having his article published and explained its relevance to some of the juvenile violence that had been in the news in recent months. He cited tragic examples in several different cities of teenagers discharging firearms at school and either intentionally targeting or randomly firing at teachers and students.

Dr. Halt concurred that the topic was timely and highly significant, but she again declined to interview him. She observed that his research had received peer review and had been rejected, and she suggested that he might be well advised to follow up on reviewers' critical comments in further investigating adolescent violence instead of attempting to publish it, as is, in the lay press. She also offered to place his name on her list of mental health professionals interested in discussing the topic of teenage violence should there be a future need for such a (gratis) interview.

> *(e) A paid advertisement relating to the psychologist's activities must be identified as such, unless it is already apparent from the context.*

(e)   Paid advertising should always be clearly identifiable as such. Do not camouflage promotional messages about your products, services, or activities as news stories or educational messages.

Vignette: Dr. Slider wrote a weekly column for the local newspaper on various topics of psychological interest: insomnia, weight control problems, sexual dysfunction, and so on. However, promotional messages about his group practice emphasizing innovative techniques, very high success rates, low fees, and a broad range of services steadily infiltrated the column's scientific message. The true purpose of this thinly disguised "informational" column was to promote his group practice and encourage readers to consider having a consultation as they learned about various psychological problems and the range of interventions offered at his clinic. Although not entirely obvious from the column's context, Dr. Slider's articles were essentially advertisements describing how treatment at his clinic would directly benefit readers. But the column was never labeled as such, and Dr. Slider justified his column with the belief that he was educating the public about various psychological problems and their remediation. However, in discussing treatment alternatives, he rarely presented the full range of options according to the current standards of care. Instead, he described only the options and interventions currently offered by him and his colleagues. By so doing, he failed to discriminate accurately between psychoeducational and promotional activities, one being didactic and the other being essentially manipulative of readers, encouraging them to seek his professional services.

3.03 Avoidance of False or Deceptive Statements

> *(a) Psychologists do not make public statements that are false, deceptive, misleading, or fraudulent, either because of what they state, convey, or suggest or because of what they omit, concerning their research, practice, or other work activities or those of persons or organizations with which they are affiliated. As examples (and not in limitation) of this standard, psychologists do not make false or deceptive statements concerning (1) their training, experience, or competence; (2) their academic degrees; (3) their credentials; (4) their institutional or association affiliations; (5) their services; (6) the scientific or clinical basis for, or results or degree of success of, their services; (7) their fees; or (8) their publications or research findings. (See also Standards 6.15, Deception in Research, and 6.18, Providing Participants With Information About the Study.)*

(a) Don't mislead or deceive others by what you say or don't say concerning (a) your training or competence, academic degrees, license or other credentials or affiliations with institutions or associations; (b) the services you offer; (c) scientific or clinical evidence of your effectiveness; (d) fees; (e) your publications or research findings; or anything else about your psychological work.

Vignette: When introducing herself to health care providers and new patients, Dr. Boaster, a recently licensed psychologist, made the following claims: She was on the staff of the local hospital, had been in practice for 7 years, and had an 85% success rate with anorectic patients.

Each of these statements was an exaggeration or was inaccurate in some way. For example, she had no formal staff affiliation with the hospital or its psychiatry department but merely attended weekly grand rounds presented by the department. Furthermore, she had only been licensed as a psychologist for 1 year, not 7 years. However she felt entitled to imply that she had been licensed to practice as a psychologist for 7 years because she had been either a pre- or postdoctoral intern for 6 years prior to her actual licensure. Finally, she had only treated a total of five anorectic patients, three of whom were still in therapy with her. All of her introductory statements were misleading to both the public and her colleagues. Dr. Boaster thought that she was engaging in reasonable ways of promoting herself in a highly competitive market. She thought that patients would be less likely to consult her for treatment if they knew of her relatively recent licensure and somewhat limited professional experience. Unfortunately, she focused more on her own self-promotion than she did on accuracy and honesty in her public statements to other health care providers and potential consumers.

> *(b) Psychologists claim as credentials for their psychological work, only degrees that (1) were earned from a regionally accredited educational institution or (2) were the basis for psychology licensure by the state in which they practice.*

(b) Do not use the title *Dr.* or claim a PhD or master's degree if your degree was earned from a school that is not regionally accredited (i.e., a school that was not formally accredited by the New England Association of Schools and Colleges, the North Central Association of Schools and Colleges, the Western Association of Schools and Colleges, or other similar regional accrediting body), unless the degree qualified you to take the licensing exam in the state in which you practice.

Vignette: Dr. Traveller earned his PhD from a school that was licensed by his home state but was not regionally accredited. After practicing for several years, he decided to move to a neighboring state with a stronger economy and attempt to establish an independent practice as a clinician and consultant.

To his surprise, the state licensing board there refused to acknowledge his PhD because he had not earned it from a regionally accredited school. Dr. Traveller argued that he had graduated from a professional school of psychology that was licensed by his home state, even though it was not regionally accredited. He added that he had achieved excellent grades during his academic career, worked under the formal supervision of a licensed psychologist for 1 year, taken the licensing exam and passed it on the first try, and then practiced independently as a psychologist for 2 years.

The licensing board was unmoved by his story, reiterating that in spite of his other accomplishments, he had not obtained his doctoral degree from a regionally accredited institution. Because the PhD he currently held clearly did not form the basis for licensure in the state because it did not meet the criteria for doctoral training there, he was not permitted to use the title. Dr. Traveller thus quickly became *Mr.* Traveller; he could not even be a candidate to retake the psychology licensing exam because the state licensing law required that all candidates have a doctoral degree from a regionally accredited institution to sit for the exam. Although discouraged, Mr. Traveller decided to formally appeal the licensing board's decision, based on his experience, prior success on the licensing exam, and independent practice in his home state.

3.04   Media Presentations

When psychologists provide advice or comment by means of public lectures, demonstrations, radio or television programs, prerecorded tapes, printed articles, mailed material, or other media, they take reasonable precautions to ensure that (1) the statements are based on appropriate psychological literature and practice, (2) the statements are otherwise consistent with this Ethics Code, and (3) the recipients of the information are not encouraged to infer that a relationship has been established with them personally.

During media presentations and whenever addressing the public in an oral address or in writing, remember the following points: (a) always be able to back up what you say; (b) make sure that you are in compliance with every other standard in this code, not just the ones in this section; and (c) don't encourage listeners, viewers, or readers to assume that you have an individualized, professional relationship with them if in fact you actually know little or nothing about them or their history.

Vignette: Dr. Duhl was a psychologist who hosted a weekly radio call-in show that regularly discussed topics concerning child development and parenting issues. She generally was careful to base her remarks on the current research in these areas, preferring to be accurate in the information she dispensed to callers. If she was asked a question that required a lengthy answer, she gave it the attention it deserved, sometimes speaking for 5 or 6 minutes at a time to provide a comprehensive reply.

After 1 month on the air, the producer of the show and the director of programming were troubled that the show's ratings were not especially high. They attempted to remedy the situation by discussing with Dr. Duhl their proposals for changing the format and content of the show in hopes of increasing the audience's interest level. They had analyzed callers' comments and concluded that many listeners were losing interest because of Dr. Duhl's tendency to focus on a single subject for each broadcast. They proposed a new format that would include brief discussions of several diverse topics per show.

They also had a number of other suggestions to "spice up" the show. They wanted Dr. Duhl to provide shorter answers than her usual lengthy, drawn-out replies. They asked that she keep her responses to under 1 minute to accommodate more callers and allow for greater audience participation. She was uncertain about how to comply with this request because she feared that she would have to give superficial treatment to some topics that required greater elaboration than 1 minute of air time.

The producer and director also mentioned Dr. Duhl's tendency to use appropriately tentative language when addressing a caller's question rather than freely giving advice or suggestions. They viewed this as "waffling" and thought that it did not meet the needs of listeners who were unsophisticated in psychological matters. They asked that she be less scholarly or "dry" in her presentation and not be so reluctant to suggest a course of action to callers. They thought she should simply "tell them what to do" to remedy a particular situation. She had intentionally resisted this temptation because she was well aware that she did not know the details of a caller's history or their immediate situation, and she did not feel competent to give advice to a caller who presented a problem in 30 seconds or less.

Finally, Dr. Duhl's superiors thought that she could enliven the discussion and further pique the interest of listeners with stories and vignettes drawn from those of actual patients from her therapy practice. She was reluctant to do this for fear of exposing the privacy of patients and breaching her ethical and legal duty to preserve confidentiality.

Dr. Duhl felt that the requests to change the format of her presentation might indeed appeal to the audience, but she did not think they were in compliance with this and other ethical standards. She was concerned about maintaining a scientific approach to her presentations, being able to support her statements, preserving the confidentiality of her patients, avoiding giving advice in the absence of a defined professional relationship with an individual (e.g., client–therapist), and refraining from making suggestions about a specific course of action without adequate information about the caller's history and circumstances. In short, Dr. Duhl felt that she could not conduct a radio presentation in the style that was being requested without compromising her ethical standards. She considered carefully the wisdom of participating in a radio program that was geared toward entertainment and eventually decided to exercise her option to withdraw from the contract with the network.

3.05 Testimonials

Psychologists do not solicit testimonials from current psychotherapy clients or patients or other persons who because of their particular circumstances are vulnerable to undue influence.

Don't ask your therapy clients, patients, or others over whom you have power or authority for permission to quote them in advertisements for your services, brochures, handouts, and so on.

Vignette: Dr. Youzem offered a weight reduction program that consisted of participation in both individual psychotherapy and a group psychoeducational approach. His results were quite good, but he had relatively few patients because managed health care companies often refused to reimburse patients for his services. In an effort to expand his practice, Dr.

Youzem asked 10 of his current patients who had maintained their healthy weight for many months if they would be willing to make a few statements endorsing his program that he could quote in a brochure to be mailed out.

All patients complied with his request, but they experienced a broad range of personal reactions. Some were happy to give testimonials; they were extremely enthusiastic about the weight they had lost and wanted to share their experience with others who wished to lose weight. However, several patients provided testimonies only because they felt unable to refuse a request from their therapist, even though they would have preferred to quietly continue their work in treatment without having to participate in any promotional activities. These patients felt somewhat coerced and used, but none of them had the assertiveness to speak up to him about their feelings. This was especially true of those who were struggling with set backs in their weight control plan and had actually begun to gain weight again. They felt as though they were unable to discuss their failures with Dr. Youzem, having provided such positive statements for his promotional brochure about their success.

Several patients experienced an increase in depression because they felt pressured to be successful in their weight loss plan and subsequently felt as though they had let their therapist down by dropping out of the program. Although they felt used by their therapist or thought he had taken advantage of his authority over them to obtain testimonials for advertising, they did not bring a complaint against him. One patient, however, wrote him a letter several months after termination indicating that she would gladly have provided a testimonial after she had completed all her therapeutic work with him. But somehow, for her, to have done so while continuing to consult with him irrevocably altered their relationship and made it impossible for her to continue in treatment.

3.06 Solicitation

> *Psychologists do not engage, directly or through agents, in uninvited in-person solicitation of business from actual or potential psychotherapy patients or clients or other persons who because of their particular circumstances are vulnerable to undue influence. However, this does not preclude attempting to implement appropriate collateral contacts with significant others for the purpose of benefiting an already engaged therapy patient.*

Don't be an "ambulance chaser" or personally invite people to begin therapy with you in settings where their judgment may be clouded by their immediate circumstances. Keep in mind that this standard doesn't rule out inviting a client's family members or significant others into your office as warranted.

Vignette: Dr. Snarem was recently licensed and had learned everything she knew about practice building from her former supervisor, Dr. Freeman, an aggressive entrepreneur with seemingly only a token concern for the welfare of her patients. Being long on creativity and energy and somewhat short on her comprehension of ethics, Dr. Snarem decided to aggressively promote her services in hopes of making personal contact with those individuals who were in immediate need of mental health services.

She printed individualized brochures addressing individuals in the midst of major life transitions who she thought might be likely candidates for therapy. Hence, she could be seen frequently distributing literature and business cards outside courtrooms where divorce and child custody litigation was going on, hospital emergency rooms, retirement communities, assisted-living centers, and any other place she could think of where people who might need her services congregated.

Dr. Snarem rapidly built up a busy practice and even surpassed her mentor, Dr. Freeman. Unfortunately, however, many of her clients could have been better served had they interviewed several therapists first, instead of beginning treatment with her. Some did not need therapy or counseling at all and would have recovered from their situational stress quite adequately with the passage of time. However, because of the emotional intensity of their life transition and the unexpected face-to-face encounter with a nurturing therapist, their judgment about beginning therapy was somewhat clouded, resulting in an inviting "short cut" to Dr. Snarem's door.

Many patients stopped therapy as abruptly as they began, once they fully understood the extent of the financial obligation. Others dropped out over a period of weeks in search of a different kind of therapist, one who was less manipulative and, in some cases, more competent and compassionate. After having paid too much money to Dr. Snarem for too long, these individuals felt exploited, as though she took advantage of their depression or panicky emotional state to initiate a therapeutic contract at a time when their objectivity and good judgment were at a minimum.

4

Therapy

4.01 Structuring the Relationship

(a) Psychologists discuss with clients or patients as early as is feasible in the therapeutic relationship appropriate issues, such as the nature and anticipated course of therapy, fees, and confidentiality. (See also Standards 1.25, Fees and Financial Arrangements, and 5.01, Discussing the Limits of Confidentiality.)

(a) Inform patients what your therapy is about and what to expect in the course of treatment early on. Discuss your fees, financial arrangements, limits of confidentiality, and theoretical orientation for starters. Consider telling them what you might want a good friend to know about the nature, structure, and anticipated course of treatment if he or she were about to consult a psychologist for the first time.

Vignette: Rosemary, a depressed 46-year-old woman with chronic pain in her lower back from a 2-year-old work injury contacted Dr. Tellem for psychotherapy and nonmedical interventions for her pain. She was expecting that one hypnotic session could relieve her suffering and hoped that antidepressant medication could alleviate her depression. Dr. Tellem explained over the phone that treatment would be longer, consisting of history taking, relaxation training, biofeedback or self-hypnotic training, psychotherapy, and possibly other interventions. He explained that his theoretical orientation was cognitive–behavioral, discussed coordinating treatment with her physician, and explained the necessity of signing a consent form. He told her the cost of therapy and indicated that because he was not listed as a provider on her managed health care plan, he would be considered an "out-of-system provider," thus it was possible that partial payments could be made by the insurer. The patient, however, would be expected to make a copayment, the exact amount of which could be determined with a telephone call to the managed health care case manager.

Rosemary was quite surprised to learn of both the anticipated duration of therapy and the cost because she had previously called Dr. Overschoot who had assured her of excellent pain relief in two or three sessions. However, she felt quite well informed by Dr. Tellem's presentation. He took the time to encourage and answer questions; after thinking it over, Rosemary decided to consult Dr. Tellem for treatment.

> *(b) When the psychologist's work with clients or patients will be supervised, the above discussion includes that fact, and the name of the supervisor, when the supervisor has legal responsibility for the case.*

(b) Always inform patients at the outset if you are under formal supervision, such as when you are working as a pre- or postdoctoral intern, fellow, psychological assistant, and so on. Give out the name of your supervisor because he or she is legally and clinically responsible for your work.

Vignette: Dr. Rhea Veel had just received her doctor of psychology (PsyD) degree and was beginning to accrue postdoctoral supervisory hours for licensure by working in a group private practice in a small midwestern town. She worked under the clinical supervision of the owner of the practice, Dr. Tellem. One of Dr. Tellem's procedures was to require all of his supervisees and employees to give new patients a handout describing the fiduciary relationships of consumer, therapist, and supervisor and other information about the psychological services offered.

Dr. Veel understood her ethical obligation to inform clients clearly that she was being supervised by Dr. Tellem and to make sure that they understood the implications of the handout that she provided. She took the time to answer their questions and present any information she thought might be helpful to their decision-making process about treatment. On several occasions, new callers declined to accept her as their therapist because they knew Dr. Tellem in various social contexts and did not want him to know about their therapy disclosures, even though they liked him as a friend and colleague. They would not have declined had Dr. Veel not released his name, and they were very grateful to have avoided a potentially embarrassing situation.

> *(c) When the therapist is a student intern, the client or patient is informed of that fact.*

(c) Always inform patients and clients if you are still in training (i.e., a practicum student, pre- or postdoctoral fellow, intern, etc.) at the outset, and give the name of your supervisor if he or she is legally responsible for you.

Vignette: A large university counseling center providing a range of psychological services to students, faculty, and staff and their families also served as a training site for the counseling and clinical psychology doctoral program and the clinical social work programs. It was not readily apparent to those seeking mental health services which staff person was a licensed mental health care practitioner, a practicum student, or an intern. For this reason, the center had a policy of distributing a printed handout to each new client describing the staff members and their credentials. In addition, practicum students and interns were required to inform new clients of their training status and the identity of their supervisor at the outset of services.

Occasionally, new clients would request a more experienced therapist than the trainee to whom they were assigned. Such requests, if they were warranted, could generally be honored, although at busier times of the year there was likely to be a waiting period of up to 4 weeks to consult with a senior staff member. However, the center's practices of informing new clients about the status of staff reduced misunderstanding about these matters.

> *(d) Psychologists make reasonable efforts to answer patients' questions and to avoid apparent misunderstandings about therapy. Whenever possible, psychologists provide oral and/or written information, using language that is reasonably understandable to the patient or client.*

(d) Anticipate patients' questions at the beginning of services. Remember, patients don't know *what they don't know* about psychotherapy, especially those who have never seen a therapist before. Many may not know what to ask or which topics to address. Help them to understand what may lie ahead by informing them in simple language or providing simple and clear handouts.

Vignette: Dr. Anne Vishen received a call from Robert, a 16-year-old high school sophomore who was having panic attacks several times a week. He thought his sanity was at risk and wondered if his burgeoning use of amphetamines might be contributing to the problem.

Dr. Vishen explained how it might be possible that street drugs could contribute to the problem but pointed out that other factors might also be involved. She described both her therapeutic approach and the possibility of involving other family members in therapy, if necessary. She brought up the subject of privacy and confidentiality and discussed how the boundaries of therapy—both in what must be held confidential and what is permitted or mandated to be disclosed—protect the client. She discussed the specific exclusions to confidentiality, those situations when she would be required to break confidentiality and notify a hospital or police department of something disclosed in therapy, such as if Robert posed a significant risk of harming himself or someone else.

After hearing Dr. Vishen's introductory comments, Robert had one question about his parents' involvement. He felt strongly that he wanted to keep his drug experimentation secret. Dr. Vishen explained that according to state law, she could use her discretion in contacting his parents and including them in his therapy; she said the two of them could discuss it and arrive at that decision collaboratively. Major considerations in including the parents would be determined by the extent to which his own drug use presented a danger to his health and safety as well as other factors to be discussed. She also informed Robert about the state law exempting his parents from having to pay her fee, unless they were included as participants in the therapy.[1]

Dr. Vishen reassured Robert that as he knew, many teens struggle with drugs and that sometimes a group therapeutic approach was an extremely useful adjunct to individual work. Robert felt well prepared for

---

[1]*Author's Note:* The reader should note that laws concerning confidentiality vary by state.

beginning counseling with Dr. Vishen and knowledgeable about the various aspects of therapy with her. He was grateful for her candor, lack of false assurances, and the fact that she fully answered all his questions and anticipated a few others. He decided to make an appointment with her as soon as she could see him.

4.02 Informed Consent to Therapy

(a) Psychologists obtain appropriate informed consent to therapy or related procedures, using language that is reasonably understandable to participants. The content of informed consent will vary depending on many circumstances; however, informed consent generally implies that the person (1) has the capacity to consent, (2) has been informed of significant information concerning the procedure, (3) has freely and without undue influence expressed consent, and (4) consent has been appropriately documented.

(a) In general, the patient should understand what you plan to offer as psychotherapy or related services and should consent to receiving them. The four parts to this rule are as follows:

1. The person must be able to understand your description and able to provide consent.
2. The person must be informed of significant aspects of the services you offer.
3. The person must freely and willingly consent to your services, without any pressure from you.
4. You must document the consent (this is done by using a form that is read and signed by the patient, by making an entry in the patient's file, or some other way).[2]

Vignette: During a telephone conversation, Dr. Sunnyview informed Janet, her new patient who was depressed and anorectic, that individual psychotherapy would rapidly provide relief for her symptoms and help her to be more productive at work. She virtually promised that treatment would be effective in nine sessions or less. This time frame was consistent with the number of sessions that had been allotted by the patient's managed care carrier, and Dr. Sunnyview wanted her patient to know that she could make a great amount of progress within that limited number of sessions. She said nothing about the possibility that depression sometimes was exacerbated during the course of therapy or the possibility that treatment might well last longer. She never discussed the need for or the logistics of seeking any required additional sessions from the managed care carrier. She did not discuss the possibility of referring her to a psychiatrist for assessment for antidepressant medication or coordinating treatment with her referring primary care physician, as might be necessary.

---

[2]See also Standard 1.25, Fees and Financial Arrangements, and 5.01, Discussing the Limits of Confidentiality.

Furthermore, Dr. Sunnyview used sophisticated psychological terms, which Janet did not understand, in describing her theoretical orientation. She said nothing about confidentiality, the possible need for hospitalization, fees, or the frequency of sessions. In fact, she expected the patient to come three times each week and pay in advance for each week's therapy, and she offered no possibility of a sliding fee or deferred payment.

When the patient appeared for her first session and learned of these expectations, she was quite disappointed because she could not afford to come as often or pay the high fee of $175 for each 45-minute session. Disappointed, she promptly dropped out of treatment and avoided contacting another therapist for several months. She felt shameful and betrayed by her meeting with Dr. Sunnyview, as though she was expected to understand in advance the financial obligation and other details of the treatment.

Not only did Dr. Sunnyview fail to inform Janet of the salient aspects of treatment and the business arrangements, she had also portrayed the therapy unrealistically, exaggerating its efficacy and grossly distorting its probable time frame. The patient was not well informed about the treatment ahead of time, and it was only after the initial session that she began to appreciate the important details of both the commitment that she was about to make with Dr. Sunnyview and its utter impossibility.

> *(b) When persons are legally incapable of giving informed consent, psychologists obtain informed permission from a legally authorized person, if such substitute consent is permitted by law.*

(b) When treating minors, those who don't understand your role or those who are not oriented to the situation because of their age (e.g., a young child, an older person with impaired memory or comprehension) or a mental impairment, be sure to obtain informed consent from their parent or legal guardian before proceeding with treatment.

Vignette: A woman contacted a psychologist about her 19-year-old son David who was schizophrenic and actively delusional. He had been hallucinating for over 1 month and was no longer able to go to his job each day. The psychologist took a brief history over the phone and presented some treatment options. These included the probability of medication and ongoing consultation with a psychiatrist and the possible need for hospitalization and involvement of other family members as a part of the treatment process.

He reviewed the range of options involving future ongoing individual and possible group psychotherapy for David as well as inpatient and outpatient programs that might be helpful. He also addressed the issue of confidentiality and its exceptions, at least in a preliminary way; he intended to present much more information about it to both mother and son later on.

The mother had several specific questions about David's diagnosis and prognosis, which the psychologist could only address in a tentative fashion, never having met or assessed the young man. After this extended telephone consultation, the mother understood, at least in a general way, how a course of treatment for David might evolve. She agreed with it as much as she was able to and decided to proceed with the treatment and bring him in for assessment and whatever therapy would be in his best interest.

> *(c) In addition, psychologists (1) inform those persons who are legally incapable of giving informed consent about the proposed interventions in a manner commensurate with the persons' psychological capacities, (2) seek their assent to those interventions, and (3) consider such persons' preferences and best interests.*

(c) When dealing with minors or those who may not understand your role, be sure to (a) inform them how you plan to intervene in their lives (e.g., assessment, counseling); (b) seek (although not necessarily obtain) their agreement about receiving your services; and (c) consider their best interests and preferences before proceeding with therapy.

Vignette: A recently remarried man brought his 8-year-old son, Alan, to a hospital outpatient clinic for treatment. Alan was having difficulty forming friendships with the other students, was getting into fights on the playground, and had been caught stealing from the teacher's room on several occasions. The boy's stepmother was often out of town on business trips and was unable to schedule a time to go to the clinic. The psychologist, Dr. Wells, who had spoken with Alan's father by phone, encouraged him to prepare his son for the meeting by telling him that he deserved to have someone special just to talk with by himself about anything that he wished. This person was to be his own special sort of counselor or coach who could meet with him each week.

The purpose of the first meeting was for all three to acquaint themselves with each other, discuss some of the background information, and arrange a mutually convenient schedule of meetings. When Dr. Wells met with Alan alone, the boy made it clear that he did not wish to be there, that he "didn't need no more counselors to talk to!" After accepting Alan's remark, Dr. Wells took this opportunity to explain how they might spend their time talking, playing games, or even drawing pictures together. She also told him that she knew he had been having a hard time in school lately, and they could talk about that. She went on to say that she would give Alan a chance to tell her how he's feeling, what he's thinking about, what he might be worried about, upset about, or even happy about. This was to be a special time each week to talk about those things—just the two of them—and if he didn't feel like talking, he could come anyway, and they could spend the time doing something else. Dr. Wells told Alan that he could help decide.

Dr. Wells also said that she might want to invite Alan's stepfather, mother, father, and stepmother in for a session sometime, but she made it clear that she would always discuss this with him first. She reviewed privacy, confidentiality, and the exceptions to these. She informed Alan that he could let her know if there was something he wanted her to keep secret, just between the two of them, or if there was something he specifically wanted her to tell his parents.

Alan was comfortable, at least for the present, in meeting with Dr. Wells. His father agreed to keep Dr. Wells apprised of behavioral changes at home and at school and any new problems or concerns that he observed. During this initial meeting, the therapist had honored her obligation to inform Alan about the nature of their contact. Whenever there was a need for change in the arrangement, such as a family meeting, Dr. Wells would first discuss this with Alan, as she had said she would. With clear communication about such fundamental issues, Alan felt secure enough to agree to a second meeting and, ultimately, many more over the course of the year.

4.03 Couple and Family Relationships

(a) When a psychologist agrees to provide services to several persons who have a relationship (such as husband and wife or parents and children), the psychologist attempts to clarify at the outset (1) which of the individuals are patients or clients and (2) the relationship the psychologist will have with each person. This clarification includes the role of the psychologist and the probable uses of the services provided or the information obtained. (See also Standard 5.01, Discussing the Limits of Confidentiality.)

(a) Identify in general what your role will be at the outset and who, specifically, is the patient if more than one person is in your office.

Vignette: Mr. and Mrs. Crandall began couples therapy with Dr. Sole after many months of conflict. Mrs. Crandall had become increasingly depressed and agitated, with periods of apparent dissociation. Mr. Crandall had been working long hours, avoiding his wife, and beginning to use alcohol on a regular basis, with increasing incidents of intoxication. Dr. Sole saw the potential need for individual psychotherapy for each of them but felt an obligation, first, to address the immediacy of their couples work.

He informed them that he saw his role as a resource to both of them and their marital relationship as the central focus of their work, even though other therapists might work differently. He made it clear that he primarily would be meeting with them as a couple. He informed them that if there was a need for individual psychotherapy, they would have the choice of continuing couples sessions with him or changing the format in some way. Mrs. Crandall wished to see Dr. Sole individually and pursue the couples sessions. He informed her that although in some cases this was possible, he thought it would pose a conflict for him because he could not function simultaneously as her individual psychotherapist and a marital therapist for the two of them. He was willing to have occasional individual sessions with her if she wished, but his theoretical framework did not allow for the extensive therapeutic intervention that she was requesting and was apparently warranted.

Shortly thereafter, Mr. Crandall asked Dr. Sole if he would also meet with their 16-year-old son. Again, Dr. Sole was willing to discuss some possibilities, such as having a single meeting with the boy or referring him to another therapist, but he was unwilling to simultaneously attempt to counsel the son and provide marital therapy. He informed the couple that therapists from other theoretical schools might agree to family therapy or, at times, collateral treatment with another family member. However, Dr. Sole had long ago found that for his style of therapy, it was essential to keep the therapeutic contract clear and simple. He did not wish to provide individual treatment to family members while carrying out marital therapy. He clearly stated the role he would play in providing services and his willingness to refer to other therapists for additional treatment if necessary.

Although initially finding his resistance to their requests frustrating, the Crandalls were ultimately grateful that he was straightforward about his role and its boundaries. They opted to continue regular biweekly sessions with him while Mrs. Crandall obtained individual treatment elsewhere.

> *(b) As soon as it becomes apparent that the psychologist may be called on to perform potentially conflicting roles (such as marital counselor to husband and wife, and then witness for one party in a divorce proceeding), the psychologist attempts to clarify and adjust, or withdraw from, roles appropriately. (See also Standard 7.03, Clarification of Role, under Forensic Activities.)*

(b) Only play one role with your patients, if possible. If marital therapy is moving in the direction of divorce, it seems possible that your clients might begin litigation, and you might be deposed or asked to reveal information about them, consider the potential for a conflict of interest. Simplify your role, and be ready to refuse requests for additional roles. Refer to others as needed!

Vignette: Dr. Superfrau, a newly licensed psychologist, had recently joined the staff of a busy community mental health center. Eager to demonstrate her competence and establish her reputation in the county, she considered accepting various members of the same family for a variety of presenting complaints. The mother first brought in her 11-year-old son for problems in school involving difficulty with reading and studying. Within 3 weeks, the mother asked Dr. Superfrau to see her 9-year-old twins, who were having difficulty sleeping through the night and seemed to have some symptoms of hyperactivity. Soon after that, she wanted to discuss with Dr. Superfrau her own sexual dysfunction because her relationship with her husband had started to deteriorate.

Within 1 month, the woman's husband telephoned Dr. Superfrau to ask if she would be willing to consult with him on an "important professional matter." He was the CEO of a large architectural firm and was seeking her assistance in coping with some interpersonal stress in the workplace. He was beginning to experience headaches, anxiety, and insomnia because ongoing conflict with several employees involving theoretical difference in the workplace was beginning to effect him. He also wanted to seek her assistance about an important personal matter. He told Dr. Superfrau that a few months earlier, he had been contacted by a 19-year-old claiming to be his son from an earlier relationship. It was true that 19 years ago he'd had such a son, whom he and the boy's mother gave up for adoption at birth, and he was well aware that a rendezvous with the young man might eventually occur. He wished to play whatever role he could as mentor but was concerned about how this new development might affect his current wife and children. He was also ambivalent about the extent of his own involvement in the boy's life at this point and the prospect of an old girlfriend, the boy's mother, reentering his life. She had also surfaced recently and was living in the same city.

Understandably, Dr. Superfrau began feeling overwhelmed with the needs of this family. Although she was competent to treat the problems presented, she saw a clear need for couples therapy in addition to the individual concerns of the members. It rapidly became too complicated for her to attempt to treat all of the family members; after presenting this case at a weekly staff meeting, she was able to see how she had overextended herself. She referred certain family members to other therapists at the agency and in the community and narrowed the scope of her work to include only the 11-year-old. This decision allowed for good confidentiality and clear lines of accountability in all the therapy relationships.

4.04 Providing Mental Health Services to Those Served by Others

In deciding whether to offer or provide services to those already receiving mental health services elsewhere, psychologists carefully consider the treatment issues and the potential patient's or client's welfare. The psychologist discusses these issues with the patient or client, or another legally authorized person on behalf of the client, in order to minimize the risk of confusion and conflict, consults with the other service providers when appropriate, and proceeds with caution and sensitivity to the therapeutic issues.

You may see patients currently consulting other therapists, but be sure to coordinate treatment and collaborate with them if it's in the patient's best interest. Therapy can become confusing and mutually sabotaging unless all parties agree to open lines of communication.

Vignette: A young woman diagnosed by Dr. Firstly with borderline personality disorder decided to secretly seek additional therapy for her panic attacks with Dr. Secundo, a reputed expert in this disorder. In her phone conversation with Dr. Secundo, she informed him that she was already seeing Dr. Firstly but was emphatic in her demand that he not collaborate with her other therapist or let her know that he also would be treating the young woman. She specifically refused to sign a consent form permitting such contact when Dr. Secundo brought up the subject.

Dr. Secundo thought that he could work effectively with the patient and that the Ethics Code now permitted such concurrent consultations with different therapists (as opposed to the previous edition of the code) as long as appropriate coordination or collaboration occurred, if needed. However, in the very first telephone call, he already was aware that problems were beginning to surface. He suspected that the young woman was engaging in manipulative behavior by prohibiting collaboration between himself and the other therapist. Furthermore, by not even wanting her primary therapist to be aware of her concurrent consultations with him, she was engaging in additional attempts to control the primary therapy, introducing a significant intervention by another therapist but keeping it secret from Dr. Firstly for her own reasons.

Dr. Secundo decided against accepting the young woman into therapy under her stipulations that collaboration with Dr. Firstly would be forbidden. He explained that the dual therapies might be confusing to her because each therapist had somewhat different theoretical orientations. He also told her that to maximize the effectiveness of her treatment, both therapists should ideally have her consent to consult with each other as needed. He further stated that he would be happy to see her in the future if she felt she could comply with these conditions.

4.05 Sexual Intimacies With Current Patients or Clients

Psychologists do not engage in sexual intimacies with current patients or clients.

Never engage in sexual activities with your current patients or clients. Also because sexual provocation is often subjectively determined, be exceedingly careful about touching or hugging your patients or any verbal or nonverbal behavior that is ambiguous and open to a sexualized interpretation.

Vignette: Camille was a 33-year-old woman married to an alcoholic who was beginning to become physically abusive. She began therapy with Dr. Mellow for the purpose of exploring how to either improve her relationship with her spouse or how to overcome her despondency and separate from him. As she progressed in therapy over the months, she became more personally secure and less compelled to seek her husband's approval and always try to please him at her own expense. She also noticed the emergence of strong feelings for Dr. Mellow and found herself thinking about him often with great gratitude and affection. She knew that Dr. Mellow was recently divorced, and she entertained the thought that he might possibly be interested in having an affair with her.

Although he had refused her invitation to meet at a nearby restaurant over a glass of wine, he seemed to have a special interest in her and had a very loving demeanor, in her opinion. After all, she reasoned, he frequently wore shirts of her favorite color and often smiled at her affectionately. One day, after a particularly difficult therapy session in which Camille revealed her loving feelings for Dr. Mellow, she gave him a slow, sensual hug at the end of the hour. Dr. Mellow found her seductiveness compelling and saw her as very physically attractive. However, he had a strong commitment to be a resource to her by remaining in the role of therapist, not by having an affair with her. He also knew well the research on erotic countertransference, that affairs with patients are generally very harmful to patients over time, and that psychologists who engage in them are frequently sued or become the target of formal ethics complaints after such relationships come to an end.

The meaning of Camille's affection for him was explored in therapy in a variety of ways and was revealed to her in a manner that helped her gain insight and resolve her erotic attachment to him. This included reviewing her immediate set of circumstances, such as the transition in her marriage, her dependency needs, and the inherent supportive behavior on the part of himself as therapist. To help maintain his objectivity, Dr. Mellow explored his own sexual feelings for Camille with a consultant, a trusted senior psychologist, and found that these sessions were extremely helpful in allowing him to continue working with his patient without being swept away by her intensity or demanding nature.

4.06 Therapy With Former Sexual Partners

Psychologists do not accept as therapy patients or clients persons with whom they have engaged in sexual intimacies.

Don't ever accept former lovers as patients no matter how much time has passed. There are usually plenty of other therapists you can refer them to who can be objective and competent. Consider that having a sexual relationship irrevocably alters your ability to provide competent therapy to a former lover.

Vignette: A pain management clinic in a local hospital referred Mr. Ecks to Dr. Helpim for nonmedical treatment of cluster headaches. After a short telephone intake, Dr. Helpim realized that this was an old boyfriend with whom she had a brief relationship during her graduate school days 20 years before. After some moments of hesitation, she agreed to accept him into treatment for biofeedback and stress management, with the private rationale that because she would not be conducting psychotherapy with him, she was not risking impaired judgment or competence. In that way, she reasoned, she would be keeping within the spirit of this ethical standard. It was true that she had been his lover years before, but she would not be offering him psychotherapy now, only biofeedback and stress management.

The two seemed to work well together for the eight biofeedback sessions, despite the significant memories for each that were triggered when Dr. Helpim would touch his head, neck, shoulders, and hands to tape on the biofeedback leads. Mr. Ecks even jokingly remarked that it seemed "just like old times" when on one occasion she asked him to remove his tie to properly attach the EMG leads to the back of his neck. That notwithstanding, the treatment progressed satisfactorily until the patient began discussing a major stressor in his life, namely, his second marriage. Exploring this life issue with her patient, Dr. Helpim realized that he was quite narcissistic and had recently developed a cocaine habit. He was happy to discuss any aspect of his life, thinking that his former girlfriend probably knew him better than anyone, and would be able to help him. She, however, found it increasingly difficult to remain objective and could see clearly that he needed (and wanted) individual psychotherapy.

As the biofeedback training drew to a close and the stress management discussions merged into therapy, she found that her patience for Mr. Ecks's self-indulgence, so characteristic in her work with other patients, was beginning to wane. At times, she had quick flashes of frustration and even anger with her patient. Sometimes he added to her frustration and feelings of conflict by discussing his complex sex life with his wife and several other women, with whom he would use cocaine. On several occasions, Mr. Ecks chose to nostalgically revisit some of their own shared intimate moments of the past, which he remembered surprisingly well. Dr. Helpim fortunately realized that no good purpose would be served by continuing to meet with this patient.

After reviewing progress and preparing for termination over his strong objections—he was just starting to look forward to these weekly sessions—she gave him the names of several colleagues to consult for individual psychotherapy. She was greatly relieved when the treatment came to a close—another sign for her that termination and referral was indeed a wise choice. She could see, with hindsight, that she never should have accepted him as a patient in the first place, even for the supposedly limited scope of carrying out biofeedback training and stress management.

4.07 Sexual Intimacies With Former Therapy Patients

(a) Psychologists do not engage in sexual intimacies with a former therapy patient or client for at least two years after cessation or termination of professional services.

(a) Assume that it is always risky and probably unwise to have sex with someone you've seen as a patient. Note, however, that if you decide to do this, you must absolutely wait for 2 full years to pass since your last professional contact before engaging in sexual intimacies. Also be aware that some states have laws specifying a different amount of posttermination time that must elapse before a sexual relationship may begin.[3]

Vignette: Dr. Roamer had been treating Julie, a 29-year-old woman with a history of childhood sexual molestation, for nearly 2 years. He was in-

---

[3]See also Standard 1.17, Multiple Relationships.

creasingly drawn to her, as he had been to numerous other patients, the longer he treated her. Her seductive way of dressing and behaving was having its effect. Julie's many years of paternal incest in childhood had resulted in her having poor boundaries, and as an adult she found herself repeatedly having affairs with men who were in a position of authority or power over her. She felt a strong sexual attraction to her therapist, and she told him so.

Dr. Roamer knew of the ethical prohibition against sex with patients but privately thought that APA had "no right" to restrict a psychologist's actions and freedom of choice to do whatever he or she pleased after terminating with a patient. After all, he reasoned, there would be no formal relationship any more after therapy, and consenting adults should be free to do whatever they agreed to do with each other.

Near the end of one session Dr. Roamer told Julie of his strong admiration and attraction for her and said that he thought he could be more help to her outside the consulting office than inside. From that moment on, their relationship was irrevocably changed. On hearing this, Julie rose from her seat, walked over to Dr. Roamer, placed her hands on his face, with her body close to his, and gazed eagerly into his eyes. They kissed a long and passionate kiss. Dr. Roamer informed her that he was "not really permitted to do this" because she was "currently a patient." At that point, she quickly suggested that she felt "cured"; indeed she felt quite exhilarated and very special that Dr. Roamer, her own psychotherapist, would fall in love with her. She told him that she had always felt a strong "spiritual connection" with him. She didn't think she really needed therapy any more anyway and preferred to meet with him under different circumstances. Dr. Roamer agreed, with some hesitation.

He thought he understood the concept of boundaries in psychotherapy and the necessity of stopping therapy completely before their relationship could go any further. Therefore, he suggested that they formally terminate their therapy relationship and meet for dinner the next night. It was on that occasion that they agreed to pursue their new and thrilling relationship.

The romance lasted approximately 10 months, during which time Dr. Roamer grew weary of Julie's depressions, neediness, and increasingly demanding behavior. The affair ended suddenly one day, with much disappointment and emotional pain for Julie. She became deeply depressed and enraged, and she ultimately attempted suicide twice over the following 3 months. During the following year, she brought a formal ethics complaint against Dr. Roamer. She charged that he had improperly terminated his therapy with her, failed to wait 2 years posttermination to begin a romantic relationship, and inflicted significant harm on her by sexualizing the relationship. She claimed that he also had violated a number of other ethical standards while he was her therapist, prior to the affair.

Dr. Roamer attempted to defend himself on the grounds that Julie was really a former patient, not a current one, and that *she* was really the one who had initiated the relationship. She was also the aggressor in sex, he added. He attempted to make the point that he felt a professional obligation to convert their therapy relationship into a love relationship because it seemed to be more "therapeutic" for her in the long run to do so.

His defense was immaterial. He had broken the 2-year rule, no matter what his rationale may have been. Of equal importance, he had shown utter disregard for the dynamics of psychotherapy and termination by essentially abandoning his therapy patient in the interest of beginning a romantic relationship. He seemed to capitalize on the significant power differential that might have been a factor in Julie's initial attraction for him but did nothing to explain, interpret, or defuse the intensity of the interaction for his patient. Instead, he chose to act on his own sexual attraction to his current patient by first converting her to a "former" patient and then disregarding the 2-year posttermination rule and agreeing to become her lover.

> *(b) Because sexual intimacies with a former therapy patient or client are so frequently harmful to the patient or client, and because such intimacies undermine public confidence in the psychology profession and thereby deter the public's use of needed services, psychologists do not engage in sexual intimacies with former therapy patients and clients even after a two-year interval except in the most unusual circumstances. The psychologist who engages in such activity after the two years following cessation or termination of treatment bears the burden of demonstrating that there has been no exploitation, in light of all relevant factors, including (1) the amount of time that has passed since therapy terminated, (2) the nature and duration of the therapy, (3) the circumstances of termination, (4) the patient's or client's personal history, (5) the patient's or client's current mental status, (6) the likelihood of adverse impact on the patient or client and others, and (7) any statements or actions made by the therapist during the course of therapy suggesting or inviting the possibility of a post-termination sexual or romantic relationship with the patient or client. (See also Standard 1.17, Multiple Relationships.)*

(b) Sex with a former patient is so fraught with complications, no matter how much time has elapsed, that you would be well advised to avoid it completely, even after 2 years. If you should develop a sexual relationship after the requisite amount of time has passed, you must be prepared to prove that you have not exploited your former patient by taking into account at least the following factors:

1. length of time since therapy ended
2. type and duration of treatment
3. circumstances of termination
4. patient's personal history
5. patient's current mental health
6. likelihood that your actions could harm the patient
7. your statements or actions during therapy suggesting a posttermination romance.

Vignette: Dr. Waerie was being consulted by Laura, a 35-year-old high school teacher and single mother of two who was grieving her father's death and suffering stress-induced headaches and backaches. The treatment consisted primarily of supportive psychotherapy, with a behavioral focus on stress management and training in progressive muscle relaxation. No Axis II disorder was present, and the patient had a good premorbid history. As the treatment progressed, Dr. Waerie found himself growing increasingly attracted to Laura. He had been recently divorced and was in the process of adapting to a new living situation away from daily contact with his children. As his sexual feelings for his patient increased, he consulted a trusted senior colleague and took a workshop on erotic countertransference, which happened to be offered at a nearby university. He was able to successfully resolve the intensity of his feelings so that he could continue treating the patient successfully. After 4 months of treatment, she terminated, very pleased with the results.

While Dr. Waerie was attending a professional conference on learning disabilities 3 years later, he encountered Laura once again. She was a high-functioning and successful teacher, was in good mental health, and was obviously very grateful to Dr. Waerie for the work he had done with her. The two agreed to get together over coffee, and Dr. Waerie found himself disclosing things to her about himself that he had never told a patient or former patient before. Up until this point, Laura actually knew very little about Dr. Waerie as a person, although she had been curious at times. The more they talked, the more they discovered their mutual attraction for each other. Their intimacy grew in the weeks that followed, but Dr. Waerie's conscience gnawed at him. He was concerned that he was possibly being exploitative of Laura because she was a former patient.

He again consulted a senior colleague, one who specialized in couples therapy, to explore the possibility that he might be abusing his power or authority as a former therapist by pursuing a relationship with Laura. He also considered having a joint meeting with the colleague if Laura was willing or possibly attending a series of workshops for couples. His focus was on equalizing any residual power differential that might have been left over from the therapy relationship 3 years before. He wished to step out of his role of "therapist" completely by openly revealing his weaknesses and foibles to Laura and exploring his personal wants and needs with her.

It would be fair to say that he took every reasonable precaution to avoid exploiting his former patient. Then and only then, he reasoned, could their developing friendship and affection for each other have the best chance of maturing into a mutually gratifying relationship, if it was to be. Nevertheless, he knew that he still might be placing himself in jeopardy if the relationship should later deteriorate and Laura feel upset about it.

4.08 Interruption of Services

(a) Psychologists make reasonable efforts to plan for facilitating care in the event that psychological services are interrupted by factors such as the psychologist's illness, death, unavailability, or relocation or by the

client's relocation or financial limitations. (See also Standard 5.09, Preserving Records and Data.)

(a) Make plans for the continuity of your patients' care in the event of a debilitating illness, a disabling accident, or your demise. Know who will take care of your patients and their records in case you become disabled, die, or decide to move to a different part of the country.

Vignette: Dr. Planner, a psychology professor at a major university who also had a part-time clinical practice, died while driving home late one night on the New York Thruway when her car was struck from behind by an intoxicated driver. This tragic loss was keenly felt by her students, colleagues, and individual and group psychotherapy patients, some of whom suffered "flashbacks" to early abandonment in life and felt panicked and depressed. Some of her patients wondered secretly if this was a suicide on the part of their therapist because she had seemed somewhat reserved and low in energy in recent months. Clearly, some of her patients were quite needy at this time, having suffered a grave loss with her death.

Fortunately, Dr. Planner had left instructions with her secretary and on her computer about how to help patients with just such a transition as well as what to do with their records. Her secretary knew that she was to contact several psychologists and activate Dr. Planner's "transition team." Some of these individuals were among her closest friends and some were simply competent colleagues who she had previously selected and instructed about the role they were to play in the event of her death or disability. Specifically, each was to be immediately "on call" for any of Dr. Planner's patients who wanted to consult them. Furthermore, they were to accept her patients into therapy (time permitting) if the patient selected them as a new therapist or handle the referral process to another therapist if the match was not good.

Those psychologists who were Dr. Planner's close friends were reminded that they should not take on this task unless they felt able to because they obviously were coping with their own grief at her loss. Indeed, two of these therapists wisely opted to be helpful "behind the scenes" with office work and records but decided they could not cope with their friend's death and simultaneously provide therapy to her grieving patients.

The team also took care to preserve the confidentiality of Dr. Planner's written records by asking patients to sign consent forms before their records were released. In some cases, patients were curious about the contents of their records, so after releasing them to another psychologist, they had a chance to sit down and review them with that therapist. These steps were methodically, rapidly, and efficiently carried out as soon as the secretary made contact with the transition team and patients. Over the course of the next several months, every patient who had consulted Dr. Planner during the previous year and had ended therapy was notified by letter of the situation. They were also referred to several other therapists in the event that they desired additional therapy.

(b) When entering into employment or contractual relationships, psychologists provide for orderly and appropriate resolution of responsibility for patient or client care in the event that the employment or contractual relationship ends, with paramount consideration given to the welfare of the patient or client.

(b) Read employment contracts and managed health care contracts carefully, so that you understand the agreement about keeping or referring patients when ending your participation in the contract. Remember, details are important. You have some ethical responsibility for the continuity of patient care.[4]

Vignette: Dr. Dawllez was the owner of the ABC Mental Health Group, Inc., a large group practice located in a metropolitan area. He had worked hard to establish contracts for his corporation as preferred providers with many managed health care organizations and had good working relationships with several nearby hospitals. He attempted to create incentives for both patients and therapists to remain attached to his practice for long periods of time. After all, he reasoned, "one could never have too much therapy."

Dr. Dawllez also fostered the notion of "institutional transference" among patients and corporations. He wanted them all to be aware of ABC's dedication and commitment to their needs over a long period of time, regardless of changes in personnel on his staff. He worked at building a good reputation for his company that would draw new patients and hold old ones, even though individual employees might come and go.

An important part of his business plan included actively discouraging his employees from continuing to see patients independently if they left ABC, regardless of whether the patients were participating in a managed care contract. Some patients had simply chosen an ABC therapist by reputation and had decided to pay for services out of pocket. Because there was no managed care contract to consider, those patients could easily follow a therapist to another location. However, if psychologists decided to leave the group practice, they were required to pay a $600 "transition fee" for each patient who continued to see them privately instead of transferring to another therapist in the group. This was a strong incentive to remain attached to the practice and keep the flow of income predictably constant. The policy of requiring a "transition fee" was specified in the employment contract signed by every employee when they were hired.

It mattered little to Dr. Dawllez whether a departing therapist was the best qualified to continue treating a given patient or whether the patient preferred to continue seeing that therapist in a different setting, having already invested much time, energy, and money in the relationship with their current psychologist. Certainly, for many patients, it would have been preferable and least disruptive for the therapy to continue in another setting with their same psychologist rather than being referred to a new in-house therapist. However, therapists who left ABC generally did not choose this alternative; the $600 fee was simply too punitive.

---

[4]See also Standard 1.27, Referrals and Fees.

Furthermore, most of Dr. Dawllez' employees did not remember signing this part of the contract when they joined the practice because it was couched in legal terms and seemed to have remote application, as though it would probably be irrelevant to their situation. This policy obviously did not support patients' freedom of choice in selecting therapists. There was also a question as to its legal propriety because the state law directly addressed this situation in a recent revision. It was only a matter of time before several therapists contacted the state licensing board about the business practices of Dr. Dawllez. They were deeply concerned that the best interests of patients were not being considered by such policies and that psychologists were effectively being financially penalized by Dawllez for attempting to comply with ethical standards in providing for the continuity of care with patients who chose to continue seeing them after leaving his practice.[5]

4.09 Terminating the Professional Relationship

(a) Psychologists do not abandon patients or clients. (See also Standard 1.25e, under Fees and Financial Arrangements.)

(a) Don't disappear from your patient's life without formally terminating treatment and providing referrals to other resources if they are needed and wanted.

Vignette: Dr. Dee Parture was a psychological assistant under the formal supervision of Dr. Cagey who had had only a minimal amount of contact with him since they began their association. Dr. Parture had been seeing one male patient for 5 months. Her patient was narcissistic, and Dr. Parture was becoming increasingly uncomfortable with his demands and the angry confrontations directed at her. Her own anxiety and avoidance began to mount with each session, but she felt obligated to continue treating the patient. She rarely had sufficient opportunity to discuss her concerns with Dr. Cagey because there were no regular supervisory sessions scheduled, and he was seemingly too involved with the administrative and business aspects of the group practice to offer her any training.

In one session with Dr. Parture, the patient began lamenting his financial status, having recently lost his job, and complained that the fee he had to pay was "unconscionably high." He stated that he had several friends who were seeing good therapists and paying a much lower fee. Troubled by his remarks and not knowing how to address them, Dr. Parture took his complaints as a clear indication that she should probably stop treating this patient and refer him to a lower cost therapist. Having had no guidance from her supervisor on this subject, she did not know how to proceed when a patient objected to paying the fee. She did not think she was at liberty to lower it and felt conflicted about how to defuse

---

[5]*Author's Note*: Laws permitting or banning payments to owners of group practices by departing psychologists who take patients with them vary from state to state.

her patient's angry feelings. As a result, she did not discuss the fee that had been set by Dr. Cagey or the patient's resentment about paying it. Instead, as the session was nearing the end, she abruptly stated that this would be the final session because it was obvious that he was unhappy with having to pay such a fee, and she could do nothing to adjust it. She also indicated that he seemed unhappy with the treatment he was receiving because he frequently engaged her in angry challenges. When her patient indicated that he did not wish to end treatment with her, she merely reaffirmed her position and, in her discomfort, even terminated the meeting a few minutes prematurely by standing up and opening the door to the office.

Several days later while discussing this case with a trusted senior clinician, Dr. Parture recognized how she had abandoned her patient because of the intensity of her own performance anxiety. She came to understand that she had not discussed his feelings about continuing or ending treatment, had not discussed the possibility of adjusting the fee temporarily until he was employed again, had not reviewed the progress and course of therapy in light of the initial goals, and had failed to give him the names of any other therapists to contact. She found that she had abruptly broken off a therapeutic process in midstream, mainly due to her own anxiety evoked by his hostile and demanding behavior. The primary lesson she learned, however, was to consult with an experienced therapist much earlier in the process whenever she began to develop apprehension about meeting with a particular patient instead of waiting until things escalated. She also discovered too late that Dr. Cagey was incompetent as a supervisor and could not be a resource to her when she needed him the most.

> *(b) Psychologists terminate a professional relationship when it becomes reasonably clear that the patient or client no longer needs the service, is not benefiting, or is being harmed by continued service.*

(b) Enough is enough! Don't provide endless therapy if the patient doesn't need it, isn't being helped in some way, or even worse is being harmed by continuing to see you.

Vignette: Dr. Chronique was seeing Mrs. LeBacque for depression and management of lumbar and thoracic pain of 8-months duration, resulting from a work injury. After 4 months of psychological intervention for pain reduction coordinated with medical treatment from a pain specialist, Mrs. LeBacque was feeling much better. Her pain symptoms had decreased by 75%, and she was working full-time again. She had also responded well to psychotherapy for depression, and her mood was much improved. She was in good mental health, had no Axis I or Axis II disorder, and was thinking of ending therapy.

Dr. Chronique was willing and interested in continuing to work with his patient, regardless of the fact that there was little the patient wished to talk about anymore in the sessions and that she had responded extremely well to treatment thus far. However, at this time his inclination was to explore other areas of interest to help evaluate and maximize her overall quality of life. Specifically, he suggested that she take a vocational inventory test, despite that she was quite pleased with her career path, and that she take the MMPI-2. He assured her that he would carefully go over all the results with her, and she might be surprised at what she would learn about herself.

As Mrs. LeBacque was somewhat dependent, she quickly deferred to her doctor's recommendations; after all, she reasoned, he had been so helpful up until now, and he knew her so well that he would know what the next appropriate step in therapy should be. The additional meeting times were becoming increasingly difficult to schedule, however; her supervisor at work eventually began to object to the time she took off to see Dr. Chronique.

Mrs. LeBacque was reluctant to bring up the subject of termination, especially because her psychologist seemed to have such a strong interest in her welfare by conducting additional testing and insisting on multiple interpretive sessions with her. When she finally did mention her desire to end therapy, she was met with assurances by Dr. Chronique that their work was not yet done, although, he assured her, she was making very good progress and soon they would be finished.

This moribund treatment dragged on for 2 more months. Finally, Mrs. LeBacque began to impulsively cancel her appointments, having a headache on one occasion and a work emergency on another. Then she went on vacation for several weeks and never called Dr. Chronique on her return. Therapy had finally stopped, without any formal termination or plan for follow-up.

Dr. Chronique continued to meet with his patient long after her treatment should have ended, causing her to spend several thousand dollars in fees for the last 3 months that were essentially unnecessary. The extension of therapy seemed be more reflective of the therapist's wishes to prolong treatment and represented a deliberate attempt on his part to do so. Concern for his patient's welfare was not the prime consideration for Dr. Chronique at this stage of his work, even though he seemed to communicate a genuine interest in the quality of her life.

> *(c) Prior to termination for whatever reason, except where precluded by the patient's or client's conduct, the psychologist discusses the patient's or client's views and needs, provides appropriate pretermination counseling, suggests alternative service providers as appropriate, and takes other reasonable steps to facilitate transfer of responsibility to another provider if the patient or client needs one immediately.*

(c) Before ending your work with patients, be sure to discuss their views about therapy, their current psychological needs, alternative resources available to them, possible referrals for different therapeutic experiences if needed, and any other matters that pertain to termination. You need not do this, however, if the patient is unavailable.

Vignette: Dr. Ender had successfully worked with Mr. and Mrs. Binwith in marital counseling for 1 year and was in the process of winding down their sessions. Before ending their contact, however, she carefully reviewed with them their presenting complaints, progress in therapy, and remaining issues to work on independently either as a couple or as individuals. They were both very pleased with the progress, and the marriage was much stronger than it had ever been.

Dr. Ender also solicited their input on the counseling process, asking for their assessment of the work, and attempted to determine if either of them had any interest in other psychological interventions. Mrs. Binwith was interested in participating in a women's group. Mr. Binwith was concerned about his career path and some impending midlife changes, which he wished to explore individually with a therapist.

Dr. Ender provided the names and phone numbers of two women's groups in the area and three therapists (both male and female). She discussed her willingness to provide information to whatever group or individual therapist they might consult, as needed. She also reviewed the need to sign a consent form if they wished her to contact a new therapist. All agreed that additional couples sessions could be scheduled in the future, if needed, and that Dr. Ender would be willing to be available as a resource for them. The session ended with a feeling of completion of badly needed work on the marriage, enthusiasm for future continued growth, and a sense of collaborative resolution for the couple and Dr. Ender.

5

Privacy and Confidentiality

5.01 Discussing the Limits of Confidentiality

(a) Psychologists discuss with persons and organizations with whom they establish a scientific or professional relationship (including, to the extent feasible, minors and their legal representatives) (1) the relevant limitations on confidentiality, including limitations where applicable in group, marital, and family therapy or in organizational consulting, and (2) the foreseeable uses of the information generated through their services.

(a) Inform patients and clients about confidentiality and its exceptions, even if you think they already know. Be sure to tell them about any limitations on confidentiality in group work, child and adolescent therapy, marital and family therapy, and organizational consulting. Also inform them about how information they reveal to you might be used in the future, such as in research, by the courts, or in any other likely way.

Vignette: Dr. Wispah, a psychologist practicing independently, discussed confidentiality and privileged communication with his new patient at the beginning of their first session. He gave her a handout he had created that described all the exceptions to confidentiality in simple language. He made sure that she understood that the law required him to break confidentiality by notifying the police or the local psychiatric emergency team if the patient ever became actively suicidal. He also explained what would happen if the patient ever communicated a serious threat of harm to another person. The state law in his particular location required him to notify the intended victim and the police.

Dr. Whispah also discussed the requirements for reporting child abuse, elder abuse, spouse abuse, and other situations where confidentiality could be or was required to be broken, even though the patient had not indicated any problems in these areas as a part of her presenting complaint. He described the information that was typically requested on the managed health care provider's outpatient treatment report and told her that this information might be requested periodically over the course of their work. Finally, he told his patient that he was carrying out a long-term research project on panic disorder and that certain information, such as paper-and-pencil tests and some of his case notes, would be a part of the data he and his colleagues were collecting. Although the patient's name would not be shared with coinvestigators, her test data and other information would. The patient was further informed that her participation in the study was optional and that there would be no adverse consequences if she chose to withdraw.

The patient manifested little concern about any of the above mentioned exceptions to confidentiality or about participating in the research protocol. However, she was intent on keeping the fact that she was consulting a psychologist a secret from her husband. Dr. Whispah assured her that even if her husband were to telephone and asked him directly about his wife's participation in therapy, he was not permitted to disclose any information about this matter without her formal consent. His patient was pleased with his response, felt well informed about all aspects of confidentiality at the outset, and was secure about proceeding with the treatment.

> *(b) Unless it is not feasible or is contraindicated, the discussion of confidentiality occurs at the outset of the relationship and thereafter as new circumstances may warrant.*

(b) Discuss confidentiality and its exceptions at the beginning of the professional contact, unless contraindicated, whether doing psychotherapy, organizational consulting, research, or any other psychological work. Also be ready to discuss confidentiality again as the situation may warrant (e.g., new intervention, entry of other individuals into the treatment, forensic work).

Vignette: Dr. Claire met with her new patient, a 49-year-old divorced woman, who complained of chronic depression and lethargy. After discussing confidentiality and its limitations, she began psychotherapy on a weekly basis. A month later, the patient had a complete physical examination, and her primary care physician diagnosed her as suffering from chronic fatigue syndrome.

At about the same time, Dr. Claire was considering referring her patient to a psychiatrist for evaluation for antidepressant medication. She was careful to discuss with her the importance of coordinating treatment with both her primary care physician and the psychiatrist who would be assessing her for antidepressants and asked her to sign consent forms releasing her to disclose information to both health care providers.

The patient had also recently begun consultations with her gynecologist about hormone replacement therapy because she was perimenopausal and was beginning to experience symptoms consistent with fluctuating hormone levels. Because Dr. Claire was well aware of the research on mood changes in perimenopausal women and the complex interactions between hormone levels and depression, she thought it was also important to discuss her patient with the gynecologist. She thoroughly discussed the rationale with her patient and obtained her formal consent before contacting the gynecologist. In the interest of keeping all health care professionals informed and promoting coordinated treatment, Dr. Claire made consistent efforts to talk with each physician about her work and the patient's progress in recovery from depression. Although this was time consuming, it was clearly in the patient's interest. Dr. Claire charged a reasonable fee for time expended on these professional consultations and had informed her patient of this policy at the outset. The patient, in turn, felt that her confidentiality was well protected by Dr. Claire and was pleased that her psychologist briefly reviewed her discussions with each physician with her during the therapy hour.

> *(c) Permission for electronic recording of interviews is secured from clients and patients.*

(c) Always ask permission to audiotape or videotape others, and get a signed consent. Even if you are carrying out research, always tell participants that you will be recording them ahead of time, unless your design prohibits this (e.g., naturalistic research) and you have carefully considered the possible risks of not informing them.

Vignette: Dr. Saver informed his new marital therapy patients that it was his usual procedure to audiotape every session. He was willing to give them the tape to listen to, each week, if they wished. He described that this would give both of them a chance to hear how they communicated and could actually help accelerate the therapy process. He explained that no one else would ever have access to the tapes and that if there ever would be future research involving the use of tapes, which were archived for a limited time, he would ask them to sign another consent form, which they would be free to reject. Although husband and wife were both agreeable to the audiotaping and did not see the need to sign a consent form, they complied with Dr. Saver's request that they do so. He also informed them that they were free to withdraw their consent at any time. By so doing, there were no misunderstandings about audiotaping, and all parties felt well informed about this aspect of the therapy process.

After 4 months of therapy, there were several sessions with a specific focus on nonverbal behavioral analysis between husband and wife, and Dr. Saver thought that videotaping could be a useful part of that work. At that point in therapy, Dr. Saver requested that the patients again sign a consent form acknowledging their permission to be videotaped. Again they complied and felt that their privacy was well protected by so doing.

5.02 Maintaining Confidentiality

> *Psychologists have a primary obligation and take reasonable precautions to respect the confidentiality rights of those with whom they work or consult, recognizing that confidentiality may be established by law, institutional rules, or professional or scientific relationships. (See also Standard 6.26, Professional Reviewers.)*

Respect the privacy of your clients, and always exercise caution in discussing your work publicly. Never reveal identifying information about them, orally or in writing, or even the fact that they consult you, without their formal consent. Make sure that you understand state and federal laws as well as the confidentiality rules of your employment setting and how they might affect your work in research, therapy, consulting, and supervisory settings, to name a few arenas.

Vignette: Dr. Claire was contacted by Tony, a 17-year-old who was reporting psychotic-like symptoms and was worried that he might not be able to complete the last marking period of his junior year in high school. Before agreeing to meet with Tony, Dr. Claire asked to speak with one of his parents because he was a minor and it is important to obtain parental consent before beginning treatment. Tony gladly complied with her request. He also volunteered that at present his whole family was meeting with a family therapist on a weekly basis and that he wanted to stop going to the sessions. He also revealed that his father was attending Alcoholics Anonymous meetings several times each week and that he wondered if he should start attending; he had heard so much about its benefits and had observed the good effects on his father.

After the first meeting with Tony, Dr. Claire decided to refer him to a psychiatrist for a medication assessment. She explained the reason for the referral to Tony and his parents and obtained both his and their signed consent permitting collaboration with the psychiatrist. She also told Tony that she would discuss the content of what was revealed to the psychiatrist to keep Tony apprised of those consultative sessions. She then sought the consent of her patient and his parents to contact the family therapist and coordinate the individual treatment with what was occurring in that setting. Tony and his parents also saw the rationale for this request and agreed to sign the consent form.

With so many mental health professionals involved in treating these family members, some of whom were minors, it was a challenging task to maintain confidentiality, requiring good boundaries and a working knowledge of relevant state laws. Dr. Claire knew the importance of collaborating regularly with certain therapists, when warranted, and Tony was in agreement with these contacts. However, she was also sensitive to her patient's unwillingness to include his parents in his therapy more than was absolutely necessary. She worked to maintain Tony's trust in her by clearly discussing the rules of confidentiality and how they applied in each case.

When Tony's pediatrician telephoned Dr. Claire to report his concern about drug abuse, she did not reveal information about her patient to the pediatrician before first contacting Tony and obtaining his consent. The potential drug abuse was of significant concern, but the psychologist rightly judged that she would jeopardize her therapeutic relationship with Tony by discussing treatment with the pediatrician behind his back. She listened to what the pediatrician had to say and his concern about Tony's safety but disclosed little to him about her patient. She then promptly telephoned Tony and asked his consent to her conversations with the pediatrician, again, so that those health care providers immediately concerned with his care could coordinate their work effectively. Again Tony complied, revealing that he was the one who had told his pediatrician about his consultations with Dr. Claire in the first place and that he had no problem with their talking with each other. He emphasized, however, that there were some topics that he wished her to keep in the consulting room, between the two of them.

On one occasion, the patient's mother telephoned to ask if Tony had mentioned that his grandmother was very angry at him for being inconsiderate the previous day. He had apparently driven her car without asking permission and, by so doing, had aggravated her hypertensive condition. Dr. Claire refused to discuss this episode extensively with his mother and suggested instead that the family therapy sessions might be a better forum, even though the next session wasn't for another 6 days. However, she was willing to schedule an extra appointment with Tony if he wished to see her sooner.

Tony was grateful that his therapist was attentive to confidentiality issues and, for the most part, informed him in advance about the nature of her disclosures to others. His trust in Dr. Claire grew, and he was comfortable remaining in treatment with her, confident that she would continue to protect his privacy in their work together.

5.03 Minimizing Intrusions on Privacy

(a) In order to minimize intrusions on privacy, psychologists include in written and oral reports, consultations, and the like, only information germane to the purpose for which the communication is made.

(a) Be parsimonious in written and oral reports, omitting all gratuitous information. Only include facts, interpretations, opinions, and so on that are directly relevant to your work.

Vignette: Dr. Lew Szlips directed the human resources office of a police department in a large midwestern city. He was involved in hiring, promoting, and terminating the employment of officers and helping to mediate disputes within the department. Unfortunately, Dr. Szlips had little ability to discriminate what information should be held in confidence and what should make its way out of the consulting room and into formal reports to supervisors and others.

On one occasion, a supervisor referred a police officer suffering from panic attacks to Dr. Szlips to discuss his disorder. In the consultation session, the officer revealed that he recently had learned that he was HIV positive, and he was gravely disturbed over this. He also discussed his homosexuality for the first time with Dr. Szlips. He reported that he was probably able to carry out his duties, but his mounting anxiety and depression were beginning to impair his concentration.

Dr. Szlips wisely referred him to an outside therapist for treatment, however he unwisely revealed too much information to the referring supervisor. In a lengthy memo, in which he presented himself as the officer's advocate, he accurately diagnosed the officer as suffering from panic attacks and depression. However, Dr. Szlips urged the supervisor to keep the officer on the job "in light of his recent discovery of his HIV status because that would tend to provide some necessary structure in his life, at a time when he may need it the most." The supervisor, who had no formal ethical duty to maintain confidentiality, casually discussed the officer's HIV status with several others on the force. Soon most officers in the precinct knew that the officer was HIV positive much sooner than the officer would have wanted this information to become public.

The response to this news was mixed. Some reacted with sympathy and provided support and encouragement to their friend. Others, who previously had been unaware that the officer was gay and did not approve, acted out their fearful and hostile feelings by avoiding and sometimes harassing him. His homophobic partner requested a transfer, and some of those whom he counted among his friends began to shun him.

Ultimately, the social climate became unbearable and the officer opted to stop working. At the very time when he indeed did need supportive relationships and predictability in his life, he found it ripped away from him because of primarily the confidentiality breach of the well-meaning but grossly inappropriate behavior of Dr. Szlips. After enduring much psychological distress, 7 months later the officer brought a formal ethics complaint and a civil suit against Dr. Szlips as compensation for his monetary losses and significant emotional suffering at work caused by the breach of confidentiality.

> *(b) Psychologists discuss confidential information obtained in clinical or consulting relationships, or evaluative data concerning patients, individual or organizational clients, students, research participants, supervisees, and employees, only for appropriate scientific or professional purposes and only with persons clearly concerned with such matters.*

(b) Reveal confidential information you've obtained while working as a therapist, consultant, supervisor, and so on only for the right reasons to those who have a scientific or professional interest in it. There should be no exceptions!

Vignette: Dr. Lew Szlips occasionally discussed some of his more interesting police evaluation cases with his friends, who were not psychologists and who had nothing to do with his work. He thought that his friends could learn something useful about human nature and the psychological stresses of carrying out this kind of work by hearing his anecdotes. Unfortunately, on several occasions, an officer's behavior had made headlines, and Dr. Szlips' friends found it easy to correctly guess the identity of the police officer involved in the case being discussed.

Dr. Szlips also taught a course on human resources at the local community college several nights each week. By way of making the lectures more appealing, he drew from his experience as a human relations consultant at the police department and presented many vignettes from his actual contacts with clients. Although he changed the details, he never bothered to tell his students this, and they thought he was revealing factual information that had been told to him in confidence.

One student, engaged to Officer O'Brien, was certain that Dr. Szlips was talking about her fiancé during one class, even though this was not the case. Many of the details of the example seemed to match his personality and behavior, and there had been no disclaimer that these were actually "changed" vignettes or, in some cases, entirely fabricated ones. Thus, this student assumed that Dr. Szlips was, indeed, disclosing factual information about her fiancé. She was upset and angry and, without even confronting her professor, decided to bring an ethics complaint to the state psychological association ethics committee. This resulted in a formal investigation by that body, requiring over 6 months to process. Dr. Szlips learned that if one is going to draw from one's professional work with clients it is wise to first get their consent, change the details enough so that they cannot be recognized, and inform the audience that the "case examples" are fictional.

5.04 Maintenance of Records

Psychologists maintain appropriate confidentiality in creating, storing, accessing, transferring, and disposing of records under their control, whether these are written, automated, or in any other medium. Psychologists maintain and dispose of records in accordance with law and in a manner that permits compliance with the requirements of this Ethics Code.

The buck stops with you in record keeping: what you write, how you store and access your records, what you do with them, and ultimately when and how you destroy them. Don't hold your secretary or your institution responsible; they are not bound by this Ethics Code, but you are.

Vignette: Dr. Current generally wrote her notes about a patient at the end of each therapy session rather than waiting hours or days, as she had done in the past. She had learned several years before, after being deposed by a divorcing husband's attorney, that what she wrote about each therapy session and patient was crucial. She knew that carelessness about records could come back to haunt her at a later time in the form of a deposition, subpoena, or a cross-examining attorney. She also felt that she was better able to maintain clinical continuity with patients by attending to this important task promptly and better able to capture the details and elements of change within the patient than if she delayed her note taking.

Having read "Record-Keeping Guidelines" (APA, 1993c) and examined other record-keeping forms, she had an accurate concept of record keeping that would facilitate the treatment process. She also knew that according to the law in her home state, patients were permitted access to their records and were entitled to receive a copy of their file if they wished. Consequently, whenever she sat down to write her notes, she would engage in the following brief fantasy: Before making any entries, her best supervisor or senior colleague was looking over one shoulder, her patient was looking over the other, an aggressive attorney was sitting across from her, and finally 12 jurors were reading every word that she wrote.

She also kept scrupulous notes of each supervisory session with her psychological assistant because she knew that she was legally and ethically responsible for the work he performed with each patient. She kept all records or summaries for 15 years, as recommended by the "Record-Keeping Guidelines" (APA, 1993c), and filed them by termination date in a locked file cabinet so that they could easily be located and destroyed when the time had elapsed.

Although she knew of colleagues who merely threw old records in the trash after tearing off the front pages with identifying information (and one environmentally minded individual who dumped them in the recycling bin downtown), she took a dim view of these practices. Even though the odds were against information that could be embarrassing or damaging to someone surfacing in a town dump or recycling bin, it *could* happen. Even one such event could have grave repercussions. Furthermore, such carelessness sent the clear message to any disinterested party who might come across casually discarded patient records that psychologists are not mindful of confidentiality, so one better be careful about what one reveals to them. To avoid such problems, Dr. Current was careful to shred or burn her obsolete files.

5.05 Disclosures

(a) Psychologists disclose confidential information without the consent of the individual only as mandated by law, or where permitted by law for a valid purpose, such as (1) to provide needed professional services to the patient or the individual or organizational client, (2) to obtain appropriate professional consultations, (3) to protect the patient or client or others from harm, or (4) to obtain payment for services, in which instance disclosure is limited to the minimum that is necessary to achieve the purpose.

(a) If your patient hasn't signed a consent form, don't disclose any information about her or him unless you are *allowed to* or *required to* by law. Otherwise, don't tell anyone anything about the recipient of your services. The law may permit disclosures for well-founded reasons with certain limitations, enabling you to (a) involuntarily hospitalize or provide other needed services, (b) get consultation or supervision from another professional, (c) protect the patient (or others) from getting hurt, or (d) collect fees for your services.

Vignette: Dr. Blunder's psychotherapy patient, Fred, signed a consent form for him to obtain medical information on his chronic back pain from his physician, Dr. Lobax. After contacting Dr. Lobax, however, Dr. Blunder was informed that Dr. Heel, a podiatrist, had treated Fred for problems with his left foot. Dr. Heel had developed an orthotic for Fred, which was helping with the back pain. Dr. Blunder thought that he should speak with the podiatrist directly rather than hear about her diagnosis and treatment from another health care provider to learn if additional podiatric treatment was being contemplated. Because he was in a rush to finish up his office work before leaving town for 1 week, he took the shortcut of telephoning Dr. Heel without first obtaining any formal consent from his patient. During their conversation, he also discussed Fred's depression and possible Axis II diagnosis.

What Dr. Blunder did not know, however, was that Dr. Heel was Fred's next door neighbor and a close friend of his patient's wife. Fred certainly would not have consented to Dr. Blunder revealing details of his psychological profile to her. When he learned about the telephone consultation, he was shocked to discover that his psychologist had broken confidentiality by contacting his podiatrist without his permission and viewed this as a gross violation of his privacy. He understood the rationale for the consultation with Dr. Lobax and had consented to it, but he saw no reason to contact a doctor who had fashioned an orthotic. Furthermore, Dr. Blunder never explained or discussed this decision with him.

If Dr. Blunder had discussed the issue with his patient, he probably would have consented, with the proviso that his psychological diagnosis be excluded from the conversation. As it was, Fred felt betrayed and exposed by his therapist and broke off treatment. This situation could have easily been avoided had Dr. Blunder not acted unilaterally in contacting the podiatrist; there was no emergency, no imminent need, and no one was at risk of being harmed. He realized too late that a seemingly innocuous consultation with another health care provider can have unexpected and damaging consequences.

> *(b) Psychologists also may disclose confidential information with the appropriate consent of the patient or the individual or organizational client (or of another legally authorized person on behalf of the patient or client), unless prohibited by law.*

(b) You are allowed to reveal information about your patient or organizational client as long as a valid consent form has been signed. Because privileged communication is often defined by state law, check with your state licensing board to determine what elements should be included in a valid release of information form.

Vignette: Allison, a 29-year-old graduate student with suicidal thoughts, had one consultation session with Dr. Caller, the owner of a small referral service. She wished to obtain the name of a female psychologist who specialized in boundary violations by psychologists. He referred her to Dr. Mae Bee and asked Allison to telephone him after the initial session to report her satisfaction with her.

Allison promptly made an appointment with Dr. Bee. In the first meeting, she learned of the psychologist's policy of contacting a patient's previous therapist to learn about that therapist's diagnostic impressions and course of treatment. Dr. Bee generally found this to be a valuable part of the history-gathering phase that was sometimes useful in validating her own diagnostic impressions. However, when asked, Allison refused to allow

Dr. Bee to contact her previous therapist, whom she had seen for over 3 years. When pressed about this, the patient became somewhat agitated and indicated that she might grant permission in the future, but for right now, she simply could not agree to it.

Dr. Bee deliberated over whether she should agree to treat Allison under these circumstances because they encouraged secrecy right from the start and might convey the impression that it was acceptable to conceal information that she considered important to the therapy. With some misgivings, she decided she would forego her usual policy this time and delay contacting the previous therapist for a little while because the patient appeared to genuinely desire treatment. The patient obviously was gravely troubled about her previous therapist.

The patient was relieved that Dr. Bee was willing to see her under these circumstances and, after several weekly sessions, felt a growing trust developing for her new therapist. However, Alison forgot to telephone Dr. Caller about her satisfaction with Dr. Bee, as he had requested. After 2 weeks, Dr. Caller himself contacted Dr. Bee to inquire if Allison had begun treatment with her. He also wished to emphasize the urgency of her situation and discuss some of the history that Allison had related about her previous therapist. Without acknowledging whether Allison had consulted her, Dr. Bee abruptly interrupted Dr. Caller, asking him if Allison had signed a consent form allowing him to disclose information about her. He reported that she had not. However, he had not conducted any therapy with her and only had been a resource for the referral, so he felt that using a consent form was an unnecessary formality. Dr. Bee disagreed with his interpretation of the ethical standards concerning confidentiality and instructed Dr. Caller about his duty to avoid releasing any information about a recipient of his services to a third party unless he held a signed consent form from that person.

Allison greatly appreciated Dr. Bee's aggressive stance in preserving her confidentiality. Within several weeks, when she felt comfortable broaching the topic, Allison was able to begin discussing the traumatic events of the previous 3 years. As it turned out, while she was working on her dissertation, she became quite depressed and began psychotherapy with one of her former professors. Their therapy relationship became quite intense, the boundaries became unclear, and ultimately it became sexualized. When her therapist broke off the relationship after the affair had lasted over 2 years, Allison became extremely depressed and had even attempted suicide. Eventually, she was able to muster enough courage to begin therapy anew following this betrayal, and she found a female therapist with Dr. Caller's assistance.

Ultimately, Dr. Bee was pleased that she did not insist on having Allison sign a release of information form immediately; it may have delayed her beginning therapy that was urgently needed. She was also pleased that she was able to abort Dr. Caller's unethical attempt to reveal her patient's history because to have done so would have been premature and would have violated Allison's privacy.

5.06 Consultations

When consulting with colleagues, (1) psychologists do not share confidential information that reasonably could lead to the identification of a patient, client, research participant, or other person or organization with whom they have a confidential relationship unless they have obtained the prior consent of the person or organization or the disclosure cannot be avoided, and (2) they share information only to the extent necessary to achieve the purposes of the consultation. (See also Standard 5.02, Maintaining Confidentiality.)

When discussing your work with colleagues, (a) never reveal the names of your patients or clients or give information that could reveal their identity without a signed consent, and (b) never reveal information unless it's relevant to the task at hand.

Vignette: In a small, rural community, five psychologists and psychiatrists routinely met every other week as a peer consultation group to discuss their clients. They were careful to avoid identifying patients by name, generally indicating only their gender, age, ethnic group (if relevant), career, marital status, and other demographic information that helped conceptualize the case. They generally would not reveal, for example, that a patient was the chair of the history department at the local university unless that fact was germane to the consultation. Although not required by this standard, in the interest of informed consent, they also had a policy of telling their patients and clients that they participated in this consultation group and disclosed the names of all the other therapists to their clients and patients. They did so to provide consumers with better confidentiality within such a small community; if patients and clients knew a particular therapist in the group in a different setting, such as the school board, work, or a personal friendship, they might not want their history discussed openly because they could easily be identified by that individual.

Informing patients and clients of the group membership the therapists essentially gave them the option of (a) requesting that their confidentiality be preserved by refraining from discussing them in the group, (b) stopping therapy, or (c) arriving at some other alternative that would be mutually agreeable. The patients felt secure that their rights to privacy were being honored when the psychologists and psychiatrists encouraged such collaborative and forthright communication about confidentiality at the outset of contact.

5.07 Confidential Information in Databases

(a) If confidential information concerning recipients of psychological services is to be entered into databases or systems of records available to persons whose access has not been consented to by the recipient, then psychologists use coding or other techniques to avoid the inclusion of personal identifiers.

(a) Remove all names and identifying information when entering research or clinical information into databases to which others may have access, unless consent has been obtained.

Vignette: Dr. Lith directed the bipolar disorder clinic at a large medical center and was also the primary investigator in a large, 10-year longitudinal study investigating variables associated with the disorder. He knew it was likely that in the future there would be requests to review his data for reanalysis or to draw on it for new research. Because he had no way of predicting the identity of these future investigators and, therefore, could not provide informed consent to his research participants (e.g., patients) in advance, he had to resort to other means of protecting their privacy. He carefully deleted all names and any other identifying information from the record before entering it into the database. He coded each entry, so that he could find the original patients, if needed, but he retained the code list in a password-protected computer file.

He also informed research participants of his methods for protecting their privacy. By adopting these measures, Dr. Lith allowed for the continuity of research and the security of his clinical patients. If there was ever a need to recontact a patient for any follow-up research, Dr. Lith would easily able to do so by accessing his code file. At that time, he could ask the patient to sign another consent form to participate in the new project, either his own or that of another investigator.

> *(b) If a research protocol approved by an institutional review board or similar body requires the inclusion of personal identifiers, such identifiers are deleted before the information is made accessible to persons other than those of whom the subject was advised.*

(b) If your research protocol has been approved by an institutional review board and it requires that you use personal identifiers, be sure to delete them before you release the data to other investigators who wish to review it.

Vignette: Three psychologists and two physicians were investigating the use of marijuana in patients with chronic pain from AIDS, cancer, and severe neck and back injuries. This was a large study, involving an experimental group of 300 individuals who had been legally purchasing and using marijuana over a 2-year period and a carefully matched control group. It required careful tracking of long-term users' names and addresses because the data was only useful if the participants of the study could be assessed for psychological and physiological changes attributable to cannabis use throughout the whole time span. There was also a possibility that the researchers would extend this longitudinal study even further and gather additional follow-up data from these same participants after many more years had elapsed; therefore, their whereabouts had to be carefully tracked after the initial data gathering was over.

After the researchers completed and published their work, they received a request from another psychologist who wished to reanalyze the data (see Standard 6.25). He believed that one of the statistical procedures had been improperly used and thought there might be some arithmetic errors because the results did not seem consistent with his own studies of long-term cannabis use. The psychologists on the research team knew of their obligation to make raw data available for reanalysis, but they also were obliged to maintain confidentiality. Unfortunately, personally identifying information was accessible along with raw scores because of the way the data had been gathered. It was essential to invest clerical time to extract names, addresses, and other identifying information from the raw data before releasing it to the requesting psychologist. This took several days of secretarial time, but it was critical to protect the privacy of the participants. The research team learned from this experience of the importance of coding their data from the outset to avoid such time and money expenditures in the future event of a similar request.

> *(c) If such deletion is not feasible, then before psychologists transfer such data to others or review such data collected by others, they take reasonable steps to determine that appropriate consent of personally identifiable individuals has been obtained.*

(c) If you cannot remove the names or identifiers, at least ask the participant to sign another consent form allowing release of the data.

Vignette: Several psychology and clinical social workers worked in an infertility clinic and were responsible for assessing couples attempting to conceive by means of a variety of medically assisted techniques. Much patient data had been accumulated over a 5-year period, including not only demographic information but also psychological testing, videotaped structured clinical interviews assessing parenting ability, the type of medical procedures used (e.g., in vitro fertilization with and without donor egg or sperm), and follow-up data about the couples' adjustment after successful or nonsuccessful attempts to conceive.

A research team from another state was conducting a metastudy on the marital stability of couples who consult fertility clinics, regardless of whether they were successful in conceiving a child. The team made contact with the psychologists and social workers on the clinic staff by sending letters to all mental health professionals who were members of the American Society for Reproductive Medicine and requested access to their databases. Because the investigation would require releasing confidential information that had already been collected to a third party, the clinic staff consulted the in-house institutional review board about to how to proceed. The staff was advised of the necessity of recontacting all couples and seeking their formal consent prior to releasing any data to other researchers. The external research team drafted the body of the letter describing the investigation and the clinic staff inviting former patients' participation in this new study added an introductory paragraph. The letter and consent forms were printed on clinic letterhead and sent to all patients who had consulted the clinic over the previous 5 years.

Only after receiving the signed consent forms by return mail did the clinic's research director proceed to release the data, including the complete videotaped interviews, to the external research team for analysis. Couples refusing to participate in the research either indicated their preference on the form and sent it back or simply failed to return the form. In this way, all patients were provided good informed consent before their privacy was further intruded on by other researchers.

5.08 Use of Confidential Information for Didactic or Other Purposes

(a) Psychologists do not disclose in their writings, lectures, or other public media, confidential, personally identifiable information concerning their patients, individual or organizational clients, students, research participants, or other recipients of their services that they obtained during the course of their work, unless the person or organization has consented in writing or unless there is other ethical or legal authorization for doing so.

(a) When writing, teaching, presenting to the media, using the Internet, or discussing your work in public, avoid using real names or even ambiguous details that could identify your client, patient, student, supervisee, research participant, or anybody else to whom you render a professional service. (You might be surprised at how clever others can be at deciphering a thinly veiled situation or guessing the identity of the person you are using in your presentation.) You are exempt from this rule if the person has consented to such a release or you have some other ethical or legal authorization to do so (e.g., mandated child abuse reporting).

Vignette: Dr. Leaky drew on his experience as a group psychotherapist in teaching a seminar at a small school of professional psychology. He frequently described actual narratives from his ongoing therapy group to students taking his group therapy course for credit. Because the therapy group was made up of graduate students and lay people from the community, he knew that there was always a risk that his classroom students could identify the people involved in his examples. Therefore, he was careful to change the names or not use names at all in his narratives. However, he usually did little or nothing in his classroom presentations to alter such important details as the subject matter discussed or change attributes such as gender, age, race, religion, or physical disability status of the group member under discussion. His examples frequently were transparent, and more than one student was able to correctly guess the identity of the individual whose story Dr. Leaky was presenting in the classroom.

On one occasion, the example used to illustrate a particular group phenomenon revealed the group member's feelings about his significant other, who, unbeknownst to Dr. Leaky, happened to be a student in his class. The feelings voiced by the young man about his girlfriend were intensely critical and angry. She was not prepared to hear this condemnation of herself in such a public setting as the classroom, where several of her friends also recognized the identities of those involved.

Dr. Leaky proved to be naive in his disregard for the privacy of others. By presenting to his students examples of group dynamics taken directly from his therapy group, he harmed many individuals in the process. Because Dr. Leaky was a senior professor on the faculty and the power differential was so strong between students and faculty, no complaints were filed about his conduct. Eventually, after they graduated from the school, several students did initiate a formal grievance because they had nothing to lose at that point.

> *(b) Ordinarily, in such scientific and professional presentations, psychologists disguise confidential information concerning such persons or organizations so that they are not individually identifiable to others and so that discussions do not cause harm to subjects who might identify themselves.*

(b) When using clinical information for educational purposes, always disguise the identity of your patient or client and inform your audience that you are doing so. Anecdotes can amplify your teaching, but they should never violate the privacy of others.

Vignette: A psychologist was invited to appear on a radio talk show with her formerly anorectic patient to discuss an innovative treatment. The format included three therapists: a psychologist, psychiatrist, and clinical social worker, with three of their own current patients discussing the history of their eating disorders and the course of treatment. She declined the invitation on the grounds that it would (a) violate the patient's confidentiality (e.g., her voice might be recognized) and (b) create a dual-role relationship (i.e. they would be partners in a media presentation in addition to the role of therapist and patient) that might impair her objectivity or impose performance pressure on the patient (see Standard 1.17).

Even though the patient was very willing to participate and the therapy was nearly completed, the psychologist knew from experience that media presentations can pose special problems for guest presenters. She knew that hosts were sometimes disingenuous and could easily create an adversarial climate on the air or foster sensationalism to attract listeners and boost ratings. She did not wish to expose her patient to such a potentially intense experience about such a delicate subject as her current psychotherapy for such a resistant disorder.

Instead, the psychologist volunteered to be interviewed alone on the same topic and was accepted by the talk show host. She promptly obtained her patient's written consent to use her therapy as a point of departure on the radio show, even though identifying details would be significantly altered. At the beginning of her interview on the air, before proceeding with her presentation, the psychologist informed the radio audience that she was changing some details of the therapy and the patient to protect her privacy. Instead of describing the patient as current, the psychologist said that she had worked with this young woman 5 years ago. She changed her patient's name and altered her age by 5 years, changed her religion, described her as an immigrant from Italy (which she was not), and gave her a different occupation. She also altered some details of her family-of-origin and childhood experiences, without changing the essential psycho-dynamics of the case. There was little chance that anyone could guess the identity of her patient after all these changes, but the seemingly anecdotal data provided a lively vehicle to describe the treatment process.

5.09 Preserving Records and Data

A psychologist makes plans in advance so that confidentiality of records and data is protected in the event of the psychologist's death, incapacity, or withdrawal from the position or practice.

Professional records and research data with personal identifiers are precious, and they must be securely maintained, regardless of your personal career path or physical health. Plan ahead for unexpected changes in the future, such as your withdrawal from practice, incapacitation, or death.

Vignette: Dr. Gardit owned a small consulting firm specializing in management–employee relations. He also occasionally taught in the business school of the local university where he carried out research.

He was scrupulous about preserving the professional records of his corporate clients. He offered each client the option of signing a consent form allowing his two partners in the firm access to the confidential records in the event of his death or incapacitation. In this way, there could be a relatively smooth transition to another consultant, if needed.

At the university, Dr. Gardit kept his research data under lock and key in the business school, with only one, trusted departmental assistant having access to it. The data and information in his computer were password protected, so that no unauthorized access could occur. He also enlisted the help of a colleague in the school of psychology, who was well acquainted with the confidentiality requirements of the Ethics Code. This person was informed of his passwords and was apprised of the procedure for working with the departmental assistant in the event of Dr. Gardit's incapacitation or death. All clients and research participants were informed in writing of the measures that Dr. Gardit had implemented at the outset of his work with them.

5.10 Ownership of Records and Data

Recognizing that ownership of records and data is governed by legal principles, psychologists take reasonable and lawful steps so that records and data remain available to the extent needed to serve the best interests of patients, individual or organizational clients, research participants, or appropriate others.

Laws controlling the ownership of patients' records vary from state to state. Know these laws, and keep your files available to serve the best interests of patients, clients, research participants, and others.

Vignette: A Hollywood actor consulting Dr. A. Procks for compulsive gambling desired to see the notes of his therapy sessions for the previous 2 months. Dr. Procks knew about privacy and confidentiality, and he thought he roughly knew state law concerning the ownership of patient records. He mistakenly believed that the therapist had complete discretion about revealing records to a patient on demand. Because he had included some hunches in his notes and some diagnostic impressions about his patient that would take some explaining, possibly damaging his rapport with the patient, he denied access to them, stating that they were "completely confidential and could not be revealed to patients." He said that he was willing to discuss what he wrote but refused to actually show them to the patient, describing them as "technical in nature and not very useful to a layman."

Several weeks later, the patient discovered from a gambling partner, who also happened to be a lawyer, that state law permitted patients access to their psychological records unless they would be harmed in some way by the disclosures therein.[1] He further learned that patients are to be notified in writing of the therapist's refusal to reveal records and the reason for it. When he mentioned this to Dr. Procks, the patient encountered a flustered reaction from a surprised and embarrassed therapist. Dr. Procks quickly invented a reason for having refused access to the records, namely, that it might interfere with the therapy and could prove hurtful to his patient. This was essentially a distortion because there was nothing in the notes that would be damaging to the patient and could not be resolved by adequate discussion in the therapy hour.

Dr. Procks eventually realized that his patient's first request to see his records had taken him by such surprise that he simply refused to deal with it, denied access to his notes, and engaged in a bit of believable confabulation. Coupled with his ignorance of the law, that action resulted in his arbitrary denial of his patient's access to the file. After this uncomfortable episode, Dr. Procks decided to attend a workshop on record keeping and confidentiality as well as other laws governing psychologists' actions at his earliest opportunity to avoid these problems in the future.

5.11 Withholding Records for Nonpayment

Psychologists may not withhold records under their control that are requested and imminently needed for a patient's or client's treatment solely because payment has not been received, except as otherwise provided by law.

Don't hold records "hostage" just because your former patient has not paid you for many months. If the records are requested and imminently needed, you must release them (with proper consent, of course).

Vignette: Dr. Neaubux had been providing treatment to a young cocaine-dependent jazz musician for 7 weeks when he suddenly stopped showing

---

[1]*Author's note:* The reader should note that laws regarding patient access to mental health records vary by state.

up for his appointments with her. Attempts to reach the young man by phone were unsuccessful, and it was clear that, for some reason, treatment was being interrupted. The patient had made small partial payments but still owed Dr. Neaubux about $575, and he had no insurance that included mental health benefits. After sending billing statements for 3 months, Dr. Neaubux concluded that there probably would be no money forthcoming, at least for the present, and that her former patient had most likely relapsed into his drug habit again.

One morning at around 7:30 a.m., her telephone answering service contacted her with an urgent call from a psychiatrist at the emergency room of the local county hospital. Her former patient had overdosed on crack cocaine and had been found unconscious in an apartment building several hours earlier. Although he had little identifying information with him, he was carrying an old appointment card of Dr. Neaubux's. The psychiatrist thought it would be useful to learn some background information on the patient, given his precarious state of health. Obviously, no consent form had been signed, but Dr. Neaubux appreciated the urgency of the situation. She agreed to speak with the psychiatrist and provided the necessary background information.

The next day, the patient was in stable condition at the hospital and had signed himself into the inpatient alcohol and drug rehabilitation unit. One of the therapists there contacted Dr. Neaubux requesting that she release some information about his course of treatment and the results of any psychological testing. The proper consent forms had been signed, and they were faxed to the psychologist's office while the original was being sent by conventional mail. Although Dr. Neaubux was tempted to avoid any involvement with this patient because he still owed her money, she knew that she had an ethical obligation to release the information that was imminently needed for his treatment. Perhaps he could have been treated without this information being released, but clearly the staff at the hospital felt that treatment would be helped with input from the former therapist. Dr. Neaubux decided to comply with the request and released the information requested.

6

Teaching, Training Supervision, Research, and Publishing

6.01 Design of Education and Training Programs

Psychologists who are responsible for education and training programs seek to ensure that the programs are competently designed, provide the proper experiences, and meet the requirements for licensure, certification, or other goals for which claims are made by the program.

If you are responsible for teaching or training, plan your program competently and deliver what you promise. Provide the proper experiences that meet the requirements for licensure, certification, or other goals that are claimed by the program.

Vignette: Dr. Anne Lighten was the director of training in the psychology department of a small university, graduating about eight students per year. Part of her responsibilities involved assuring that students obtained the proper amount of practicum supervision while matriculating in the program and seeing that they had access to suitable internships. She routinely informed students in their last year about all the internship opportunities within the state and encouraged students to apply to any of them.

One year, an unfortunate situation was encountered by a recent PhD who was registered with the state as a psychological assistant under the supervision of a licensed psychologist within a large group practice. This particular supervisor, the infamous Dr. Cagey, actually had two psychological assistants in addition to his busy practice and administrative duties. He had little time to devote to proper supervision and frequently skimped on the requirement that psychologists spend at least 1 hour per week in face-to-face meetings with the supervisee. Sometimes he would meet his trainees over lunch at a busy restaurant, even though the distractions were many and the possibility for confidentiality breaches were significant.

Dr. Lighten learned of these substandard supervisory practices from the psychological assistant. She judged that Dr. Cagey was effectively putting consumers at risk while providing a poor learning environment for trainees. This not only constituted poor mentoring but was in violation of the state law mandating a minimum number of supervisory hours as a prerequisite for the state licensing examination.

Although the internship setting of Dr. Cagey's practice was not formally affilliated with the training program at her university, there had been sufficient informal connections for a long time to warrant concern by Dr. Lighten under this ethical standard. For over 12 years, she had been encouraging graduates to apply for his psychological assistantships and felt that he played an important role in the postgraduate training of her students. Now, as his practice grew, he seemingly was providing incompetent supervision and apparently could no longer make a significant contribution to the mentoring of the postdoctoral students. When Dr. Lighten raised her concerns with Dr. Cagey, he ultimately turned a deaf ear and refused to alter his supervision practices. With reluctance, she removed his name from her list of internships. Out of concern for his substandard supervisory practices and the ultimate impact on supervisees from other academic programs, she weighed the merits of either contacting the state psychological association's program for impaired psychologists, which did outreach work, or the state board of psychology regarding his formal status as a supervisor. In light of the potential for serious harm to patients who were consulting unlicensed and undersupervised therapists and because of Dr. Cagey's blatant resistance to her feedback, Dr. Lighten felt obligated to notify the state licensing board.

6.02 Descriptions of Education and Training Programs

> *(a) Psychologists responsible for education and training programs seek to ensure that there is a current and accurate description of the program content, training goals and objectives, and requirements that must be met for satisfactory completion of the program. This information must be made readily available to all interested parties.*

(a) If you are responsible for education or training programs, be sure to have an accurate and up-to-date description in the catalog or brochure of the content, goals, objectives, and requirements of the program. This must be readily available to anyone who requests a copy.[1]

Vignette: Dr. Scruplo chaired the psychology department at a large university. As a part of his responsibilities, he and several colleagues reviewed and edited all brochures, departmental publicity, and the annual course catalog. He was dedicated to promulgating a philosophy of the department that was generally reflective of its faculty, mission, and goals. He made consistent attempts each year to modify the printed materials to accurately reflect the content areas of the department as well as its goals and objectives.

He was fastidious about ensuring that prerequisite academic experience and all requirements for the master's and doctoral programs were described comprehensively with a clear explanation of the required core

---

[1]Compare this standard to Standard 3.03.

subjects within the program. For clinical and counseling psychology programs, the course catalog listed the faculty members, their specialty areas, and internship requirements. He provided careful guidance on the content of their descriptions to optimize students' understanding about a course offering prior to enrolling in it. Also he and his colleagues made consistent attempts to review and update this information on an as-needed basis. In short, Dr. Scruplo consistently upheld a high standard of providing clear, accurate, and comprehensive descriptions of the psychology department's mission, goals, and objectives.

He devoted much energy to this important project each year by both personally reviewing the material and delegating and coordinating the efforts of other faculty members involved.

> *(b) Psychologists seek to ensure that statements concerning their course outlines are accurate and not misleading, particularly regarding the subject matter to be covered, bases for evaluating progress, and the nature of course experiences. (See also Standard 3.03, Avoidance of False or Deceptive Statements.)*

(b) Try to be accurate in all descriptions of the courses you teach. Tell students at the outset about the expectations of the course, and be candid about the subject matter, the bases for evaluating progress, and the types of experiences to be anticipated.

Vignette: Dr. Lernit taught the chemical dependency course at a nearby campus of her state's school of professional psychology and decided to include an experiential aspect she had never required before. She planned to ask all students to attend three different 12-step meetings, visit three different bars (that they did not already frequent), and walk or drive in the daytime through a part of town that was notorious for drug dealing. Unfortunately, she forgot to mention this new requirement in the school catalog or to indicate on the course syllabus that students would also be required to write about these experiences in a 10-page paper.

When Dr. Lernit gave this assignment 2 months into the course, many students objected. Several students were quite fearful of driving through the drug dealers' part of town because the area had a reputation for violent crimes and car jackings. They objected on the grounds that it was excessively risky, stating that they never would have enrolled in this course had they known about the requirement at the outset. Several other students objected to the time it would take to visit the bars and 12-step meetings and to write a 10-page paper as well. They worked part time and could not find the extra hours to fit in this requirement, without advance notice. Another student had strong religious convictions prohibiting the use of alcohol and much apprehension about visiting bars.

Dr. Lernit began to see the problems she had created by "springing" this experiential assignment on the class without first having provided some description in the school catalog. She listened to her students' objections and decided to drop the requirement. After making appropriate modifications that reduced any substantial risk to her students, she included the requirement in the next semester's course and made sure that she put a description of it in the school catalog.

> *(c) To the degree to which they exercise control, psychologists responsible for announcements, catalogs, brochures, or advertisements describing workshops, seminars, or other non-degree-granting educational programs ensure that they accurately describe the audience for which the program is intended, the educational objectives, the presenters, and the fees involved.*

(c) Even if you are teaching in a nondegree program (e.g., weekend workshop or seminar), you still must accurately describe the intended audience, educational objectives, presenters, and cost in brochures, catalogs, and advertisements.

Vignette: Four clinicians offered a 2-day seminar in biofeedback training for migraine headache patients. In the printed announcement, which appeared in professional journals and was mailed out to health care professionals, they stated the cost of the seminar and indicated that the workshop should be attended by licensed psychologists, psychiatrists, or other health care practitioners whose legal scope of practice included the use of biofeedback and who were already trained in its basic applications.

In the announcement, the clinicians described the educational objectives of the seminar and the topic areas that would be included. They also outlined how much time would be allocated to each topic, whether the meetings were plenary sessions or smaller group presentations, and to what degree instruction could be individualized. They described how each participant would have some exposure to the more sophisticated biofeedback equipment, with some "hands-on" experience on the second day of training. Finally, they made it clear that attendees could have follow-up supervision of their clinical work by any of the four presenters or other experienced practitioners. As a part of their participation in the seminar, they were entitled to be formally referred to supervising health care practitioners available in their city of origin who were experienced in biofeedback training. The teaching team took great care to develop a brochure and journal announcement that was accurate, comprehensive, and concise and that provided an excellent basis on which prospective trainees could make a decision about attending.

6.03 Accuracy and Objectivity in Teaching

> *(a) When engaged in teaching or training, psychologists present psychological information accurately and with a reasonable degree of objectivity.*

(a) When teaching or training, be sure to be accurate and objective. Avoid distorting or biasing the material in favor of your own theoretical orientation without basis. Be aware of your own blind spots.

Vignette: An assistant professor, well known for his preference for cognitive–behavioral psychotherapy, was teaching a survey course to beginning graduate students that exposed them to various theories of psychotherapy. Over the 12-week quarter, he covered eight different theoretical approaches in individual psychotherapy. However, he devoted over half his lectures to the cognitive–behavioral approach because, as he put it, "this is really the only theory of therapy that students need to know to be competent." The other seven theories of psychotherapy were compressed into the remaining few weeks of the quarter.

He regaled his students with many fascinating case histories drawn from his clinical work and did not hesitate to point out how his own expertise and creativity within this theoretical framework was a critical factor to these successful outcomes. Unfortunately, the professor did not use scientific principles in assessing his own clinical work and often drew unwarranted conclusions from his patient outcomes. As an example, he presented the history of a patient he was treating who was in remission from breast cancer for 11 months after comprehensive treatment at a local hospital. The woman had consulted him originally for depression 5 months before and had indeed experienced substantial elevation in her mood, which resulted in more active engagement with her family and friends. However, the therapist's inference was that her cancer remission was due chiefly to the therapy provided by him rather than her medical treatment.

Using such a case as an example of the profound efficacy of cognitive–behavioral psychotherapy in his graduate seminar exemplified this professor's bias and poor judgment as well as his blatant disregard for the empirical basis on which psychologists must rely in their work. It was also potentially dangerous to imply in a training setting that a psychotherapeutic intervention alone was preferable to medical intervention for an illness as significant as breast cancer. Some naive students were indeed impressed by his lectures, whereas others were disappointed and frustrated that they had selected a survey course and were receiving what essentially amounted to propaganda for one theoretical school of thought.

> *(b) When engaged in teaching or training, psychologists recognize the power they hold over students or supervisees and therefore make reasonable efforts to avoid engaging in conduct that is personally demeaning to students or supervisees. (See also Standards 1.09, Respecting Others, and 1.12, Other Harassment.)*

(b) Acknowledge the power and influence that you hold over students when teaching or training. Never demean or personally undermine students in any way.

Vignette: Dr. Blaster was a training supervisor at a veterans' hospital and taught in the doctoral program of a large university nearby. He had been on the faculty for over 30 years and, in recent years, was finding it difficult to cope with a student body that was becoming increasingly diverse in many ways, such as theoretical orientation, age, ethnicity, and sexual orientation, to name a few areas.

Dr. Blaster found it impossible to treat all students fairly, at times reverting to personal and subtle unwarranted criticism. For example, his complete disregard for students who had a strong interest in behavioral theories of psychology was well known. He made pointed and sarcastic remarks about these students and their pursuit of "quick-fix therapy" as an example of their lack of sophistication about the importance of unconscious motivation. He was also judgmental about students who smoked or drank alcohol and could be heard making humiliating or hostile comments about these individuals.

During supervisory sessions, Dr. Blaster sometimes became aloof, somewhat sarcastic, and even punitive in his attitude toward his supervisees if they favored a psychological intervention with which he disagreed. Instead of engaging them in a scholarly discussion of the merits or drawbacks of various theoretical approaches, he tended to become resentful or hostile, making critical remarks intended to demean or humiliate rather than to educate.

Because of his seniority in the hospital and at the university, Dr. Blaster acted with virtual impunity. Students feared his power and rarely complained, and fellow colleagues, viewing him as unlikely to change his ways for the most part, simply tolerated his behavior without ever confronting him.

One year, a small group of students who felt particularly distressed about by his behavior decided to take formal action against Dr. Blaster, but they resolved to wait until they had completed their dissertations and formally graduated from the program to avoid any possibility of retribution by him or his colleagues. They brought formal complaints to the university and hospital administration, the APA Ethics Committee, and the state board of psychology and were able to present much documentation and many witnesses to support their allegations of his chronic hostile and demeaning behavior toward students.

6.04 Limitation on Teaching

Psychologists do not teach the use of techniques or procedures that require specialized training, licensure, or expertise, including but not limited to hypnosis, biofeedback, and projective techniques, to individuals who lack the prerequisite training, legal scope of practice, or expertise.

Don't teach psychological techniques such as hypnosis, biofeedback training, or assessment to anyone who is not qualified to use them because of a lack of training, licensing or credentials, or legal scope of practice.

Vignette: Dr. Teachawl noticed a decline in her clinical practice because in part of the impact of managed health care and was seeking ways to augment her income. Because she was quite experienced in the use of hypnosis and had recently begun to do some forensic work, she thought she might creatively combine the two. She knew that lawyers frequently worked with individuals who were suffering major life transitions and sometimes may have even exacerbated emotional conflict in the course of their work, such as during divorce litigation. She thought that lawyers might increase their attractiveness to clients by offering the service of reducing anxiety and stress for their clients in addition to carrying out their legal work.

She decided to offer a workshop at the state bar association annual convention on progressive muscle relaxation, diaphragmatic breathing, and self-hypnosis training. She also decided to offer training in memory enhancement with hypnosis for use with clients because she had some experience that she thought was valid. However, Dr. Teachawl had little knowledge about the risks of the hypnotic contamination of memory or implanting of ideas, and she did not mention the possibility of these problems in her training sessions. For those attorneys who were skittish about using hypnosis, she suggested that they could merely think of it as "guided imagery" and told them they need not worry about practicing psychology because no license is required for guided imagery work. She also failed to address psychological history taking, diagnostic screening for hypnosis, or the problems than can occur with those who have certain mental disorders and should probably not be subjected to hypnosis, even by a competent mental health provider.

Several lawyers were quite intrigued with her teaching and immediately implemented it with some of their most troubled clients, both victims and witnesses of violent crimes. The results in several cases were destructive, characterized by panic attacks in the attorney's office, flashbacks to traumatic episodes (both recent and in the distant past), and other events that the attorneys were ill prepared to handle. In many of these cases, the clients discharged their attorneys when they discovered that a psychological technique was being used inappropriately. Some experienced subsequent depression and other symptoms that were elicited by the crude attempts at hypnosis by the lawyers.

The attorneys who used the techniques were surprised and troubled by these adverse reactions and dismayed that Dr. Teachawl did not apprise them of the possible risks of using hypnosis in her training session. To the contrary, she explained, she had presented hypnosis as a benign and powerful tool, easily learned and broadly applicable. Several lawyers brought formal complaints against Dr. Teachawl for her inept and unethical teaching of a psychological technique that ultimately resulted in harm to their clients.

6.05 Assessing Student and Supervisee Performance

(a) In academic and supervisory relationships, psychologists establish an appropriate process for providing feedback to students and supervisees.

(a) Always have a well-defined and efficient process for giving feedback to students and supervisees about their performance.

Vignette: Whenever Dr. Monitor taught a course, she was careful to inform students on the first day of class about course requirements and grading criteria. She also informed them that class participation would be an important part of the grading process because it was a means of informally assessing students' grasp of the material.

She kept regular office hours several days each week, and she informed students that they could make appointments to consult with her or drop by for a nonscheduled chat. She gave out her email address to encourage dialogue with students, although she made it clear that this was for academic purposes and not for socializing. She also informed students that they were required to meet with her individually at least once during the second half of the semester to discuss their progress and performance to date.

Students knew clearly from the beginning of the class of how to meet their professor's expectations, and those who needed additional support or structure were able to obtain it in a timely fashion. There were rarely any major disappointments about grades at the end of the semester, and students felt well informed about the ongoing quality of their performance in this course.

> *(b) Psychologists evaluate students and supervisees on the basis of their actual performance on relevant and established program requirements.*

(b) Base grades and evaluations on how a student or supervisee actually performs, according to program requirements or criteria.

Vignette: Many professors on the faculty of a small professional school of psychology routinely were overly generous in their grading practices. In keeping with the unspoken policy of the school, once a student was accepted into the doctoral program, he or she would most certainly graduate, regardless of their academic performance. The financial success of the institution was held at a higher priority than academic excellence, and student tuitions constituted the major share of the school's income.

Students who put forth a great amount of effort and were especially competent generally earned *As*. However, students who were clearly unqualified to continue in the program earned *Bs* and even *As*, on occasion, if they supplemented their academic work with clerical work in the department. Many of the students who were "strung along" eventually experienced significant problems in their academic careers, including inadequate performance in postdoctoral internships or inability to pass the state licensing examination, even with repeated attempts. They would likely have fared better had they been "weeded out" sooner and encouraged to pursue other career paths.

One senior faculty member had the integrity to resist the school's unspoken rules and base student evaluations on academic performance instead of extraneous factors. Because of her values and educational philosophy, she gave some students low passing or even failing grades at times in various core courses, thus threatening their academic status at the school. Over time, this professor was pressured by the administration to comply with the grading policy of her peers and to bear in mind that her salary was being paid by those very students who were about to fail out of the program.

Unwilling to yield to the social pressure, she ultimately left the professional school, unfortunately, because the prevailing climate was antithetical to her values. On her departure, she brought formal complaints against the dean and several faculty members for their pervasive and persistent ethical violations concerning student evaluation practices.

6.06 Planning Research

(a) Psychologists design, conduct, and report research in accordance with recognized standards of scientific competence and ethical research.

(a) Plan, carry out, and report the results of your research according to recognized scientific and ethical standards, such as this Ethics Code and other APA guidelines and standards, relevant documents of other professions in interdisciplinary research, National Institutes for Health documents, and institutional review boards, to name a few.

Vignette: Even though Dr. Solo, an independent practitioner with no university or hospital affiliation, had many contracts with managed care companies, his income began to decline. Consequently, he decided to pursue research demonstrating the efficacy of his form of short-term psychotherapy, thinking it would benefit his marketability and result in increased referrals from enthusiastic case managers. He developed a research protocol for measuring treatment outcome but had little or no familiarity about the current research in this area. He had never read any of APA's ethical standards pertaining to research with human participants and had not done any research since graduate school, many years before.

His research design included him as the only therapist, attempting to use different theoretical orientations with various patients, even though his area of demonstrated clinical competence was confined to one particular school of psychotherapy. Attempting to randomize his patient–research participants, he assigned new patients into one of three different groups and provided different kinds of therapy to each group, one of them being his recently developed short-term treatment paradigm. He used a short scale for assessing anxiety and depression, obtaining pretest and posttest measures to analyze. When he had accumulated data on 15 patients in each group over a period of 6 months, he ended his research and began to analyze the data.

Dr. Solo failed to comply with even the most basic recognized scientific standards in carrying out his research. He never informed his patients that he was involving them in a research project because he thought this might prejudice their participation. His basic research design was flawed in that he was the only therapist involved in the study, thereby increasing the likelihood of researcher bias and therapist incompetence in administering different modes of psychotherapy. He had a small number of participants, and his analysis of the data was based on inappropriate statistical techniques, both resulting in conclusions that were not valid.

His clinical judgment during the data-gathering phase of his project seemed to be somewhat impaired. He overlooked some suicidal warning signs of an alcoholic young man and failed to provide him with badly needed treatment, presumably in the interest of maintaining objectivity in carrying out the research project and retaining him as a participant in the research. Unfortunately, this patient's depression increased significantly, resulting in an unsuccessful suicide attempt. There were other incidents where the patients, who were unaware of their own participation in the research project, were permitted to deteriorate in the interest of maintaining the research protocol.

Dr. Solo's research was essentially worthless. It lacked scientific rigor and proved nothing about his hypothesis concerning the efficiency of his novel therapeutic approach. Moreover, his methods resulted in harm to several patients. Because they never provided informed consent about participating at the outset, they could not be given options to withdraw from their assigned treatment group if they wished later on. In the interest of promoting his practice to managed health care by quickly generating research data, Dr. Solo revealed his ignorance and disregard for the fundamental tenets of his profession concerning scientific and clinical practices.

> *(b) Psychologists plan their research so as to minimize the possibility that results will be misleading.*

(b) Plan your research so as to minimize the chances that the interpretations will be misleading.

Vignette: Dr. Will Garble was frequently interviewed on TV talk shows and in the print media for his ideas and theories concerning psychoneuroimmunology and psychological interventions that strengthened the body's immune system. He presented and discussed the results of his scientific research, which seemed to demonstrate that chronic pain, chronic illness, and fatal diseases are accompanied and even preceded by negative cognitions.

He had developed an instrument purporting to assess patients' cognitions about their own health and physical functioning. He demonstrated that as patients' health improved, their scores on this instrument increased significantly, thereby validating his theory that good physical health was virtually wholly dependent on one's cognitions. How one thought about oneself determined the robustness of one's immune function and tendency to recover from or succumb to pain and illness. He also used several conventional personality inventories that never had been standardized for chronically ill patients and assessed patients at various stages of health and illness.

Dr. Garble never validated or standardized his own instrument; neither did he use control and experimental groups to reach his conclusions. Although the contribution of patients' cognitions to failing health and subsequent recovery may have been an important scientific question to address, it was not investigated in a manner consistent with scientific principles. Furthermore, he appeared to make the mistaken assumption that events coinciding in time are necessarily causally related (i.e., *post hoc ergo propter hoc* = "after something, therefore, because of it"). His "results" were misleading because he had not gathered data on patients' cognitions preceding their illness or onset of chronic pain while he attempted to make inferences about the impact of cognitions on the etiology of illness, pain, and recovery. His research results were open to significant misinterpretation, both by himself and by those in the media to whom he was presenting them, but they were eagerly reported by journalists. It seemed as though he "proved" what he wanted to prove, with little regard for scientific rigor or conventional research design and methodology, using instead short cuts and abrogation of the scientific method.

> *(c) In planning research, psychologists consider its ethical acceptability under the Ethics Code. If an ethical issue is unclear, psychologists seek to resolve the issue through consultation with institutional review boards, animal care and use committees, peer consultations, or other proper mechanisms.*

(c) Make sure that your research protocol meets all ethical standards that apply. If you are uncertain, consult others such as an institutional review board, animal care and use committee, experienced researchers, or other resources.

Vignette: Dr. Solo was conducting research of an unorthodox sort with his own patients to prove the efficacy of a new style of therapy, as mentioned above. He never informed them that they were to be involved in research when they began therapy with him, and he deliberately withheld constructive interventions from some patients who were in need of them to preserve the research model.

Dr. Claire learned of Dr. Solo's unusual clinical research indirectly when two of his research participant–patients consulted her about his odd style of conducting psychotherapy. She obtained their formal consent to speak with him and then proceeded to contact him.

Dr. Solo was willing to discuss his work with her. But he was highly resistant to her collegial suggestions that he provide his patients with informed consent about their participation in his research instead of carrying it out covertly and her recommendation that he follow other well-accepted research practices. She urged him to consult with a senior professor at a nearby university who was well known in the professional community to review his research design. However, Dr. Solo reasoned that an academician could not fully appreciate the issues facing a clinician dealing with the constraints of the managed health care system and the pressure to develop brief-term interventions.

When Dr. Claire then suggested that he might be eligible to submit his research protocol for review by the institutional review board of a local teaching hospital, she was met with more resistance: "What would they know? They're only concerned with hospital issues!" Clearly, Dr. Solo was disinterested in her feedback about his research or clinical practices, but Dr. Claire persevered in attempting to have an influence. She gave him a copy of the Ethics Code with relevant standards highlighted, excerpts from the National Institutes of Health's (Title 45, 1991) *Code of Federal Regulations* (the NIH Institutional Review Board guidebook) pertaining to informed consent, and a copy of the *Belmont Report* (National Commission for the Protection of Human Subjects of Biomedical and Behavioral Research, 1979). These publications addressed issues concerning informed consent, deception, research participant welfare, experimenter bias, and experimenter duties and responsibilities, to name a few areas of concern. Dr. Solo remained unimpressed, however. Because his research did not involve any federal grant money, he concluded that he was not under the jurisdiction of the National Institutes of Health or its standards.

Dr. Solo was beginning to resent Dr. Claire's suggestions that he was conducting research less than competently and viewed her attempts to influence him as intrusive and inappropriate. Feeling exasperated with her persistence, he made a veiled threat that she had no right to interfere with how he conducted his business and that she had better stop harassing him, or else he would resort to legal action. Dr. Claire then refrained from any further attempts to contact him and proceeded to notify the state board of psychology of his actions.

> *(d) Psychologists take reasonable steps to implement appropriate protections for the rights and welfare of human participants, other persons affected by the research, and the welfare of animal subjects.*

(d) Preserve the rights and welfare of your research participants: animals, people, and those who will ultimately be affected by your investigation.

Vignette: Dr. Loosey was the principal investigator in a study concerning state-dependent learning. His research participants were randomly distributed by gender, age, ethnicity, education level, and socioeconomic status. His methodology included the use of brief video clips, using both professional actors and selected footage from television newscasts designed to elicit various affective reactions in participants immediately prior to exposure to learning trials. The videos included situations that would evoke boredom, anger, sadness, guilt, and fear.

To preserve the naiveté of the participants, Dr. Loosey provided little information in the informed consent concerning the content of the videotapes. Unfortunately, several of the research participants were veterans of the Vietnam and Gulf Wars who were suffering from untreated posttraumatic stress disorder (PTSD). The video scenes inducing fear caused significant reactions, in some cases producing strong sympathetic nervous system arousal with flashbacks to earlier traumatic episodes. This exacerbated their PTSD symptoms, resulting in nightmares in the weeks following their participation, increased depression, and a variety of other somatic, cognitive, affective, and behavioral symptoms.

Had these individuals been informed at the outset that their participation would include viewing videotapes of situations that could be upsetting or anxiety arousing, they may well have refused to participate in the first place. Or if they had agreed to participate, at least they would have felt that they had been properly warned in advance. They would have been able to make an informed choice to proceed with their role in the research instead of feeling misled by a psychologist who provided poor informed consent and exposed them to situations that resulted in harm.

6.07 Responsibility

(a) Psychologists conduct research competently and with due concern for the dignity and welfare of the participants.

(a) Carry out investigations competently. Be knowledgeable about your research area and the nature of the population under study, and be sure to treat all human participants with dignity and concern for their safety.

Vignette: Dr. Fitless was carrying out a large study on gay Asian men in terms of their endorsement of safe sexual practices, lifestyles, occupational stability, and personality characteristics as measured by various instruments of assessment. Dr. Fitless was neither Asian nor gay, although he held himself to be neutral, objective, and sufficiently knowledgeable to carry out this investigation. In fact, however, his knowledge of the Chinese, Japanese, Korean, and Southeast Asian cultures was limited to 6 months of providing clinical services to members of these groups and one brief training seminar.

The assessment instruments he chose had not been standardized on the population for which he intended to use them. The questionnaire he developed concerning sexual practices was also quickly constructed and had never been used in a pilot study, raising some questions of its usefulness and appropriateness. When he trained his 10 assistants, who were to carry out personal interviews with each research participant, he failed to devote adequate time to providing information about some cultural habits, values, and areas of sensitivity that would be useful in the face-to-face assessments.

As a result, the data gathering was flawed and the results and conclusions of the study were compromised. Furthermore, some of the research participants were treated with discourtesy and disregard for their deeply held values, resulting in their refusal to continue in the research. This could have been an important study had the principal investigator been more knowledgeable about the population he had investigated or attempted to consult those who were.

(b) Psychologists are responsible for the ethical conduct of research conducted by them or by others under their supervision or control.

(b) You have the ultimate responsibility for others' performance when delegating research tasks. Always be alert to the ethical conduct of your assistants.

Vignette: Dr. Fitless was researching "safe sex" practices and a variety of related lifestyle variables among gay Asian men by means of objective measures and personal interviews. He trained his research assistants to carry out the interviews and discussed the importance of maintaining standardization in format and content when administering the interview.

One of the student assistants, Victor, was not experienced in conducting research and decided to take some shortcuts in the way he carried out the personal interviews. He altered the wording of some questions that he thought were somewhat difficult to understand and failed to inform Dr. Fitless of the changes he had made. Also to shorten the time required to administer the questionnaire, he omitted some of the questions when he thought he could accurately infer the individual's responses. Finally, he characteristically added a few questions that reflected his own personal curiosity or prurient interests rather than any scientific or scholarly aim; these inappropriate questions were often rather intrusive in nature and caused discomfort in many research participants.

This young man also demonstrated a disregard for the boundaries and personal distance that would normally be required of the role he played as a research assistant. He became romantically attracted to one of the participants in the study and soon found himself in a sexual relationship with him. He discussed much of the research protocol with him while the participant was still involved in the study, thus further compromising the participant's naiveté about the study's objectives.

It was clear that Dr. Fitless had failed to anticipate Victor's sexual indiscretions and utter disregard for standardized data gathering. His failure to provide ongoing supervision during the year of data gathering also compounded the problem. Victor's nonstandardized interviews and unprofessional conduct culminated in a relationship with one participant and ultimately affected the quality of the data. Dr. Fitless remained accountable for the misconduct of his assistant, even though Victor was not a psychologist and Dr. Fitless was unaware of it while it occurred.

(c) Researchers and assistants are permitted to perform only those tasks for which they are appropriately trained and prepared.

(c) Only attempt research tasks for which you and your assistants are adequately trained and prepared.

Vignette: Dr. Klinish planned to explore psychophysiological changes in research participants who recalled vivid memories with accompanying positive and negative emotions and how these states correlated with certain personality measures. He had never attempted any research before but was experienced as a clinician providing biofeedback training to patients with a broad variety of complaints. He intended to measure peripheral vasodilatation and contraction of the frontalis (forehead) muscle and trapezius (upper back) muscle in response to mood changes elicited by the recalled memories. To do so, he planned to use thermal and EMG biofeedback equipment.

His four assistants were master's level graduate students who were naive about biofeedback equipment. But Dr. Klinish thought they could be easily trained to carry out the experimental procedures. Attaching the thermal sensors to the finger and EMG sensors to the forehead was relatively simple, and the assistants seemed to quickly grasp the methodology. However, locating the precise placement for proper attachment to the specific trapezius muscles was considerably more demanding. Dr. Klinish attempted to train his assistants to use measuring techniques from a standard text in the field of electrode placement in EMG biofeedback, showing them diagrams and anatomy drawings to help quantify the proper placement. In addition, he taught his students palpation techniques for the shoulder blade and neck areas by demonstrating on several volunteers. He told them that with practice they could eventually rely on the "feel" of the muscle to isolate it. The assistants became confident in their abilities after a brief period of training, despite their lack of formal education about anatomy or physiology. They quickly learned how to read the instruments and record their observations in a systematic fashion, although they had little understanding about what they were actually measuring.

When it came time to begin gathering data, three of the assistants performed with great variability. They had relied on palpating the muscles of the research participants rather than using a precise measurement technique because they considered the measuring techniques to be cumbersome. They rapidly developed a reliance on palpation alone to locate the muscles to be monitored. As a result, there was little consistency in attaching the EMG sensors in a standardized way because depending exclusively on the feel of locating a tense muscle did not yield sufficient precision for the research protocol.

Several weeks of data collection had gone by before Dr. Klinish discovered the "short cuts" that were being used by his assistants. He realized that there was little standardization in EMG electrode placement, possibly because of his ambiguous instructions during the training of his assistants.

In relying solely on the judgment of his assistants without actually assessing their developing competence, Dr. Klinish failed to devote sufficient attention to their training. He did not adequately emphasize the importance of relying on objective measurements by means of consistent placement of the biofeedback sensors either. His failure to fully understand the principles and procedures involved in competent research of this kind resulted in inadequate training and monitoring of his assistants. Although his method of palpating the tense muscles may have been useful in the clinical setting, this technique did not meet the strict criteria for data gathering in the research setting.

(d) As part of the process of development and implementation of research projects, psychologists consult those with expertise concerning any special population under investigation or most likely to be affected.

(d) When preparing to begin your research, consult those who are in a position to know about the likely impact of your work on the groups that you are studying. This includes experts in the field or individuals who are members of the population under study.

Vignette: A psychologist was contemplating conducting a study in her home state investigating the effects of various psychotherapeutic interventions with women who had sought refuge from domestic violence in shelters. Although the psychologist had never lived in a shelter, she had been married to an abusive man and knew the grave risks that women encounter in such long-term relationships. She was also well aware of several bills to provide badly needed financial support to women's shelters that had repeatedly failed in the state legislature, and she hoped to obtain data demonstrating the short- and long-term efficacy of certain interventions.

Because of her lack of experience with this phenomenon, she interviewed women staying in different shelters before she began to collect data. She also interviewed paid employees, volunteers, hospital staff (e.g., emergency room physicians, nurses, social workers), police officers, psychotherapists, and even the parents of some of the women. By so doing, she adequately prepared herself to investigate this population and the psychotherapeutic means by which they could best be helped. She knew that her research was likely to have a significant impact on the care and rehabilitation of battered women, hence her responsibility was to be as familiar with this population as she could at the outset.

She found that the process of learning about the special attributes of this group and those associated with them assisted her in formulating and refining the research protocol and helped cue her about new areas to investigate. She knew that by doing so she was minimizing the chances that the investigation itself or its results would be harmful to the research participants.

6.08 Compliance With Law and Standards

Psychologists plan and conduct research in a manner consistent with federal and state law and regulations, as well as professional standards governing the conduct of research, and particularly those standards governing research with human participants and animal subjects.

Know and obey all federal and state laws and regulations that may affect your research. Observe all standards and guidelines of your professional organizations before beginning your research, particularly those addressing human participants and animal subjects, even if they slow you down, are inconvenient to implement, or may increase cost.

Vignette: Several psychologists were researching the effects of exposure to fear-evoking motion picture excerpts on college students as measured by changes in physiological responses. The experimental group consisted of students who claimed to remember traumatic experiences from their preadolescent years, such as child abuse, traumatic divorce, and so on. The protocol included noninvasive measures, such as heart rate and EEG monitors, and invasive measures, such as venipunctures, for monitoring changes in levels of plasma cortisol and other hormones.

Before beginning the research, the team thoroughly reviewed the relevant literature to ascertain whether this was an appropriate area of study with research to support such a design. They also weighed the relevance of meaningful findings about such physiological changes in young adults with a history of trauma. Specifically, what would be the value of these findings, and how could they actually contribute to benefiting trauma survivors and others in the future? Did the potential value of the research merit inflicting minor psychological and physiological discomfort on research participants?

To adequately address these questions, the investigators thoroughly reviewed relevant documents available from their local institutional review board. These included NIH's (Title 45, 1991) *Code of Federal Regulations*, published by the Office for Protection of Research Ethics in the Department of Health and Human Services. They also reviewed the *Belmont Report* (National Commission, 1979), which was useful in addressing such broad ethical principles as respect for people, beneficence, and justice. Finally, they examined several relatively brief publications, such as the *Declaration of Helsinki* (World Medical Association, 1989/1991) and the *Nuremberg Code* (*Trials of War Criminals Before the Nuremberg Military Tribunals Under Control Council Law*, 1949), which were more general in nature but still informative about fundamental ethical concepts concerning research with humans. By studying these publications, the researchers were able to make wise decisions about their research design, which ultimately required very few modifications when it was reviewed by their institutional review board.

6.09 Institutional Approval

Psychologists obtain from host institutions or organizations appropriate approval prior to conducting research, and they provide accurate information about their research proposals. They conduct the research in accordance with the approved research protocol.

Get permission from the host institution before you begin your research. This means obtaining formal consent from hospitals (research involving patients), schools or colleges (research involving teachers or students), factories or places of business (research involving employees), police departments (research involving police officers), and so on before you actually approach individuals and begin collecting data. Be accurate in disclosing the details of your research proposal (e.g., goals, design, intrusiveness or risk to participants, confidentiality issues, possible benefits to the host institution, other matters that would affect cooperation). Don't make significant changes after your proposal has been approved without again submitting them to the host institution for review.

Vignette: A research team consisting of two child psychologists and several computer software engineers developed a protocol for researching the impact of a carefully designed sequence of videogames on aggressive behavior in junior high school boys. They contacted the superintendent's office in an inner-city school district to present their research rationale and methodology. After being referred to the assistant superintendent for curriculum and the human research committee of the school district, they proceeded to discuss the research.

They informed the district officials that participating in the study could benefit students whose behavior was provocative or violent and indirectly benefit the school. They explained that students would be told that they were being asked to evaluate a series of new videogames emphasizing intellectual resourcefulness instead of violence and that their feedback could be useful to the developers of the games. This was essentially true because the games were designed to expose participants in the experimental group to a sequence of social conflict situations where cleverness, intellectual creativity, and negotiation were reinforced but the use of brute force was not. The researchers explained to the administration that their mild deception—presenting games to be evaluated instead of inviting the cooperation of participants—was a means of increasing participation in the project.

They explained that the entire project would span approximately 2 months, with three 45-minute game sessions each week at the end of the school day and occasional discussion groups. Pretesting and posttesting would be carried out by using a computer-administered instrument to assess aggressiveness and self-esteem. Confidentiality would be managed by allowing students to select their own password and fictitious names, so the students' true identity would never be tracked by the computer. Informed consent would be addressed by means of signed parental and student consent forms. Debriefing at the end of the study would consist of presenting group data to students and their parents from pre- and posttesting and performance on various simulations that reinforced nonviolent behavior.

After learning about all the details of the proposal, the assistant superintendent and the human research committee consulted with the three junior high school principals in the district, each of whom had an opportunity to raise questions and concerns of the researchers. The administrators were invited to ask about any aspect of the research that was unclear or problematical. The researchers, in kind, responded to queries in a clear and comprehensive fashion, always encouraging a scholarly discussion of the details of the research and their implications. The dialogue was thorough, the school officials were satisfied that they had been given a chance to adequately scrutinize the research protocol to make an intelligent decision as to its suitability for their schools, and each agreed to allow the study to take place in their school.

6.10 Research Responsibilities

Prior to conducting research (except research involving only anonymous surveys, naturalistic observations, or similar research), psychologists enter into an agreement with participants that clarifies the nature of the research and the responsibilities of each party.

Before gathering data, tell participants what the research is about, what will happen to them, and who has which obligations to whom. This does not apply to unobtrusive research, however, such as anonymous surveys, naturalistic observations, and so on.

Vignette: Dr. Dee Seaver was carrying out research on the effects of various interventions with elementary and secondary schoolchildren who were diagnosed with attention deficit hyperactivity disorder. In her letter to parents and children inviting their participation, she made it clear that interviews and paper-and-pencil testing would constitute part of the research and be the basis of assignment of participants to control and experimental groups.

However, Dr. Seaver failed to inform the participants of some important information that might have affected their willingness to participate. This included the fact that there would be repeated interviews of parents and children on weekends over a 6-month period and that the behavioral intervention for some participants would require up to 5 minutes daily and necessitated detailed record keeping. Dr. Seaver made it clear that she and her associates would be available for consultation during certain hours each day to answer unanticipated questions about the research, particularly regarding methodology of parental behavioral intervention and record keeping.

The unfortunate result of Dr. Seaver's failure to inform the participants about some of the crucial details about their role and the required time commitment to the project was a high drop-out rate. Many who participated could not give the time and energy required for the research, and they found it necessary to withdraw after several weeks or months. Some of these problems could have been averted had Dr. Seaver comprehensively described what would be required of the participants at the outset instead of providing only partially accurate information.

6.11 Informed Consent to Research

(a) Psychologists use language that is reasonably understandable to research participants in obtaining their appropriate informed consent (except as provided in Standard 6.12, Dispensing With Informed Consent). Such informed consent is appropriately documented.

(a) When informing research participants about what will be expected of them, use simple English in addition to any technical language that may be required. Also document the consent procedure by use of forms or other appropriate records.

Vignette: A psychologist who was investigating PTSD and perceptual modalities of coding the distressing events developed an informed consent statement that he thought was comprehensive and concise. In the interest of saving time when creating the form, he simply copied many sentences from his grant proposal, verbatim, and added a few more sentences that addressed the expectations and requirements of participants. His opening paragraph read as follows:

> This study will investigate the cognitive mapping and etiology of symptoms associated with posttraumatic stress disorder. It will examine the intensity of visual and auditory evoked potentials and concurrent subjective strength of eidetic imagery.

Although this was not language that was easily understood by laymen, it did accurately convey a description of the research.

In discussing his research with one of his associates, Dr. Eron Kawshen, the principal investigator mentioned how he had created the consent form. After reading the form, Dr. Kawshen had some concern about the abstruse language, and he pointed out that few laypeople would have the foggiest idea about what they were consenting to. Furthermore, he warned his colleague that many participants would probably drop out of the research before their participation was over, once they realized what it involved, because of apprehension about flashbacks to their own traumatic events.

Fortunately, the researcher was persuaded to alter his opening paragraph in the consent form. With Dr. Kawshen's editorial help, it then read as follows:

> This study will investigate the ways in which people store memories of traumatic experiences in their past and the intensity of each sense that is a part of that memory (e.g., vision, hearing, smell, touch, physical sensations). It will also attempt to examine the vividness of visual imagery that is experienced by the person when he or she is asked to recall the event in question.

Although this did not constitute the form in its entirety, as an opening paragraph it was much more understandable than the original version.

> *(b) Using language that is reasonably understandable to participants, psychologists inform participants of the nature of the research; they inform participants that they are free to participate or to decline to participate or to withdraw from the research; they explain the foreseeable consequences of declining or withdrawing; they inform participants of significant factors that may be expected to influence their willingness to participate (such as risks, discomfort, adverse effects, or limitations on confidentiality, except as provided in Standard 6.15, Deception in Research); and they explain other aspects about which the prospective participants inquire.*

(b) Have a thorough informed consent form written in simple language, and have each participant read, understand, and sign it before beginning to collect data. Be sure to comply with the basic requirements of this ethical standard, including (a) describing the nature of the research, (b) ensuring voluntary participation, (c) informing about any consequences of declining or withdrawing from the research, (d) disclosing all factors that would influence one's willingness to participate, and (e) answering questions raised by prospective participants forthrightly and accurately (without compromising their naiveté, as necessary). Although not mandated by this standard, it is also important to comply with additional requirements by institutional review boards or other relevant professional or regulatory agencies when creating an informed consent form (e.g., National Institutes of Health, ethics codes of professional associations other than APA or the American Psychological Society in the case of multidisciplinary research).

An informed consent form should include the following elements:

1. *Description of the research.* Describe the nature of the research and what will be expected of participants. What is the subject of the investigation? Why is it important? What will be expected of the participants in terms of time, effort, risk, and so on? Will there be compensation of some sort?

2. *Voluntary participation.* Tell potential participants that participation is completely voluntary, and that they may drop out of the project at any time without being penalized or discriminated against in any way. Make certain there is no subtle pressure to participate, such as gaining the favor (and grade bonus) of a professor. Indicate the procedure for withdrawing from the research.

3. *Consequences of refusing to participate or dropping out.* Inform participants if there will be any consequences of declining to participate or withdrawing from the project once it is underway. For example, if a student enrolled in Psychology 101 refuses to participate, will he or she be required to complete another project instead, such as a paper or presentation, to get comparable credit? Is there the potential for adverse affects to withdrawing, such as losing out on the opportunity for debriefing, if desired? Will "drop outs" forfeit their entitlement to receiving compensation or inducements for participating that were offered at the outset (e.g., money, psychological products or services)? Will participants who withdraw still be entitled to receive a copy of the results of research, if they wish?

4. *Information that would affect one's willingness to participate.* Tell potential participants about everything that would likely affect their willingness to participate in the research. Are there any physical or psychological risks, discomfort, or adverse affects? Will they experience stress, medication effects, unpleasant emotional or physical sensations, pain, sleep deprivation, sexual arousal, or any other negative affects? Will there be unpleasant psychosocial effects or experiences that might be offensive to one's gender, ethnic roots, religious beliefs, or other fundamental traits or values that one holds dear? Are there any limitations on confidentiality or privacy, such as the use of videotaping? Tell all that would make

a difference in their willingness to participate. However, you don't have to compromise prospective participants' naiveté if it is essential for the research.

5. *Answering questions raised by participants.* Answer questions by potential participants candidly and clearly without distorting, minimizing, exaggerating, or omitting important information. Remember, potential participants do not always know which questions to ask; they don't know what they don't know about the research underway. How can you allay concerns of participants without giving false reassurances? How can you be sure that a potential participant, particularly children or those who are in some way impaired, understand your answers? Are your answers framed in simple language to be easily understood by those with less education or who speak English as a second language? When is an individual sufficiently informed, in your opinion, to make a sound decision about whether to participate in your study?

> *(c) When psychologists conduct research with individuals such as students or subordinates, psychologists take special care to protect the prospective participants from adverse consequences of declining or withdrawing from participation.*

(c) Don't be punitive in any way toward students, clients, or anyone else in a "one-down" power position if they refuse to participate in your research or decide to withdraw from it. You might urgently need participants, but always remember that participation in research must be *voluntary*. (This not only protects others but may improve the quality of your results too.)

Vignette: Dr. Will Smite was a full professor engaged in full-time teaching and research. He frequently would expect undergraduate and graduate students to be participants in projects in his research. In return, he would invite them to monthly dinners at his home and informal seminars at the university on a variety of topics. He also regularly assisted graduate students in locating satisfactory internship settings and other professional opportunities. It was well known in the psychology department that refusal to participate in his research meant that one's name would be removed from the guest list of his monthly dinners and informal seminars.

Furthermore and of some ethical concern, Dr. Smite refused to assist trainees who declined to participate in his research to obtain internships; on the contrary, he would base his decisions on internship and job placement primarily on the extent of the students' research participation. It was his practice to help place students in the best internships who were eager to serve as research participants repeatedly in different investigations, regardless of their relative competence as compared with other students in competition for a limited number of openings. His letters of reference for students were strongly influenced by these same factors, namely, how much they volunteered to be a research participant, not their actual strengths or appropriateness for the internship.

Dr. Smite was clearly engaging in punitive tactics for those who declined to participate or dropped out of his research projects. Unfortunately, no students complained, fearing even greater retribution on the part of this man who seemed to hold such power and authority over their work at the university and professional futures.

> *(d) When research participation is a course requirement or opportunity for extra credit, the prospective participant is given the choice of equitable alternative activities.*

(d) When offering research participation as a course requirement or extra credit opportunity, always allow students to decline and give them a choice of an equitable alternative project (e.g., research paper, presentation, participation in a different research project).

Vignette: A professor who was carrying out research requiring a large sample recruited students from one of his introductory psychology classes. His consent form revealed that the time required would not exceed 3 hours and that they would receive credit toward their final grade for participation in the study. He offered an alternative to students who did not wish to participate; but hoping to increasing their motivation, he required every nonparticipating student to write a 15-page paper on a topic related to his research.

Several students objected to this alternative, arguing that it was punitive. They claimed that writing a good research paper of that length would require considerably longer than the 3 hours expected of the research participants. Furthermore, the effort in writing such a paper involved very different skills and was far more demanding intellectually than merely participating in a research project. One student summed up the prevailing sentiments of his peers by declaring that he would "be damned if he was going to write a research paper that would contribute to his professor's review of the literature section for his journal article." He viewed the professor's alternative assignment as self-serving, unreasonable, and exploitative, particularly in view of the time that would be required to write a high-quality paper. The professor was unyielding in his requirement, however, and the students felt they had no other recourse than to complain to the chair of the psychology department or appropriate graduate school office.

> *(e) For persons who are legally incapable of giving informed consent, psychologists nevertheless (1) provide an appropriate explanation, (2) obtain the participant's assent, and (3) obtain appropriate permission from a legally authorized person, if such substitute consent is permitted by law.*

(e) When conducting research with children, people with mental disabilities, impaired older people, or others who cannot legally give consent, you still are obliged to do the following: (a) explain the research project to them anyway, as simply as possible; (b) obtain their agreement to cooperate, even though they may not fully understand; then,

(c) fully disclose your research to the responsible parent or legal guardian, according to the rules of Standard 6.11, and obtain their formal consent, before proceeding with the research.

Vignette: Dr. Anne Gram was interested in studying memory in children ranging in age from 5 to 8 years. She was examining free and cued recall of events as influenced by interrogatory bias, coercive persuasion on the part of the examiner, various types of misinformation, and inherent suggestibility of the child. Before she began, she discussed the study with the children and informed them that she would be testing their memory for events. She told them that some of them would be allowed to play with toys, others would watch television (videotapes), and then they would be asked some questions. This was done in a way to preserve their naiveté for the tasks. They were also told that they would probably enjoy the experience but that they did not have to participate if they did not wish to.

After the children assented, Dr. Gram spoke to the parents, informing them about the essence of the research; its goal to examine the phenomena of distortion of memory of recent events, repression, and confabulation in young children; and the rationale for the research, which was to help assess the validity of children's testimony who have been asked to provide details of their traumatic experiences when there have been allegations of child abuse. She explained that there would be little or no risk, that participation was completely voluntary, and that the child could drop out of the project at any point.

After asking their own questions about the research and receiving answers to their satisfaction, most parents agreed to allow their child to participate in the research. Parents were also encouraged to ask additional questions or explore any other concerns that might arise during the course of the research. With that in mind, Dr. Gram also made herself accessible to any parent who might have reservations about continuing after the data gathering had begun.

6.12 Dispensing With Informed Consent

Before determining that planned research (such as research involving only anonymous questionnaires, naturalistic observations, or certain kinds of archival research) does not require the informed consent of research participants, psychologists consider applicable regulations and institutional review board requirements, and they consult with colleagues as appropriate.

In certain planned research (e.g., anonymous questionnaires, naturalistic observations, certain kinds of archival research), don't automatically assume that informed consent is not needed. Always consider the effect of your research on participants, however slight you think it may be. Be sure to review any (a) applicable regulations (e.g., professional guidelines, NIH rules), (b) institutional review board requirements, and (c) relevant input from your colleagues before omitting informed consent.

Vignette: Dr. Seeker was investigating the psychological effects on partners who survived an AIDS-related death of a loved one. The independent variables he was exploring were length of time the patient was HIV positive, course of AIDS-related symptoms, duration of the relationship, financial stability, and family of origin support, to name a few. Dr. Seeker developed a questionnaire that addressed these issues and planned to distribute it in a nonrandom fashion at various locations throughout San Francisco (CA). He thought that it was unnecessary to seek respondents' informed consent because their participation consisted merely of completing an anonymous questionnaire, and he did not view this as a formal intervention or see it as posing any risk to those who would reply.

However, after discussing his research design and questionnaire with a gay male colleague who had personal experience in losing his partner, Dr. Seeker began to appreciate the potential for creating distress in others by simply exposing them to certain questions. It was likely that for some survivors the experience of responding to the questionnaire could possibly help bring further understanding, resolution, or peace of mind or even stimulate them to consult a counselor to further explore their feelings. For others who had made little progress processing their grief, guilt, anger, and other dysphoric feelings, the mere act of responding to probing questions about thoughts, feelings, and behavior concerning a highly stressful and protracted period of suffering and loss could rekindle feelings of bereavement and pain. It could exacerbate negative feelings, contribute to depression, and interfere with the individual's fragile psychological defenses and functioning, depending on their mental health at the time they completed the questionnaire.

Dr. Seeker began to understand that he could not necessarily predict the effect that responding to the questionnaire items could have on individuals. Therefore, in response to advice from his colleague, he created an informed consent sheet in which he described the nature of the questionnaire items and the range of possible effects that participating in this research might have on respondents. His colleague previewed the consent form and agreed that an individual could now freely make an intelligent decision at the outset about whether to participate in the research with less risk of adverse effect than only responding to the items without understanding their nature.

6.13 Informed Consent in Research Filming or Recording

> *Psychologists obtain informed consent from research participants prior to filming or recording them in any form, unless the research involves simply naturalistic observations in public places and it is not anticipated that the recording will be used in a manner that could cause personal identification or harm.*

Always obtain research participants' informed consent before audio- or videotaping because people may be identified by their voice or image. You do not need informed consent, however, when doing naturalistic research in public places and the recording will not be used in a way that would reveal identities or could otherwise harm people.

Vignette: Dr. Philmore, who was teaching a seminar in group psychotherapy for advanced doctoral students, was planning to videotape a colleague's group therapy sessions for both didactic and research purposes. He was investigating nonverbal communication, both facial and postural, and measurable changes in these behaviors over the duration of the group. For this purpose, he had trained five doctoral students to serve as raters and view videotape segments and record their observations.

Dr. Philmore was aware of the ethical standard requiring informed consent by research participants when videotaping and was careful to inform them in advance of the fact that they would be taped. Unfortunately, he provided a rather narrow informed consent, neglecting to describe the intended audience of the videotape or provide the general rationale for taping. He also neglected to mention that trained raters would be viewing the tape. When several of the potential research participants raised questions about who would see the tape, it became clear to Dr. Philmore that important elements of the consent had been omitted. He quickly provided the names of all the raters and discovered, to his surprise, that an unanticipated problem immediately surfaced. By coincidence, two of the group therapy clients lived in the same large graduate student housing complex as one of the raters. Although not friends, the rater was known to both of them, and neither person wished to expose himself to this particular individual by means of participating in the videotape segments.

The two group therapy clients were distressed that the so-called informed consent had neglected to reveal such an important fact as the identity of the raters and confronted the group therapist with their feelings. The group therapist relayed this information to Dr. Philmore, who realized that not only was his consent form flawed, but his plan to videotape a therapy group and show segments to students also might be flawed because students might recognize other students on the tape. After gaining an appreciation of the potential risks to confidentiality by engaging in such a practice, he elected to refrain from showing the videotape to his class.

Coincidences happen all too often, even in larger communities, and the most unlikely circumstances can sometimes pose real risks to individuals' privacy and confidentiality. Dr. Philmore promptly took measures to guard against any further omissions in his consent form with a careful revision that provided much better protection to future patients and research participants.

6.14 Offering Inducements for Research Participants

> *(a) In offering professional services as an inducement to obtain research participants, psychologists make clear the nature of the services, as well as the risks, obligations, and limitations. (See also Standard 1.18, Barter [With Patients or Clients].)*

(a) When encouraging others to participate in research by offering professional services (e.g., receiving limited counseling services, receiving assessment interpretations), be sure to be candid about your services, including risks, obligations, and limitations. *Risks* includes the possibility that someone might be distressed after learning of their scores or performance on some aspect of the research. *Obligations* means that you must clearly state your intended responsibilities, such as providing a specific service, number of counseling sessions, and so on. *Limitations* refers to the scope of services that are being offered. Obligations do not go on forever, so be clear that there is a specific end to the researchers' responsibility.

Vignette: A researcher examining the effects of a variety of individual and group interventions for obese individuals extending over a 6-month period offered the inducement of individual consultations at the conclusion of the series of group meetings. The experimental groups included didactic, therapeutic, and pharmacological interventions. The rationale was that for some, the group experiences could elicit strong feelings, including depression and anxiety, and these might be remedied by individual sessions at the conclusion of the study. There were 30 men and women in each of the four groups (three experimental and one control), and predictably, some did experience dysphoric feelings over the course of the investigation. In fact, for a few, the promise of individual consultations at the end was the main reason they continued to participate in the study.

At the conclusion of the study, the researcher attempted to make good on her promise but was dismayed to find that over 25 participants wished to follow up with individual consultations. Furthermore, some of them expected to have an ongoing series of meetings or individual psychotherapy because the consent form had clearly stated that "the researcher and her assistants will be available for individual consultations following the conclusion of the study to help group members resolve any distressing feelings resulting from participation in the project." The consent form had given no limit on time or the number of individual consultations. Such a vague and open-ended statement was an invitation for some group members to feel entitled to have many sessions, essentially beginning a course of brief-term psychotherapy.

Ultimately, the research team spent many more hours providing support and therapy than they had ever intended and found that they were obligated to make several referrals for individual psychotherapy to comply with providing the inducement promised in the informed consent.

> *(b) Psychologists do not offer excessive or inappropriate financial or other inducements to obtain research participants, particularly when it might tend to coerce participation.*

(b) Don't offer extreme or inappropriate incentives for participating in research. Your participant may feel coerced and your research data may ultimately be compromised.

Vignette: Dr. Aufermuch taught at a small school for professional psychology and was having difficulty obtaining enough students to volunteer for his research projects. Because he was very intent on conducting research, he had to be quite creative in inducing students to come forth. He developed several plans that he felt would significantly increase students' motivation to participate in his research, requiring approximately 4 hours of their time.

First, he waived the final examination and awarded the equivalent of an automatic *A* on the test to students enrolled in his course if they volunteered for both projects. Second, for other students in the school who were not enrolled in his course, he offered money drawn from grant funds for a different project that had not been expended. He paid each student $45 per project (over $20 per hour) for being a research participant; this was over three times the hourly minimum wage.

Finally, he offered a 1-night stay in his time-shared condominium in Las Vegas (NV) to those who volunteered to be in both projects and provided help in rating the results. Dr. Aufermuch had little comprehension of this ethical standard that prohibits researchers from offering excessively large inducements to research participants. By so doing, he risked the possibility of a conflict of interest, placing research participants more in the role of "employee" or "partner" than volunteer for a scientific study. By offering inducements that were so overwhelmingly attractive to a graduate student population, he may have also compromised the validity of his data by essentially "buying" research participants who would have an interest in attempting to help prove his research hypothesis as they understood it.

6.15 Deception in Research

(a) Psychologists do not conduct a study involving deception unless they have determined that the use of deceptive techniques is justified by the study's prospective scientific, educational, or applied value and that equally effective alternative procedures that do not use deception are not feasible.

(a) Never deceive your research participants unless the investigation warrants it and there is no other way to obtain the results. Do not mislead, lie, or use any deceptive techniques, unless they are justified by the prospective value of the research in one of these areas: (a) *scientific* (e.g., it is a significant contribution to the knowledge base), (b) *educational* (e.g., it is of benefit to individuals or society), or (c) *applied* (e.g., it has application to industrial and organizational settings, environmental psychology, or direct implications for the ways in which psychologists intervene in others' lives).

Vignette: Dr. Nares, interested in investigating the effects of a new fast-acting, antianxiety medication that could be self-administered through a nose spray, developed a design that required deception. He wished to compare the effect of the new medication with a placebo in a randomized, double-blind study. As part of an experiment supposedly measuring perceptual acuity and cognitive ability as a function of aging, participants were required to fill out a health history questionnaire and undergo a brief medical examination. Physiological measures, blood chemistry, and subjective reports would yield the data on state anxiety and any changes therein. Each participant was then falsely informed that he or she had an irregular heartbeat, slightly elevated blood pressure, and other indicators of a vascular or neurological disorder in preparation for the nose spray antianxiety drug.

The institutional review board evaluating the protocol rejected it on the grounds that the prospective scientific value of the research did not merit deceiving participants about such a significant matter as their own current medical status or risk of mortality. Furthermore, it argued that there were alternate ways to investigate this anxiety-alleviating product without putting individuals at risk. One way to test the medication would be to seek individuals who already experienced the symptoms of anxiety or to seek those in naturally occurring anxiety-arousing settings, such as in hospitals, with medical patients who had just received accurate "bad news" about their health status (e.g., HIV positive diagnosis). It might require more effort and ingenuity on the part of Dr. Nares and his team to select a particular setting that would yield cooperative and anxious participants, but doing so would not require putting people needlessly at risk of being deceived and suffering concomitant intense emotional and physiological reactions.

> *(b) Psychologists never deceive research participants about significant aspects that would affect their willingness to participate, such as physical risks, discomfort, or unpleasant emotional experiences.*

(b) Never deceive potential research participants about a part of the study that would affect their willingness to become involved (e.g., physical risks, discomfort, unpleasant emotional experience).

Vignette: Dr. Parshall placed an ad in the newspaper for healthy volunteers to test the effects of physical exercise on a variety of psychological measures and interventions. Participants were offered $100 if they completed the study. Unfortunately, Dr. Parshall neglected to inform participants responding to the ad that they would be required to visit the laboratory facility regularly to achieve a consistent amount of exertion across participants. He also failed to inform them that they might be assigned to experimental groups where hypnosis, biofeedback training, and other interventions might be used as independent variables, necessitating meetings at certain times of the day. In addition, potential participants were not informed accurately of the approximate total amount of time that would be required of them. Finally, they were told that the amount of exercise would be "easily tolerated by most people" on a regular basis. However, the protocol called for participants to spend anywhere from 20 to 60 minutes on alternating days performing fairly rigorous exercise.

Because he failed to disclose these details about the research requirements, the investigator lost many prospective research participants after they learned what they were expected to do. Many did not wish to visit the facility so often for such long periods of exercise and viewed this obligation as a significant hardship. Some had philosophical or religious objections to the use of hypnosis or did not wish to participate in "mind control" experiments. Of that subgroup, some had previous aversive experiences with hypnosis in therapy settings, such as lingering posthypnotic effects of unpleasant sensations or memories from early life events, and did not wish to risk reexperiencing them.

Those who withdrew from the study regretted that they had wasted nearly an hour of their time, with no monetary compensation, before learning of the actual requirements for physical exercise and hypnosis. They felt that they should have been informed of the expectations for their participation at the outset because the study requirements obviously affected their willingness to participate and could easily have been disclosed without compromising their naiveté as participants.

> *(c) Any other deception that is an integral feature of the design and conduct of an experiment must be explained to participants as early as is feasible, preferably at the conclusion of their participation, but no later than at the conclusion of the research. (See also Standard 6.18, Providing Participants With Information About the Study.)*

(c) Debrief participants as early as possible about any deceptions used during their participation. Participants can usually be debriefed at the end of their involvement in the research.

Vignette: Dr. Jekyl had used deception in a protocol involving the giving of false medical statistics (e.g., cardiac functioning, blood pressure) to participants. He had originally planned to have a group debriefing session at the end of each week so that all participants for that week of data gathering would convene and learn of the deception at once. He reasoned that all participants who were deceived about their own cardiac functioning and blood pressure to increase anxiety would receive an in-depth description of the rationale for the deceptions inherent in the research at the same time. All questions could be easily addressed at one time, and he would not have to repeat the same presentation many times for each individual. Furthermore, he thought, by prolonging the deception for up to a week, he could obtain a more realistic appraisal of long-term effects of the antianxiety nasal spray while anxiety-evoking cognitions were allowed to remain in place.

Dr. Jekyl neglected to adequately consider that by prolonging the deception of having given false information about participants' own medical statistics, he was also prolonging the anxiety or suffering of these participants. He could just as easily have adhered to the requirement of this standard by debriefing participants at the conclusion of their individual participation in the study rather than scheduling a group debriefing session at his convenience at the end of each week. Because deception in the protocol was revealed to be gratuitous and potentially harmful to participants by the institutional review board, the project involving planned group debriefings was not approved.

6.16 Sharing and Utilizing Data

Psychologists inform research participants of their anticipated sharing or further use of personally identifiable research data and of the possibility of unanticipated future uses.

Be sure to tell research participants if you plan to share your data with others, and inform them of any other plans you have for using the data in the future.

Vignette: Dr. Willa Cher was conducting research on group therapy for adolescent and adult anorectic women. Her protocol called for videotaping each group therapy session and using trained raters to evaluate certain verbal and nonverbal behaviors in response to the group therapists' interventions. She obtained the patients' consent in advance, informing them that (a) every meeting would be videotaped and (b) raters would be viewing and evaluating the tapes. She even provided the names of all the raters so that there would be no "surprises" and gave every group member the chance to refuse to participate if she knew the rater in another context or for any other reason.

Unfortunately, she neglected to inform the women that she intended to share her data with the staff of an eating disorders unit in a nearby psychiatric hospital. She also failed to tell them that she planned to use the videotapes in training mental health professionals. Three of the women were "treatment failures" at the psychiatric hospital who'd had some unpleasant experiences with staff members there; they did not wish to have anything further to do with the unit and certainly would have been opposed to having personal identifying information about their group experiences released.

When it became clear after four meetings that Dr. Cher intended to share data in these ways, the three women voiced their strong opposition to her plan. Some other group members objected to using the tapes to train therapists, unless they knew their identity in advance; they had participated in psychotherapy with numerous therapists in the community over a 10-year period, with mixed results, and did not wish to reveal details of their current therapy to them.

Dr. Cher could easily remove the women's objective test data from the pool in accordance with their wishes, but it would pose significant logistical and procedural problems to comply with their request to delete their images and voices from the videotapes. After all, it had been her plan to not only release the data to other researchers but also to help train mental health workers at the hospital and in the community by using excerpts from the actual therapy group videotapes.

Although some group members were not opposed to such sharing of data and use of the tapes, they all would have preferred to have known of her plans at the outset. The researcher was now faced with several choices, each of which had drawbacks. Either she could alter her research design and intentions for using the tapes for training purposes, or she could maintain her plans and request group members who objected to withdraw from the group, truncating their therapy and risking harm to them through abandonment. All this could have been avoided had she provided thorough informed consent about her intentions for sharing her data and results at the outset, thus weeding out those individuals in advance who did not wish to be part of such a project.

6.17 Minimizing Invasiveness

In conducting research, psychologists interfere with the participants or milieu from which data are collected only in a manner that is warranted by an appropriate research design and that is consistent with psychologists' roles as scientific investigators.

Minimize intrusion into the lives and settings of research participants when you're collecting data. Don't indulge in nonscientific curiosity by seeking information over and above that which is needed for your study.

Vignette: Dr. I. M. Low was attempting to research grief reactions of 500 individuals who had recently lost a spouse or close friend to sudden death. He planned to use a variety of criteria for tracking changes in mood, thought process, and activity level for 1 year following the death. He was attempting to ascertain the spontaneous coping techniques used by survivors and why some move through the grieving process more swiftly and productively than others.

His design consisted of four parts: (a) repeated objective testing, (b) personal interviews, (c) monitoring changes in health status, and (d) monitoring changes in financial status that might have ensued from the sudden loss of a primary income producer over a period of 1 year following the death.

Dr. Low also required each participant to keep a daily journal, logging their tearfulness, private thoughts, physical activity, sleep, and sexual behavior. Although he did not intend to analyze these journal entries or use them in any way as a part of his investigation—as he thought it unwieldy to do so with such a large sample—he was curious about these aspects of his participants' lives. His reason for exploring such areas was more personally than scientifically motivated. He had suffered a tragic loss several years before—his wife had died in a mountain climbing accident—and he had been unable to accept her death and go on with his life. He hoped to learn from the success of others about processing such a loss by reading their daily journals.

Although Dr. Low had selected a research question that was worthy of scientific investigation, he developed a design that was unnecessarily intrusive and placed a needless burden on research participants who were already experiencing significant personal distress. His motivation for including the requirement to make daily journal entries was based on his own desire to resolve a personal tragedy in his life rather than to make a contribution to scientific knowledge. By indulging his personal needs and unresolved grief about his wife's death, he gratuitously intruded into the private lives of many people who volunteered to be research participants during a time of intense personal loss and grieving. The investigation could well have been completed by simply adhering to the four parts of the design that would have provided usable data. Alternatively, he could have developed a means of analyzing and using journal entries that would be less intrusive or collected on a less frequent basis. Furthermore, it is likely that with a less invasive design, many more research participants would have agreed to remain a part of the study instead of dropping out of the study, as was the case. Dr. Low would have been better served by consulting a competent therapist or seeking some other therapeutic experience to help him with grieving instead of using unwitting research participants to attempt to resolve his own loss.

6.18 Providing Participants With Information About the Study

> *(a) Psychologists provide a prompt opportunity for participants to obtain appropriate information about the nature, results, and conclusions of the research, and psychologists attempt to correct any misconceptions that participants may have.*

(a) Provide all research participants with a prompt opportunity to learn about the nature, results, and conclusions of the research after they've completed their role, and address any misconceptions that they may have.

Vignette: Dr. Philmore carried out research involving the rating of videotapes of group psychotherapy sessions, and he was well aware of the importance of providing participants with information about the study at the conclusion. After the psychotherapy group members were videotaped, all the data were analyzed, and the results and conclusions of the study were written, Dr. Philmore made his abstract available to the participants. He presented his research hypothesis: focusing on changes in nonverbal communication (facial expression, body posture, movement, etc.) and changes in verbal behavior (volume, pitch, pace, inflection, etc.) as a function of participation in a therapy group. He also described in lay terms the nature of his research hypotheses so that participants could understand the goal of the investigation.

Dr. Philmore also made himself available for individual consultations with any participants who had specific questions about the research. He wanted to be certain that he had communicated his ideas clearly and that there were no misconceptions in the minds of the participants about the research or their role in it.

Several participants had questions that went beyond the research; specifically, they sought information about their own individual ratings and what their nonverbal behavior in the group had communicated. Dr. Philmore was unwilling to review the videotapes or individual ratings with those participants because that would have constituted a major time commitment and was beyond the scope of his promise to provide information about the study. However, he did agree to spend some time educating them about basic principles of nonverbal communication and providing some generic information that seemed to meet their needs.

> *(b) If scientific or humane values justify delaying or withholding this information, psychologists take reasonable measures to reduce the risk of harm.*

(b) If there is a good reason to delay informing participants about your study, such as preserving the naiveté of future participants or sensitivity to their feelings, you may do so. But be sure to at least minimize any possible harm to them in the process.

Vignette: Dr. Kara Taker planned to investigate psychosocial variables that might affect the longevity of terminally ill patients. Her sample included HIV patients who were suffering advanced clinical symptoms and cancer patients who had particularly aggressive forms of the disease. Her independent variables were the amount of love and emotional support available from a partner, family of origin, friends, and caretakers. She used objective measures and brief personal interviews to assess the quantity and quality of social support present (e.g., frequency and length of visits, topics discussed in depth, physical and sexual contact).

Some earlier research supported the importance of these variables in prolonging and improving the quality of life of the patient. Dr. Taker believed that patients who had little or no social support might be at greater risk for dying sooner. She reasoned that little purpose would be served by revealing the true nature and goals of this research to dying patients. In fact, she thought that there was a reasonable risk of some patients becoming further depressed on learning of the possibility of a further shortened life span. She decided to avoid providing direct information about the study to the patients themselves. Patients and others were simply told at the outset that the project focused on individuals who had a chronic illness and the methods they used to cope with pain, isolation, and dysphoric feelings.

When patients died, Dr. Taker provided their families or those who had legal responsibility for them additional information about the research. Care was taken to avoid blaming or inducing feelings of guilt or wrongdoing in those family members and helpers who were able to offer only limited social support. By preserving the naiveté of dying patients, the researcher avoided inflicting additional pain and suffering on some of them but was able to obtain important data that might have significant implications for others diagnosed with serious diseases.

6.19 Honoring Commitments

> *Psychologists take reasonable measures to honor all commitments they have made to research participants.*

Keep all commitments you have made with research participants after the project is over. Do what you promised to do.

Vignette: Dr. U. N. Line was conducting research on the influence of computer technology and the use of the Internet on psychotherapy. His independent variables consisted of various interactive settings, such as face-to-face therapy, video conferencing, email, and self-help style (interactive) "chat rooms." Each participant, an actual client seeking counseling, was promised a IBM-compatible or MacIntosh version of "Dr. Cyberpsych," an application that had been developed for an earlier study involving psychotherapy by computer and was currently undergoing further study by other researchers.

About 4 months into the project, Dr. Line learned of research results indicating that use of Dr. Cyberpsych could actually exacerbate depression in some patients. He discovered, much to his chagrin, in several cases that patients behaved in a self-destructive manner after extended and frequent sessions with the computer software.

Dr. Line was in a quandary. Ethically, he felt he should no longer offer this application to research participants as an incentive for participating in his project because he knew that some individuals in his samples could be at risk of being harmed. However, he also had an obligation to make good on his promise to give them *something* for their cooperation; they were investing many hours as research participants and expected to receive a copy of Dr. Cyberpsych at the conclusion.

After consulting with some colleagues in the instructional technology department, Dr. Line evolved a creative solution to his dilemma. He learned about an entertaining prototype of a recently developed computerized educational game for young adults that would never be available to the public in its current form. The creator of the game was a friend of Dr. Line and agreed to make copies available for him to distribute to his research participants in place of Dr. Cyberpsych. Dr. Line also wrote a short statement explaining the predicament and provided information about the recent research that resulted in the recall of the problematical application.

Dr. Line learned an important lesson: He was too hasty in offering Dr. Cyberpsych as an inducement for participation in research before the application's strengths, weaknesses, and risks to certain individuals had been thoroughly assessed. Fortunately, he was able to provide research participants with computer software, as promised, although it was a different application than originally described. It was only due to the coincidence of the availability of his colleague's educational game (and goodwill) that he was able to reward participants for their time and energy with an incentive that was similar to that which had been promised.

6.20 Care and Use of Animals in Research

(a) Psychologists who conduct research involving animals treat them humanely.

(a) Treat your animal subjects humanely.

Vignette: Dr. Terry Aire, a researcher at a small university, was attentive to all federal rules and regulations as well as APA's (1993a) ethical standards and guidelines pertaining to animal care and treatment. She even supported practices in her laboratory that were not required but were considered humane treatment in light of current knowledge about animals and their needs. An example of this was her treatment of animals who were not currently being used for research purposes. She had just completed a project involving the acquisition of new learning in rats that required a regulated feeding schedule resulting in a consistent weight of 90% of normal. As she was about to take a 2-week vacation and it would be an additional week until the next research would begin with the same rats, she gave instructions to Erich, her research assistant, about caring for them during this time. Specifically, she asked him to remove the rats from the restricted feeding schedule and return them to a free-feeding schedule, allowing them to gain up to 25 grams in weight. She knew that this would necessitate allowing additional time to attain the reduced weight, once again, before beginining the next experiment. However, in the interest of treating the animals humanely in the interim, although not required by any standard or regulation, she reverted to the feeding schedule that was less aversive to them.

Erich followed Dr. Aire's instructions 4 days each week, when he was at the university. However, he delegated the weekend responsibilities to Jake, an experienced animal care worker who had recently joined the staff from another university. In carrying out the instructions, Jake provided a large amount of food for the rats on Friday night and did not look in on the animals again until early Monday morning. This was the way he had always attended to animals that were on an unregulated eating schedule at the previous animal laboratory where he had worked for many years.

One Sunday afternoon when Erich happened to be on the campus he decided to drop in to the laboratory to check on the animals. He noticed that they were out of food and that the water supply was low. He promptly contacted Jake, who informed him that this was his usual procedure of caring for the animals over the weekend that were on a free-feeding schedule. Erich told Jake that Dr. Aire considered risking running out of food on Sunday, as had just happened, to be a hardship for the animals and that he was to monitor their supply daily on the weekends. Jake agreed to follow this schedule, even though he felt that it was almost "too" humane.

There were other practices in Dr. Aire's laboratory that also seemed overly scrupulous to Jake, compared with the outdated practices in his previous work setting. In the vivarium that housed the rats, mice, and birds, all lights were on a 12-hour timer to simulate day and night. Where he had previously worked, the lights always remained on because "that was the way things had always been done there"; some researchers wanted the animals not to entrain on lights that go on and off but on the time of the daily experimental session. Even though Dr. Aire knew that U.S. Department of Agriculture (USDA) requirements did not cover rats, mice, and birds, she also knew from research on chronobiology that it was potentially distressful on the animals never to experience darkness.

Finally, in her work with monkeys, Dr. Aire was familiar with the USDA requirements mandating enriched environments for the animals. This might mean providing the monkeys with a toy to promote play or psychological well-being while in the cage. Jake had cared for monkeys before and was not particularly concerned about the quality of the toy provided for the animals. But Dr. Aire told him about the research that clearly informed scientists about preferred toys for monkeys and which type of toy was relatively useless in contributing to an enriched environment for the animals. She knew the value of remaining current in the research of the animal she was working with and creating a living environment that adequately reflected their needs, over and above the mandated standards.

> *(b) Psychologists acquire, care for, use, and dispose of animals in compliance with current federal, state, and local laws and regulations, and with professional standards.*

(b) In purchasing, caring for, using, and disposing of animals, be sure to observe federal, state, and local laws and regulations as well as the standards of any other professional associations to which you belong.

Vignette: Dr. Snatcher usually purchased animals through his university's Research Animals Resource Unit, which had well-established business relationships with animal dealers across the country. He was aware of the *Guide for the Care and Use of Laboratory Animals* (Institute of Laboratory Animal Resources, 1996) and the regulations of the USDA. However, he routinely engaged in some practices that were not in compliance with all the regulations, thinking that they were creative and harmless ways of dealing with some of the common problems encountered by animal researchers.

For example, at the conclusion of research with mice, rats, and pigeons when there was no further planned use for the animals, he would commonly release them into a nearby woods. He thought that the animals would fare better in a natural setting than by remaining cooped up in their cages for long periods of time. However, by releasing the animals in this way, he was exposing them to greater risk; they had been born and raised in captivity and had no experience fending for themselves in the wild. In spite of his benevolent intentions, Dr. Snatcher was actually increasing the risk that the animals would be harmed by predators, extreme weather conditions, infection, and disease. It would have been more humane to have them euthanized appropriately, according to the standards of the American Veterinary Association, or to make arrangements with other researchers to make use of the animals if consistent with institutional policies.

Dr. Snatcher also had begun acquiring animals in rather creative ways over the past year, using a variety of sources instead of licensed vendors. For example, he had a good friend who owned several animal petting zoos in three nearby cities. This resulted in a regular supply of rabbits, marmosetts, and capuchins for his research; he could regularly be seen driving his modified pick-up truck with the young animals in the back. He also occasionally carried his pet dogs and cats in the same truck, and sometimes he transported racoons, opossums, and other garden nuisances to remote places for drop off. Unfortunately he did not disinfect the truck cages adequately, and the resulting contamination placed the animals to be used for research at a high risk of infection. On occasion, these animals also brought diseases from the petting zoo into the existing colonies of Dr. Snatcher's laboratory, causing illness in other animals that sometimes resulted in death. This had obvious implications for the research because animals that are in poor health tend to behave differently, thus compromising the integrity of the research data.

When he consulted his friends who sat on the university's Institutional Animal Care and Use Committee about the recurring problem of illness among his animals, he was told that it was probably due to his unusual way of procuring and transporting the new animals. The committee members were alarmed about his methods and informed him that they were contrary to the university's guidelines and USDA regulations. The committee had been somewhat lax in carrying out its federally mandated duties. However, when he approached the members directly in obvious need of guidance, they provided it and resolved to arange better oversight of animal procurement in the institution from that point on.

> *(c) Psychologists trained in research methods and experienced in the care of laboratory animals supervise all procedures involving animals and are responsible for ensuring appropriate consideration of their comfort, health, and humane treatment.*

(c) Supervise every procedure involving your animals to assure competence and humane treatment by assistants and caretakers.

Vignette: Dr. Perry Gawn and his colleagues were investigating whether electric current administered by means of an implanted electrode in the spinal cord altered the reactivity to different types of pain in rats. The rats were derived from the Holtzman Company stock and were bred at the university's Research Animal Resource Unit. Because his research involved the administering of different kinds of painful stimuli to his animal subjects, Dr. Gawn was particularly fastidious about closely adhering to all ethical and federal standards and knew that his university's Institutional Animal Care and Use Committee would take a particular interest in closely scrutinizing every aspect of his protocol. His research would have major implications for the treatment of chronic pain in humans who were disabled by their suffering and unable to obtain sustained relief by any other means.

Dr. Gawn took great care in teaching his graduate students and research assistants exactly how to use each piece of equipment and handle the animals according to currently held principles (Iversen & Lattal,

1991). He first trained them in the handling of rats and thoroughly supervised their desensitization to the animals. The assistants were then carefully shown how to prepare the rats for the experiment, which included placing them in a plexiglas restraint box.

He carefully instructed them in the use of the computer software controlling the amperage to administer through the implanted electrodes to guarantee standardization in treatment. He also scrupulously reviewed the various aversive stimuli to use in the research, such as chemical, thermal, or electrical, and the methodology of delivering the stimuli to the rats. Finally, he took great care in teaching them observational methods for assessing pain reactivity in the rats, including tail flicks and other motor reactivity.

In supervising his research assistants, Dr. Gawn was methodical, comprehensive, and compassionate. He encouraged his collaborators and assistants to ask for guidance when needed rather than to risk harming animals or compromising the data collection. He even requested that they telephone him at home if they had any questions that needed immediate attention. He would randomly monitor their activities and had well-established procedures for being contacted if problems developed. In this way of teaching and supervising in an ongoing way, he maximized the chances that the rats would be well attended, the data gathering would be standardized, and the assistants would be well qualified to carry out their duties. The meticulous way in which Dr. Gawn conducted his research resulted in an extensive contribution to the field that did not have to be repeated and that required less suffering for the animals and less financial cost in the long run.

> *(d) Psychologists ensure that all individuals using animals under their supervision have received instruction in research methods and in the care, maintenance, and handling of the species being used, to the extent appropriate to their role.*

(d) Consistent with their role, every assistant should be well trained and competent in research methods and the care, maintenance, and handling of the kind of animal being used.

Vignette: Dr. Hatta Skip was conducting a behavioral pharmacological study on rats requiring repetitive blood sampling. While she was in the middle of training her postdoctoral fellows, she had a family crisis that necessitated her leaving town for a short while. Unfortunately this resulted in inadequate instruction on techniques for drawing blood and how to handle the animals during the procedures. She also failed to educate her assistants adequately about the importance of maintaining antiseptic procedures, including the use of proper restraint procedures and inhalational anaesthetics.

Fortunately, most of the postdoctoral fellows were already competent in these procedures because they'd had much previous experience with research on rats. However, one assistant had virtually no experience in drawing blood from rats. He made many errors, such as disregarding the importance of antiseptic procedures and reusing needles, resulting in the spread of infection to many of the animals. Because he lacked knowledge in proper handling of the rats, he was bitten and ended up dropping or even throwing the rats at times.

His incompetence did not come to the attention of Dr. Skip until several weeks had gone by when two other postdoctoral fellows felt compelled to bring his incompetence to her attention. As it turned out, the assistant had misrepresented his experience to Dr. Skip when he originally interviewed for the position. Furthermore, he had a long history of addiction to opiates, from a chronic pain condition, and his primary reason for wanting to work in an animal lab was to gain access to a variety of drugs. Dr. Skip discovered that he had been diverting drugs from the laboratory stock for his own personal use.

Because Dr. Skip mistakenly assumed competence in all her assistants and had failed to properly train and supervise them in the application of standardized techniques, she lost five animals to infection. Thus, she lost time and accumulated data that was essentially unusable, necessitating restarting some of the animals in the experimental conditions. The assistant had also subjected many animals to needless suffering due to the improper techniques resulting in pain and infection. Because the assistant was incompetent and Dr. Skip provided him inadequate training at the outset, the animals, the assistant, and ultimately the research project itself were harmed.

> *(e) Responsibilities and activities of individuals assisting in a research project are consistent with their respective competencies.*

(e) All research assistants must be competent to perform at whatever level of responsibility is required of them.

Vignette: Dr. Will Phillin was investigating visual discrimination and cognition in pigeons and had thoroughly trained his two research assistants to help him. Each was working in an area commensurate with his or her abilities and experience level. George worked primarily with the computer, interfacing it with the display equipment and complex learning environment and managing the actual data collection. Liza worked with the pigeons, connecting sensors and orienting the animals to each of the tasks they faced.

After working on the project for 4 weeks, Liza had a skiing accident and, unfortunately, was unable to continue her part of the work. Dr. Phillin needed to locate another assistant, but his department was very small and there were no other graduate students who were skilled and available. Although Dr. Phillin was well aware that any assistant would have to meet the standards of the protocol that had been approved by the Institutional Animal Care and Use Committee, he was tempted to take a short cut because he was under pressure to complete the research in time for pending tenure decisions. He had come to know Tim, the animal care worker who had maintained all the animals in the laboratory for several years quite well, and he decided to ask him to "pinch hit" and take Liza's place in working with the pigeons. He was available, obviously familiar and comfortable with the pigeons, and interested in earning some extra income.

After attempting to instruct Tim about the research and emphasizing the importance of standardized procedures with each animal on every task, Dr. Phillin monitored him closely for several days as he ran subjects. Tim seemed to grasp the concepts and master the procedures quickly and easily adapted to his new role in the lab. However, 1 week later, when he was on his own, he was finding it difficult to maintain the rigorous schedule and scrupulously standardized procedures that were expected of him. His concern and genuine affection for the pigeons interfered with his objectivity. He found it virtually impossible to participate in activities that would be frustrating to the pigeons, and any deprivation or minor discomfort that was part of the protocol was distressing to him.

After struggling with these conflicts and the personal temptation to make things easier for the "little guys" by changing the protocol, Tim decided that he could no longer continue to play this new role. He went to Dr. Phillin and announced that he must withdraw from the project. An animal care worker he could be, but a researcher he was not. Dr. Phillin then realized that his wishful thinking and urgency to move ahead with the project had blinded him to the importance of maintaining ethical standards and the problems that can develop when relying on an assistant who is not competent. He was grateful, however, that Tim was able to confront his own personal conflict about continuing the research honestly and reveal it openly rather than further compromise the protocol by doing a half-hearted job collecting data.

> *(f) Psychologists make reasonable efforts to minimize the discomfort, infection, illness, and pain of animal subjects.*

(f) Be sure to minimize animals' discomfort, infection, illness, and suffering.

Vignette: In a long research project using macaque monkeys, Dr. Rex Emplery was fastidious in his care for and supervision of the animals, going great lengths to minimize any discomfort, illness, and suffering. He thoroughly reviewed pertinent sections of the USDA regulations pertaining to the Animal Welfare Act (Title 9, 1992) and the *Guide for the Care and Use of Laboratory Animals* (Institute of Laboratory Animal Resources, 1996) with his assistants and animal care workers. These documents describe in detail the standards for indoor and outdoor housing facilities, mobile housing facilities, environment enhancement to promote psychological well-being, transportation requirements, and of course such basics as feeding, watering, and sanitation requirements.

Because Dr. Emplery housed the animals in facilities that were under his authority, as approved by the Institutional Animal Care and Use Committee, he was well aware of his responsibility to meet the standards of the Code of Federal Regulations. Although he knew that his assistants and animal care workers were somewhat experienced, he still felt an obligation to review some of the standards with them to maximize the chances that the monkeys would remain healthy and robust for the duration of his research and would not suffer needlessly.

In particular, he was concerned about temperature control and ventilation of the cages because the university was having significant problems in these areas. He found it necessary to closely monitor these conditions and, at times, to be in regular contact with the maintenance staff during summer and winter. There had also been problems with the automatic light timers in the past and some laxness in replacing light bulbs when they burned out. Such illumination variability could possibly affect the performance of the monkeys, and Dr. Emplery wanted to take no chances in increasing threats to the validity of his data.

He also was concerned about the general cleanliness of the cages, feeding and watering on a strict schedule, and control of disease. If the cages were not cleaned on a regular schedule and the bedding changed as needed, which occasionally happened over extended weekends or during vacations while the regular staff was away, he was quick to see that these lapses were corrected. He also exhorted his staff to be vigilant about unusual behavior or symptoms that might signify illness in the animals. By seeing to it that skin and other diseases were promptly diagnosed and treated, Dr. Emplery minimized the likelihood of contagion within the colony and, ultimately, any negative impact on his data collection.

Indeed, he was a model of concern for the health and welfare of his animals. Some might say he was excessive in his attention to some of the minor aspects of animal care. However, because of his vigilance and ongoing supervision of others responsible for the monkeys, he was able to complete his research in a timely fashion with healthy animals and valid data.

> *(g) A procedure subjecting animals to pain, stress, or privation, is used only when an alternative procedure is unavailable and the goal is justified by its prospective scientific, educational, or applied value.*

(g) Never conduct research exposing animals to pain, stress, or privation, unless there are no alternative procedures that address the same research question and the goal is justified by its prospective scientific, educational, or applied value.

Vignette: A child psychologist, child psychiatrist, endocrine neurologist, and several geneticists were engaged in planning a large research project focusing on the long-term cognitive and behavioral effects on dogs of repeated exposure to aversive stimuli during early developmental stages. The study was intended to be an animal analogue for child abuse, namely, its effects on various physiological systems (e.g., endocrine, neurological) and implications for long-term psychopharmacological treatment once the animal reached maturity. The investigators used dogs of various ages, from 1 month to 3 years of age, and measured stress hormones, such as adrenocorticotropic hormone, prolactin, and plasma catecholamines, as a means of quantifying the animals' stress reactions. At various stages of their growth and then at maturity, the dogs in the experimental groups received two new medications; one increased the availability of certain neurotransmitters (e.g., seratonin, dopamine) and the other was a genetically engineered drug directly affecting the DNA of several sympathetic nervous system target organs, somewhat reducing their reactivity to adrenalin. The results of this investigation would have major implications for decisions about long-term medication of adults who had been severely abused as children.

It was of prime consideration to ascertain the minimal threshold values of current intensity and duration that would evoke a stress reaction of sufficient magnitude to produce hormonal changes but not so aversive as to inflict needless suffering on the animals for no additional return on the data. A major consideration of the hospital's Institutional Animal Care and Use Committee was that the animals not be exposed to unnecessary pain. The researchers presented the rationale that using a carefully titrated electric current was the simplest and most precise way to obtain the hormonal and neurological changes necessary for testing the research hypotheses: A carefully controlled electric shock in the developing dogs would constitute an approximate physiological equivalent of recurring severe abuse in a child by evoking similar arousal of the organism's sympathetic nervous system and its target organs (e.g., heart, gastrointestinal system). The ultimate prospective value of the research was its potential contribution to the psychopharmacological treatment of adults who had suffered severe child abuse at various developmental stages and were at risk for a lifetime of increased anxiety, depression, and possibly suicide.

To ascertain the optimal range of electric current stimuli, the team had relied largely on their earlier research and those of other investigators that assessed the changes in stress hormone output as a function of varying amperage with dogs of different ages. They also carried out additional research for this particular study to establish the optimal amount of electric shock for each animal by age and weight. It was critically important that optimal current values be achieved for obtaining useful data without inflicting unnecessary pain or discomfort on the animals. Too little current would simply be uncomfortable but would not elevate hormone levels sufficiently, and too much shock would cause unnecessary suffering in the animals. The team was hopeful that their protocol would be approved by the hospital's Institutional Animal Care and Use Committee and the Institutional Review Board because its prospective applied value was significant. They felt that there was no other way to obtain this data, and they had taken great care to minimize the suffering of the animals.

(h) Surgical procedures are performed under appropriate anesthesia; techniques to avoid infection and minimize pain are followed during and after surgery.

(h) When performing surgery, use up-to-date methods for anesthesia and analgesia, including postoperative analgesia, that are appropriate for the species. Prevent infections by performing the surgery under aseptic conditions and with antibiotics as needed.

Vignette: Dr. Crest had a good reputation for maintaining high standards in her laboratory, in conformance with the *Guide for the Care and Use of Laboratory Animals* (Institute of Laboratory Animal Resources, 1996). Unannounced visits to her research facility by inspectors from the USDA never revealed any violations or improper procedures. It was her habit to provide comprehensive instruction to her research assistants, and she was particularly scrupulous in supervising them during invasive procedures, such as implanting electrodes, collecting body fluids, or surgery.

Her laboratory personnel consistently observed standard anesthetic and aseptic procedures, and as a result, the animals had a very low infection rate and recovered quickly from invasive procedures with a minimum of discomfort or suffering. She also encouraged her staff to be vigilant about preoperative care, postoperative pain, and the proper use of analgesics. She sought consultations with the veterinary staff on an as-needed basis and encouraged her assistants to do likewise. In this way, she was able to remain current about the proper type and dose of analgesics and tranquilizers consistent with the species being used and the research objectives.

Because of Dr. Crest's firm convictions and scrupulous observance of animal research standards, her university enjoyed full accreditation by the Council on Accreditation of the American Association for the Accreditation of Laboratory Animal Care. Over the years, many generations of research assistants learned from Dr. Crest's deeply held and well-informed philosophy of humane treatment of animal subjects.

> *(i) When it is appropriate that the animal's life be terminated, it is done rapidly, with an effort to minimize pain, and in accordance with accepted procedures.*

(i) If you or someone with whom you work must terminate an animal's life, do it rapidly and painlessly in accordance with existing standards and guidelines.

Vignette: In research requiring the ultimate sacrificing of rats to examine brain tissue, Dr. Black was considering the options to select a method that was quick and painless. In keeping with the protocol, however, it was essential to euthanize the animals without significant risk of damaging brain tissue. As a part of providing mentoring on the topic of euthanizing animals to his postdoctoral fellow, Arthur, Dr. Black asked him to formally study the variety of techniques available. Specifically, he asked Arthur to research and justify the various methods of euthanasia to increase his understanding of the procedures and rationales from the ground up rather than simply blindly following what others have done.

Arthur was already well aware of the regulations of his university's Institutional Animal Care and Use Committee, and he knew that the committee would have to approve any methods of terminating an animal's life because this was a federally funded project. He was also aware of the NIH standards concerning the broad array of euthanizing agents. He found the American Veterinary Medical Association's (AVMA) "Report of the AVMA Panel on Euthanasia" (1986), which provided a thorough review of the subject, most useful in his considerations. This document reviews in depth the characteristics and relative merits of using each of the three major methods of euthanizing animals: (a) hypoxic agents (e.g., carbon monoxide, curariform drugs, nitrogen inhalation), (b) direct neuron depressing agents (e.g., anesthetic gases, barbiturates, chloral hydrate), and (c) physical agents (e.g., decapitation, exsanguination, rapid freezing). To minimize the animals' suffering, Arthur learned that the most preferable method was one that would induce a rapid loss of consciousness prior to death, lest the rats be incapacitated and conscious and increasingly anxious and distressed. He learned that drugs such as curare or succinylcholine used in isolation were prohibited because they paralyzed the animal, including respiratory muscles; thus, the animal could experience pain and panic while it suffocated. He also learned that agents that blocked apprehension and pain perception first, such as chloroform or barbiturates, were preferable because they brought death rapidly following a quick loss of consciousness. There were many factors to be considered in this final phase of the project that were new to Arthur and required knowledge of the effects of various methods and consideration of the animal species involved.

After reviewing the results of Arthur's research, Dr. Black asked him to participate in consultations on the merits of several different methods with a veterinarian and with another psychologist to be certain that their knowledge was current. Dr. Black and Arthur finally agreed on a method of euthanizing the rats that was quick and painless, posed little risk to brain tissue for analysis, was relatively safe to administer, and was aesthetically acceptable to laboratory personnel. They were satisfied that they had devoted ample time and energy to this important aspect of the protocol, lest the animals suffer unnecessarily at the conclusion of the research.

6.21 Reporting of Results

(a) Psychologists do not fabricate data or falsify results in their publications.

(a) Never fabricate data or falsify results in publications reporting your research results.

Vignette: Dr. Will Alter and a colleague were investigating changes in positron emission tomography (PET) brain scans of young children viewing violent cartoons and playing certain types of on-line videogames. This was a timely and important study. But for Dr. Alter, there was some urgency because this was his final year before tenure evaluation and he badly needed additional publications in refereed journals if he was to remain on the faculty. He thought that the publication of his results would have more impact if his data revealed greater statistical significance than was actually the case. Thus, unbeknownst to his coinvestigator, he altered the PET-scan data of several children to yield such an increase.

Fortunately, Dr. Alter's coinvestigator, Dr. Noyu Dohnt, was reviewing the data one night and discovered the anomalies, much to his surprise and disappointment. After confronting his colleague about the erroneous data, he prevailed on Dr. Alter to abandon his plan and maintain the integrity of the study, even though it might have less of an impact on the scientific community. At least it would be veridical, would not corrupt the psychology knowledge base, and would likely spawn other studies, which might lead to more significant findings.

This painful confrontation and its sequelae strained the professional and personal relationship of the two scientists. For many days, Dr. Dohnt wondered if he should report his coinvestigator to an ethics committee because altering data was such a fundamental abrogation of the responsibilities of a researcher and a violation to the science of psychology. Although Dr. Alter had never modified data or distorted results in any previous research, his judgment for the present was obviously impaired, and possibly he would require monitoring in the future. Dr. Dohnt wondered if he could ever trust his friend again and discussed the matter with him in great depth. Dr. Alter realized in the course of these discussions that for many months, he had been suffering significant depression that was extensively clouding his judgment. He admitted to suicidal thoughts of late and feared that his career was about to take a major turn for the worse by not being granted tenure.

As a result of this crisis and Dr. Dohnt's continuing confrontation and concern about his friend, Dr. Alter decided to begin consultations with a psychotherapist to address his depression. Because it was obvious to Dr. Dohnt that Dr. Alter was deeply troubled by his own uncharacteristic behavior and was taking active steps to remedy the situation by consulting a therapist, Dr. Dohnt considered it unnecessary to bring a formal complaint to an ethics committee; he carefully reviewed Standards 8.04 and 8.05 of the Ethics Code in making this decision, however.

> *(b) If psychologists discover significant errors in their published data, they take reasonable steps to correct such errors in a correction, retraction, erratum, or other appropriate publication means.*

(b) If you find significant mistakes in your publications, make attempts to correct them and publicize the correction, if possible.

Vignette: Dr. Rhea Tell had recently concluded a 10-year study on weight loss with moderately obese adults. She presented her results at APA's Annual Convention and was pleased with the attention accorded her research by colleagues and the mass media. She was rather dismayed, however, to read the sensationalistic claims presented by a newspaper reporter who attended her presentation. Significant exaggerations were printed in the paper, and all the disclaimers and qualifications that were an important part of her presentation concerning demographics of the participants and details of the interventions had been omitted.

Dr. Tell telephoned the newspaper the next day with her complaint and was met with reluctance by the reporter to make any changes. She persisted in her argument that the newspaper was essentially printing erroneous information, and the reporter finally agreed to print a correction on the following day. Because an abbreviated form of the newspaper was also published on the Internet each day, it too had to be corrected.

Unfortunately, Dr. Tell had less success attempting to correct errors in a short television interview. The journalist conducting the interview, Ms. Kutten Paste, misstated the conclusions of the study and deleted much of what the psychologist said in the service of adhering to the station's policy of relying primarily on brief sound bites. Many of her statements were taken out of context and juxtaposed, presenting a significant distortion of her basic research. Although Dr. Tell was able to contact Ms. Paste, she could not convince her to include more of the interview or present a correction of the misstatements; she informed Dr. Tell that there was "simply too much news breaking that day" to accommodate her request. Attempts to contact Ms. Paste's supervisor were equally unsuccessful to correct the situation. Although disappointed that she had little control over the broadcast, she was satisfied that she at least had made a serious attempt to correct the situation, as ethically required.

Another error occurred when her study was published in a refereed journal 1 year later. The statistics were grossly wrong because several decimal points had been misplaced and two lines of text were missing in one paragraph. She had been too busy to personally review the proofs of the article sent to her prior to publication and had delegated that task to her secretary, who failed to catch the errors. She promptly contacted the publisher; in the subsequent issue, an erratum was printed correcting these errors. Dr. Tell learned the important lesson that some tasks are too important to delegate to others, no matter how busy one might be.

6.22 Plagiarism

Psychologists do not present substantial portions or elements of another's work or data as their own, even if the other work or data source is cited occasionally.

Always cite your sources; do not pass off another's concepts, data, text, and so on as your own whether in print, in presentations, on the Internet, or anywhere else.[2]

Vignette: Dr. Cribwell routinely performed psychological assessments for a large medical practice specializing in chronic disorders, such as chronic

---

[2]See also 2.08, Test Scoring and Interpretation Services.

fatigue syndrome, myofascial pains, and autoimmune disorders. He relied on several standard objective instruments and generally sent them to automated scoring services to obtain profiles and a printed narrative report. When writing psychological reports to be included in patients' medical records, he would typically use entire paragraphs verbatim from the computerized narrative that he received back from the scoring service, but it never occurred to him to cite the source. He paid no attention to the bold print at the bottom of the printout stating that the narrative report was copyrighted material. By integrating it into his psychological report and claiming authorship, Dr. Cribwell was violating both the APA Ethics Code and copyright laws.

He also occasionally did research in his area of specialty and relied heavily on Internet resources, such as several electronic journals. When he used information and data from these journals in his writings, he never ascribed authorship because he assumed that anything available on the World Wide Web was in the public domain and thus freely available to subscribers to use as they pleased, without citation. He did not realize that the obligation to cite one's sources includes on-line journals.

Fortunately, a colleague contacted Dr. Cribwell and informed him about his obligation to comply with the ethical standards concerning plagiarism and suggested he review the laws concerning intellectual property. He also referred his colleague to sections of the APA publication manual (APA, 1994b) that address plagiarism. He further reminded him that the rights to scholarly work generally belonged to the author or the publisher, regardless of the medium in which it was published (e.g., journal, book, Internet), even though, admittedly, there was still uncertainty concerning the ownership of material that was electronically published. In any case, the ethical standards prevail, and one should never claim authorship of material that was written by another.

6.23 Publication Credit

(a) Psychologists take responsibility and credit, including authorship credit, only for work they have actually performed or to which they have contributed.

(a) Take authorship credit and responsibility only for the work that you actually performed or to which you contributed.

Vignette: Dr. Shadow was the owner of an employee assistance program and had a long-standing practice of publishing a monthly newsletter that was sent to all contracting employees having access to psychological services. Although her name appeared as the author of such articles as "Burnout in the Workplace" and "Getting Along With Your Supervisor," she never actually contributed any text to the newsletter. Instead, she had delegated that responsibility to several of her staff members and was so busy with administrative responsibilities that she rarely saw the draft of the newsletter before it went to print. Occasionally, she scanned the column under her own name, but she never wrote any material for it.

Sometimes she would submit a column from the newsletter to her state psychological association monthly publication. Again, her name would appear as the author when in fact she had written none of the text. More egregiously, she sometimes used "ghost writers" on her staff to create articles for publication in electronic journals on the Internet. She commissioned several colleagues to investigate topics relating to clinical services in a managed health care setting, but aside from specifying the focus of the research, she did not participate in any other aspects. She was listed as sole author, and the writers on her staff who performed the research and did the writing were not listed at all. They did receive monetary compensation for their efforts, however. Everyone involved was content with the business arrangement, even though Dr. Shadow was consistently violating an important ethical standard. When another psychologist in the office became aware of her apparent disregard for this standard, she called her attention to it. Dr. Shadow was surprised to learn that her practices were considered unethical; she took steps to conform to this standard by ceasing to falsely claim publication credit.

> (b) Principal authorship and other publication credits accurately reflect the relative scientific or professional contributions of the individuals involved, regardless of their relative status. Mere possession of an institutional position, such as Department Chair, does not justify authorship credit. Minor contributions to the research or to the writing for publications are appropriately acknowledged, such as in footnotes or in an introductory statement.

(b) Only claim publication credit that reflects what you actually contributed to the group effort. Just because you may chair the department, run the laboratory, contribute to research funding, or obtain research participants does not mean that you are automatically entitled to be listed as an author. But minor contributors should be acknowledged in a footnote or some other way.

Vignette: Dr. I. M. Sun chaired the psychology department at a nearby university but had little familiarity with the standards concerning authorship credit. He was conducting interdisciplinary research involving opiate dependence among amputee patients suffering phantom limb pain in collaboration with several physicians on staff at the neurology clinic of a local hospital. In his methodology, he relied heavily on the wisdom and experience of two widely published junior colleagues in the psychology department, namely, a statistician and a specialist in chronic pain. He also spent many hours conferring with the director of the hospital's chemical dependency unit in addition to the two physicians on the pain clinic staff. Each of these individuals played a key role, in one way or another, in helping shape the research design, formulate hypotheses, select instruments of assessment, obtain research participants, and analyze the data. Each of them also contributed text to the journal article; without their cooperation, the project would not have happened.

Each participant considered him- or herself to be a coinvestigator, even though there was no formal agreement in advance about the listing of authorship credit. Dr. Sun, however, had different ideas about publication credit. Because he chaired the department, conceived the study, and felt that he did most of the work, he listed himself as principal author, with the two physicians as his junior authors. The psychology colleagues and director of the chemical dependency unit were relegated to a 3-line footnote of acknowledgment.

When they reviewed the proofs of the article and discovered that they were not listed as authors, these three individuals were understandably quite disgruntled. They confronted Dr. Sun about his lack of fairness in failing to list them as coauthors. Dr. Sun, however, responded that they had no claim to joint authorship because they played a comparatively small role in the project and had no part in authoring the grant that funded the project. It took the consultation of two senior faculty members, an in-house grievance, and the threat of a formal ethics complaint to bring about a partial eclipse of Dr. Sun and to convince him to share authorship credit among all contributors to the project.

> *(c) A student is usually listed as principal author on any multiple-authored article that is substantially based on the student's dissertation or thesis.*

(c) Principal authorship is usually reserved for a student in a publication that is mainly based on his or her thesis or doctoral dissertation.

Vignette: Dr. Meefurst had chaired many dissertation committees over the course of his academic career. Generally, he would assist the student in publishing research results based on his or her dissertation and would provide guidance about which journals to consider in submitting it for publication. Dr. Meefurst also made his secretarial staff available for editing and revising a student's articles, as needed. Often he would collaborate with the student in writing an article for publication based chiefly on the student's dissertation.

In return for all these efforts, Dr. Meefurst felt entitled to list himself as the primary author of the articles based primarily on his students' dissertations. If a student raised a question about this, Dr. Meefurst pointed out that it had always been his custom to list himself as the primary author, which was a perfectly acceptable practice. In response to further questioning, Dr. Meefurst reminded the student that without all of his support and clerical assistance, which greatly promoted the student's work, it never would have reached the publishable stage in such a short time. Any additional confrontation would be met with subtle reminders that a student is essentially powerless within an academic setting and is quite vulnerable to losing out on important professional opportunities in the future. Because of this very perception of powerlessness, few students ever objected or raised a formal complaint.

One particularly assertive student, who was inappropriately listed as a second author by Dr. Meefurst, her former dissertation chair, had studied the 1992 revision of the Ethics Code thoroughly and was well aware that his customary assumption of primary authorship was open to question. Although she was grateful for the help he had given her in the course of writing her dissertation, she felt that she should have been listed as the primary investigator on the paper submitted for publication. She waited until all her work at the university was completed, her degree was awarded, and she was well established in her postdoctoral internship. Then, knowing that the APA Ethics Committee statute of limitations allowed her 5 years from the time the alleged misconduct occurred until the complaint was received (APA, 1996a), she formally initiated a complaint against the man who had formerly chaired her dissertation committee. By so doing, she not only began a process of formal scrutinizing of Dr. Meefurst's conduct but also set an example for other graduate students who were being discriminated against by being robbed of due principal authorship credit.

6.24 Duplicate Publication of Data

Psychologists do not publish, as original data, data that have been previously published. This does not preclude republishing data when they are accompanied by proper acknowledgment.

Only publish your original data as *original* once. When referring to your findings in subsequent writings, you must cite the original publication, even though it is your own work.

Vignette: In 1996, Dr. Overnover published a seminal paper about his brief inventory for assessing psychological distress and physical pain as distinct entities in patients coping with chronic illness. He introduced normative data with samples representing adequate diversity in gender, age, ethnicity, and other variables. He was so enthusiastic that later in the year he submitted for publication to a non-APA journal another article that relied heavily on the already published data about his inventory with only slight modifications to the items of the inventory, but he never cited the original 1996 publication. He introduced his instrument of assessment again "for the first time" with the second article that was published.

By failing to cite the original source (i.e., his own 1996 publication), he gave the false impression that the inventory was new. It would have been simple enough to cite his earlier work. However, Dr. Overnover thought it was unnecessary to do so. Because it was his own data, he thought that he bore no responsibility to cite the earlier publication; it was impossible to plagiarize from oneself or so he thought. However, his practice made it difficult for other researchers to track the natural evolution of the inventory or to know which version they were using in attempting to carry out further clinical research. If he had simply complied with the ethical standard that forbids duplicate publication of data, he would have cleared up any potential confusion for readers.

6.25 Sharing Data

After research results are published, psychologists do not withhold the data on which their conclusions are based from other competent professionals who seek to verify the substantive claims through reanalysis and who intend to use such data only for that purpose, provided that the confidentiality of the participants can be protected and unless legal rights concerning proprietary data preclude their release.

Be prepared to yield your raw data to other researchers who wish to recheck your analyses and verify your claims. If legal rights concerning proprietary data or confidentiality concerns preclude this, however, you do not have to release the data. (Note: APA journals require you to keep your data for reanalysis for 5 years.)

Vignette: A consultant for a major telephone company was asked to carry out research on the subject of consumers' preferences for and competence in accessing email and the Internet through new kinds of cordless and cellular phones. She did a comprehensive study involving questionnaire, personal interview, and use of hardware prototypes. Because her work had implications beyond the research and development needs of the telephone company she had contracted with, she decided to publish her results in a professional journal also.

Within a few months of publication, Dr. Dubius, a psychologist, contacted her for the purpose of reviewing her data and statistical analysis. He questioned her methodology and did not believe her claims concerning the pervasiveness of computer avoidance to be valid, particularly by women, those in older age groups, and those who were disabled in some way, such as those who are chronically ill or hearing impaired.

The consultant would gladly have released her data as requested by Dr. Dubius, but her research was "owned" by the telephone company, who legally held the proprietary rights. By contracting with the company in the first place, she had agreed to keep her data "in house." She could present or publish her general results and conclusions as she did—with permission from the phone company—but she was not permitted to reveal the raw data in its entirety or the protocols developed for the research. As indicated in this standard, her ethical obligation to retain her data and yield it for reanalysis was secondary to her legal obligation to honor the contract she had with the phone company.

6.26 Professional Reviewers

Psychologists who review material submitted for publication, grant, or other research proposal review respect the confidentiality of and the proprietary rights in such information of those who submitted it.

If you review or screen the work of others, such as papers for publication or grant proposals, resist the temptation to use the newly submitted information for any purpose whatsoever. It is to be evaluated by you and then returned or destroyed. In other words, act as if the content does not exist until it is published.

Vignette: Dr. Will Uzit was asked to review a paper submitted for publication in a non-APA hypnosis journal. Because he was an expert in the application of hypnosis as an adjunctive technique for some patients in the treatment of PTSD and the paper explored the validity of repressed memory for traumatic events, he seemed to be a logical choice as one of the three reviewers. While reading the paper, Dr. Uzit became interested in the authors' area of research, namely, the use of PET scans for assessing the accuracy of long-term memory for traumatic episodes, regardless of the patient's subjective belief that a particular trauma, in fact, did occur. Although much additional research remained to be done, the preliminary data was promising.

Dr. Uzit reviewed this well-written manuscript and suggested some minor editorial changes only. In his evaluation, the paper successfully met the journal's criteria for outstanding and scientific professional merit; the topic was timely and appropriate for the journal, it was written in a highly scholarly fashion, the review of the literature was comprehensive, and the design and statistical analyses were exemplary.

About 2 weeks after reviewing the paper, Dr. Uzit was invited to participate on a small panel for a major TV network presentation entitled "Child Abuse and Repressed Memory—What Can You Believe?" During the taping of the 2-hour show, the discussion became heated, including ad hominem attacks. Dr. Uzit became somewhat agitated and, in the heat of debate, attempted to defend his rigid views on the subject by citing the study that he had recently reviewed for publication. He referred to "new and important research involving PET scans that yields hard scientific data validating that patients do, in fact, remember exactly what happened to them in the past." He not only disregarded the confidentiality and proprietary rights of the author in citing this study, he also misstated the results, leaving out qualifying and cautionary comments.

After the show aired, two journalists from major newspapers telephoned Dr. Uzit for interviews. By this time, he had recovered his objectivity and declined their requests, realizing the error he had made on the air by citing a study that was not yet published. He knew that in his eagerness to take a shortcut in educating the public and championing his cause, he had violated important property rights of another psychologist and, with his show of poor judgment, diminished his own credibility among his peers. As it happened, the authors of the paper had seen the broadcast and rightly suspected that Dr. Uzit was citing their work, even though it had not yet been published. They brought a formal ethics complaint against Dr. Uzit for his transgression.

7

Forensic Activities

7.01 Professionalism

Psychologists who perform forensic functions, such as assessments, interviews, consultations, reports, or expert testimony, must comply with all other provisions of this Ethics Code to the extent that they apply to such activities. In addition, psychologists base their forensic work on appropriate knowledge of and competence in the areas underlying such work, including specialized knowledge concerning special populations. (See also Standards 1.06, Basis for Scientific and Professional Judgments; 1.08, Human Differences; 1.15, Misuse of Psychologists' Influence; and 1.23, Documentation of Professional and Scientific Work.)

When conducting forensic work, such as giving expert testimony, carrying out assessments, writing reports, and providing advice to attorneys, remember that every standard in this code still applies to what you do (e.g., boundaries of competence, maintaining confidentiality, describing the nature and results of psychological services, avoiding harm, multiple relationships). Base your work (e.g., all your oral and written statements) on competence in the areas under consideration and appropriately specialized knowledge about the people or groups that are involved. Only make statements about subject matters that you actually are qualified to address.

Vignette: For several years, Dr. Bee Leevitt had served as a consultant to attorneys in a cluster of several midwestern towns and provided expert testimony in a variety of cases. She was considered to be a useful resource within the legal community and was sought out with increasing frequency by plaintiffs' attorneys in civil suits against psychologists for malpractice, harassment, multiple roles and conflict of interest, and matters of professional competence. However, she had little formal training in forensics, and she did not fully understand that in carrying out forensic work she was required to comply with every standard of the Ethics Code to the same degree as in her clinical work.

Nonetheless, Dr. Leevitt had agreed to become a consultant to Mr. Will Gogettum, the lawyer for the plaintiff in a civil suit against a therapist who had used hypnosis with a patient with a dual diagnosis of dissociative disorder and PTSD (delayed onset). There were also some pediatric hospital records that seemed to lend validity to the woman's memories of abuse by her stepfather many years before, although they were not considered to be conclusive. The patient was generally pleased with her therapist and the progress of therapy and had no interest in bringing a lawsuit against her stepfather. However, her parents were quite unhappy with the therapist and the family turmoil that resulted from the daughter's disclosures to them about the alleged abuse. They decided to initiate a lawsuit against her therapist for using hypnosis as a part of treatment, supposedly creating childhood memories of sexual abuse.

Although Dr. Leevitt had treated several patients with PTSD herself, she had never seen a patient with a dissociative disorder, nor been formally trained in the use of hypnosis. She was familiar in a superficial way with the literature on memory. But she had little appreciation for the distinctions between cued and free recall, memory for specific details as opposed to general impressions, somatic representation of memory, and most of the current research in this area. She believed that patients always distort memories of abuse significantly when hypnosis is used and that hypnotic testimony should never be accepted as even partially valid or used as grounds for seeking corroborative evidence of childhood abuse. When testifying as an expert, she seemed to be advocating dogmatically for her theoretical position rather than presenting her views in an appropriately scientific and tentative manner.

In accepting the role of consultant to Mr. Gogettum, Dr. Leevitt advised him to question the validity of the testimony by the psychologist who had used hypnosis with the patient, regardless of his technical competence or level of experience. Simply the use of hypnosis, she claimed, was sufficient grounds for mistrusting the patient's memory. Furthermore, because the patient's own testimony contained some historically inaccurate statements, Dr. Leevitt argued that it was inherently flawed and therefore none of the memories could be considered reliable or valid. She asserted that either the therapist must have contaminated his patient's recall by his suggestive questioning in hypnosis or the young woman was unconsciously distorting the truth for her own psychological reasons, perhaps to bring a civil suit against her stepfather at some time in the future and obtain monetary compensation for abuse she supposedly suffered at his hands. In either case, the psychologist pointed out, the woman should not be believed, and the case should be dropped for lack of evidence.

Dr. Leevitt did not know that she was making statements and recommendations that were outside her area of expertise concerning the accuracy and validity of memory in either a hypnotic or nonhypnotic context. Although carrying out forensic work, she was still obliged to remain within her area of competence and to make statements that were based on current research or her own clinical experience. Even when dubbed an "expert witness," she was still ethically obliged to determine the limits of her areas of expertise, remembering that the term *expert witness* is a legal one, not a psychological one. Attorneys and others were likely to attribute competence to her that, in fact, she might not possess.

She should not have been serving in an advisory role to lawyers due to her lack of relevant scientific knowledge and clinical experience. It was only a matter of time until a psychologist knowledgeable about the research in these areas would be retained as an expert for the opposing side and would bring a formal complaint against Dr. Leevitt for her incompetence and lack of professionalism.

7.02 Forensic Assessments

(a) Psychologists' forensic assessments, recommendations, and reports are based on information and techniques (including personal interviews of the individual, when appropriate) sufficient to provide appropriate substantiation for their findings. (See also Standards 1.03, Professional and Scientific Relationship; 1.23, Documentation of Professional and Scientific Work; 2.01, Evaluation, Diagnosis, and Interventions in Professional Context; and 2.05, Interpreting Assessment Results.)

(a) Be able to substantiate what you say in all forensic work, whether performing assessments, making formal recommendations, or writing reports. Base your work on adequate information, proper techniques, and personal interviews of the individual (when appropriate). Don't present hunches or guesses as if they were facts.

Vignette: Dr. Noah Count, who had a practice in a rural area, was contacted by an attorney representing an injured employee in a worker's compensation case. His client was injured in a serious fall while working in a furniture factory and suffered from chronic headaches, neck pain, and chronic fatigue for 8 months. The worker began litigation against his employer and as part of the process was required to submit to a psychological examination by a qualified mental health professional. Dr. Count was the only licensed psychologist in town, but he was not experienced in diagnosing or treating patients with chronic pain. Nevertheless, he agreed to perform the assessment as the expert witness for the defense. The counsel for the furniture company was attempting to demonstrate that the plaintiff was malingering and had a long history of chronic depression and alcohol dependence prior to the accident.

Due to his lack of experience in these matters, Dr. Count unfortunately selected instruments of assessment that were inappropriate for a chronic pain patient and yielded questionably useful results. He was aware that the instruments were inappropriate for this purpose but believed that, because he had administered them many times over a number of years, his "internal norms" would suffice. He felt he did not have time to learn about other instruments of assessment even if they might have been more appropriate. He justified his choice by reasoning that his assessment of the employee would be more valid if he used instruments with which he was familiar rather than new instruments, even though they may have had better validity for the task at hand.

The clinical interview of the man confirmed the existence of a major depressive disorder but did not rule out other Axis I disorders or malingering. Nevertheless, he wrote a report and testified to the effect that the plaintiff was excessively hypochondriachal, suffered from a conversion disorder manifesting in chronic pain, and would certainly be capable of carrying out his old job in the furniture factory if he could only recover from his dependence on alcohol. Although alcohol dependence fit prominently in the employee's profile, it was not necessarily the only factor preventing his return to work. The patient also required treatment for his chronic pain by means of medical and psychological interventions. In dismissing the pain as psychogenic and attributing it to a conversion disorder, the psychologist was doing him a disservice.

Dr. Count's impressions and hunches about the plaintiff were presented as factual, without disclaimers or the tentative language that is important when diagnostic validity may be questionable. Dr. Count also lacked an adequate scientific or clinical basis to support his expert testimony, using instruments of assessment that were not appropriate for the situation. However, his testimony was considered important in the overall evaluation of the plaintiff, and it had a strong undermining effect on his case. Not only was Dr. Count practicing outside his area of expertise, his actions made a material difference in the outcome of the lawsuit, resulting in discrediting the plaintiff and immense financial loss for him and his large family.

> *(b) Except as noted in (c), below, psychologists provide written or oral forensic reports or testimony of the psychological characteristics of an individual only after they have conducted an examination of the individual adequate to support their statements or conclusions.*

(b) Whenever you testify or write a psychological report about someone you have assessed, make sure that your comments, judgments, and recommendations are based on an examination of the person(s) that is sufficient to support them (unless this is impossible; see Standard 7.02c, following).

Vignette: Dr. Wurst was asked to perform a child custody assessment by Mrs. Ethel Scarlett, a divorcing mother of two who was a frequent marijuana user. Her estranged husband was the chief financial officer of a steel manufacturing company and regularly worked over 85 hours per week. Dr. Wurst had assessed several other families in her brief forensic career with the mentoring of a former supervisor, but she was not accustomed to the intensity and acrimony of this high-conflict divorce proceeding nor prepared for the array of problems it presented. Mr. Scarlett had moved out several months before, and recently threatened to harm his wife and kidnap the children if things did not go his way. He had been attempting to gain legal and physical custody of his children. Fearful of her husband's threats, Mrs. Scarlett called the police for support on more than one occasion, and was considering seeking a restraining order to insure maximum safety for herself and her children.

Under these circumstances, Dr. Wurst did her best to formally evaluate the individuals involved, using proper instruments of assessment and personal interviews. Because Mr. Scarlett was difficult to contact due both to his frequent business traveling and his hostile interpersonal demeanor, she never had a face-to-face structured interview with him as part of the total assessment. In her written report to the court presenting her assessment of Mr. and Mrs. Scarlett and their children, she provided the summarized results and conclusions from psychological testing, collateral information from other sources (neighbors, teachers, etc.), and personal interviewing that she had carried out. However, she never revealed in her report that she had never personally assessed Mr. Scarlett. It wasn't until the cross examination when Mr. Scarlett's attorney raised the issue of her failure to interview Mr. Scarlett and the resulting prejudicial assessment and recommendations in favor of the wife that the problem of the inadequate assessment surfaced.

Dr. Wurst appreciated the seriousness of her lapse in judgment in dispensing with a face-to-face interview with a difficult individual and agreed that the assessment was not comprehensive and had not been competently performed. Because she had not performed a personal assessment of Mr. Scarlet, she should not have made any statements about his parenting skills, nor about the relative parenting capability of Mr. and Mrs. Scarlet. She also realized, belatedly, that she should have informed the court during her direct examination about her failure to have assessed Mr. Scarlett personally instead of waiting for the cross examination for it to come to light.

> *(c) When, despite reasonable efforts, such an examination is not feasible, psychologists clarify the impact of their limited information on the reliability and validity of their reports and testimony, and they appropriately limit the nature and extent of their conclusions or recommendations.*

(c) If circumstances prevent you from personally examining an individual, advise the court of how the validity, reliability, and relevance of your comments are diminished. Limit the scope of your conclusions and recommendations accordingly, and don't make statements that go beyond your data about the person or situation.

Vignette: In a child custody case, Dr. Wurst was intent on personally assessing every family member, and not relying on the statements of others or a blind review of psychological testing in forming her opinions. In this unusual case, Samantha and Dolly, two lesbian women raising a 3-year-old boy, were in the process of separating. They had been together for 9 years, and each wanted to retain full physical and legal custody of the child.

Dr. Wurst was able to meet with Samantha, but she found it impossible to arrange a face-to-face meeting with Dolly in order to have an interview and administer psychological tests. In fact, Dolly's attorney had recommended that his client avoid Dr. Wurst's assessment because she was actively alcoholic and had a belligerent interpersonal style. He feared that Dr. Wurst's assessment might adversely affect Dolly's chances at obtaining access to the child. Besides, he had retained his own expert witness, Dr. Overschoot, to assess Dolly, and was pleased that his psychological report failed to mention her alcohol dependence or place his client in a bad light whatsoever. The only data about Dolly that Dr. Wurst was successful in obtaining were interviews with those who knew her and a parenting abilities checklist, which he had administered over the telephone. Unfortunately, little or no standardization data existed for lesbian parents with this particular instrument.

When it came time for Dr. Wurst to testify, she responded conservatively to questions about Dolly. She made clear that (a) she had never met the woman; (b) she did not perform a comprehensive assessment; (c) her only sources of information about Dolly were Samantha, several friends, neighbors, and two teachers at their son's day-care center; and (d) the data from the Parenting Abilities Checklist, which probably had questionable validity given the lack norms for gay populations and the fact that it was administered over the telephone. She made these points clear in her psychological report, her deposition, and her court testimony.

When asked pointed questions about Dolly, she was cautious in responding, usually replying that she lacked sufficient data to answer the question. Though the attorneys strongly encouraged her to reach conclusions about Dolly's parenting ability, based on the data that *was* available, Dr. Wurst was steadfast in her resolve, and avoided the temptation to offer opinions or conclusions that could not be substantiated by the data. She wisely remained within her area of competence, even though there was little she had to say about Dolly that was based on her own assessment.

7.03 Clarification of Role

In most circumstances, psychologists avoid performing multiple and potentially conflicting roles in forensic matters. When psychologists may be called on to serve in more than one role in a legal proceeding—for example, as consultant or expert for one party or for the court and as a fact witness—they clarify role expectations and the extent of confidentiality in advance to the extent feasible, and thereafter as changes occur, in order to avoid compromising their professional judgment and objectivity and in order to avoid misleading others regarding their role.

Have a clearly defined role in forensic matters, and avoid multiple and conflicting professional roles. This includes potential conflicts of interest involving a former role, concurrent role, or a likely future role that you might play with a consumer. Are you an individual or couples therapist, fact witness or expert witness, therapist or assessor, advocate or therapist, and so on? Accurately inform others about the professional capacity that you intend to assume and any potential threats to competence, objectivity, confidentiality, or any other aspect of your professional service that might result from it. Be aware that these may affect how you testify and even what fees you may charge.

Vignette: Mrs. Hert had suffered a lumbar vertebral fracture and ensuing back and leg pain for over 2 years from tripping backwards over a plant at her office. As an adjunct to her medical treatment, she had been referred to Dr. Omni for training in biofeedback and cognitive–behavioral therapy for management of chronic pain. She was also diagnosed with a borderline personality disorder and was suffering much depression and marital distress. Dr. Omni had provided marital therapy for 4 months concurrent with her individual therapy in an attempt to reduce the intense stress in her patient's marriage relationship.

After being declared *permanent and stationary* by her physician—meaning that she was unlikely to make any significant improvements—Mrs. Hert initiated litigation against her employer for her injury, depression, opiate addiction from pain medication, and ultimate deterioration of her marriage. Her attorney deposed Dr. Omni as her treating psychologist to attest to her psychological and marital distress. The defense strategy consisted chiefly of invalidating any claims that her current problems were related causally to the injury she sustained 2 years before. At issue was separating the effects of the injury from the effects of her preexisting personality disorder and attempting to identify which was primarily responsible for exacerbating depression, opiate addiction, inability to work, and ultimate breakup of her marriage.

Dr. Omni found himself in the increasingly difficult position of not only providing testimony about his patient's suffering, but also serving as an assessor of the faltering marriage and an expert witness on the diagnosis and treatment of borderline personality disorder per se. In response to questions about secondary gain for chronic pain patients and the traits of patients who have borderline personality disorder, Dr. Omni presented his professional opinions. Unfortunately, when his client heard his testimony, she felt quite hurt by his view that a significant amount of her pain and suffering was psychogenic in nature, due largely to the secondary gain of all the additional attention she was receiving from family members rather than to her back injury alone. Mrs. Hert was also very distressed to learn through his assessment that much of the marital breakdown was due to deficits within herself and was not chiefly due to her back injury and subsequent pain and dysfunction.

By agreeing to serve as an expert witness in the treatment of borderline personality disorder for the plaintiff's attorney while also playing the role of the plaintiff's current individual therapist and former marital therapist, Dr. Omni significantly complicated the therapeutic relationship with his client, adding to her distress. He would have been well advised originally not to provide marital therapy, given the complexity of her history, and to have informed the attorney that he could not serve as an expert witness about this particular Axis II disorder because it could place him in a conflict of interest, reduce his objectivity, and impair his professional relationship with his current patient, the plaintiff. He failed to clearly establish professional boundaries during the early treatment phase and compounded the problem when litigation began by refusing to restrict the roles he was expected to play to those that would not be in conflict with each other.

7.04 Truthfulness and Candor

(a) In forensic testimony and reports, psychologists testify truthfully, honestly, and candidly and, consistent with applicable legal procedures, describe fairly the bases for their testimony and conclusions.

(a) Be accurate, honest, and candid when providing forensic testimony and reports, consistent with applicable legal procedures. Never "slant" or distort the truth. Also as required, be ready to give the bases for your testimony and conclusions (e.g., test data, clinical interview, research findings).

Vignette: Dr. Willa Syst provided court-ordered marital therapy to Mr. and Mrs. Bear, a high-conflict young couple, because Mr. Bear had assaulted his wife several weeks before being ordered to meet with her. Their stormy 3-year marriage had been characterized by Mr. Bear's alcohol abuse and multiple violent encounters. During that period, Mrs. Bear had called 911 three times when Mr. Bear had struck her repeatedly, deliberately driven recklessly to frighten her, and threatened to wreck the house and harm their infant daughter while he was in an alcoholic rage. As a result of charges filed by Mrs. Bear against her husband, Mr. Bear was required to address his alcohol dependency and angry rages by participating in psychological counseling, both individual and marital, and by following all recommendations of his therapist, Dr. Syst.

After 2 months of treatment, Dr. Syst was asked to provide a progress report for Mrs. Bear's attorney. The attorney had litigated many similar cases and created a graphic scenario of the severe legal consequences that might befall Mr. Bear if he did not show progress in his treatment. Dr. Syst learned of the monetary fine and possible jail sentence that awaited her client if he did not develop more adaptive behavior and she did not note improvement in Mr. Bear in the progress report.

Dr. Syst had taken a genuine liking to both Mr. and Mrs. Bear and felt sympathy for them, as she herself had alcoholic parents and she knew well of the mood swings and chaotic changes that were characteristic of such a family. Her objectivity as a psychologist began to fade slightly because she felt her motivation imperceptibly moving toward an advocacy role for her patients rather than a therapeutic one. She wanted them to succeed in therapy and, furthermore, wanted to give a stronger appearance of the progress to date than was actually the case.

In the interest of retaining Mr. Bear in treatment and helping him avoid the dire legal consequences, Dr. Syst wrote an unrealistically positive report of the changes he had made to date. A review of the facts revealed a very different picture, however, indicating that Mr. Bear had actually failed to carry through with his therapy commitments in several important ways. He had promised to enroll in an alcohol treatment program, but as of yet had failed to find one that matched his unusual work hours. His commitment to attend Alcoholics Anonymous meetings regularly and take an anger management class lasted a short time; he attended only two meetings over a 6-week period, supposedly due to conflicts with his work schedule. In spite of this, Dr. Syst thought he was genuinely committed to treatment and had made some significant gains in insight. She feared all this would be jeopardized if she wrote a wholly accurate report. She thought that presenting only the positive side would keep him invested on couples work and increase the likelihood that his mental health would improve over time.

Unfortunately, her decision to be only partially accurate in reporting Mr. Bear's progress, combined with the lawyer's skilled advocacy, resulted in the court dropping the requirement for Mr. Bear to remain in treatment. It seemed clear from Dr. Syst's letter that the client was in compliance with all requirements for his treatment program to date. But 3 weeks after Dr. Syst's report and the resulting cessation of the legal coercion to consult with a psychologist, Mr. Bear dropped out of therapy and shortly afterwards had a resurgence of violent behavior.

As a result of this experience, Dr. Syst gained an appreciation of her own blind spots, her overeagerness to help those in crisis, and the extent to which they impaired her objectivity. She noted how her denial of the facts about Mr. Bear's failure to follow the therapy regimen was a major factor in writing a distorted report to the attorney. She considered beginning psychotherapy, seeking supervision for her forensic practice, and obtaining additional training in forensic psychology to enhance her skills and avoid a reoccurrence of such impaired judgment in the future.

> *(b) Whenever necessary to avoid misleading, psychologists acknowledge the limits of their data or conclusions.*

(b) To avoid misleading others, acknowledge the limits of your data and sources, and don't draw premature conclusions. Also admit when you are uncertain or don't know the answer rather than inventing "facts" on the spot that seem to address the issue.

Vignette: Robert, a 26-year-old gay man, consulted Dr. Morphius to explore the possibilities of altering his sexual orientation. Dr. Morphius had given assurances over the telephone that converting to heterosexuality was successful "more often than not" as long as the patient was "highly motivated and willing to go the distance in treatment." After 6 months of therapy sessions and over nearly $3,000 in fees, much of which was willingly paid by the patient's parents, Robert was no closer to realizing his goal than before. As a result, he became increasingly depressed and agitated and reached a point of hopelessness about ever changing his sexual orientation. He concluded that Dr. Morphius's assurances were false, at least for him, and that his treatment could not benefit him in any significant way.

Robert dropped out of therapy, consulted a different psychologist, and 5 months later initiated a civil suit against Dr. Morphius for malpractice. Dr. Morphius and his attorney were able to locate an expert witness, Dr. Speakwell, who was willing to support his theories about altering sexual orientation in psychotherapy. During his deposition, Dr. Speakwell was asked about the empirical basis for his conclusion that psychotherapy was beneficial in altering one's sexual orientation. He replied that there was little research by others that he could cite, but the type of therapy both he and Dr. Morphius use was unequivocally novel and had been quite successful, as his "clinical research and publications demonstrated."

On closer examination, it was not so obvious that Dr. Speakwell could adequately support his claims, either by suitable clinical experience or empirical research. He submitted his publications for review by counsel several days after his deposition was taken. His clinical research on the topic consisted of two articles that generally addressed the topic, which he had written for his state psychological association's quarterly newsletter the previous year, and a handout describing his treatment modality that he routinely gave to patients who were discontent with their sexual orientation. His only relevant clinical experience consisted of Dr. Speakwell having successfully helped a young bisexual man to become more predominantly heterosexual in his behavior, as he had desired. However, there was no attempt at posttermination follow-up and no evidence that Dr. Speakwell or Dr. Morphius were using a psychological therapy that essentially "converted" gay men and lesbians to being heterosexual, as he had claimed.

When he was called to testify about the validity of his remarks concerning therapy for changing one's sexual orientation, Dr. Speakwell had the firm obligation to qualify his statements, as needed, regarding his own clinical work and its apparent success. Instead, he misrepresented his competence at the outset. Furthermore, while testifying in court, he continued to make misleading statements; did not qualify and state the limitations of his clinical data (i.e., that he had only treated one patient—a bisexual man with no follow-up); and drew unwarranted conclusions for the court, going well beyond any supporting research or clinical data. Dr. Speakwell learned, with much anguish later on in the litigation, that acknowledging the limits of one's data and conclusions was of fundamental importance and that failing to do so carried major legal consequences.

7.05 Prior Relationships

A prior professional relationship with a party does not preclude psychologists from testifying as fact witnesses or from testifying to their services to the extent permitted by applicable law. Psychologists appropriately take into account ways in which the prior relationship might affect their professional objectivity or opinions and disclose the potential conflict to the relevant parties.

Even though you've been someone's therapist or consultant in the past, a colleague, or a friend, you could still be asked to testify as a fact witness in court about their case. Know how your objectivity and competence may be affected, however, and openly acknowledge this and any conflict of interest in court or at a deposition.

Vignette: Dr. John Splitter had done a series of workshops on communication, stress management, and other topics for the journalists and other staff members of a large publishing company that owned several newspapers and popular magazines. He had also provided individual consultation to management over a period of 4 years. He was well acquainted with each of the managers and supervisors in this company and was familiar with the ongoing personnel issues both within and between departments.

Near the end of the fiscal year, the CFO began to exhibit some peculiar behavioral problems, and employees were complaining about his transgressions and poor judgment. He began to sexually harass female employees. He refused to listen to feedback from other staff members, and he manifested increasingly poor judgment about monetary matters. He was finally asked to take a mandatory medical leave and pursue individual counseling for a brief period of time. However, when he returned 1 month later, he showed no substantial improvement in his functioning. He was offered a small severance package and was asked to leave the organization altogether 3 months later.

Saddened and angry at this turn of events, the former CFO promptly brought a civil suit against the company for wrongful termination. As part of the plaintiff's strategy, his attorney deposed Dr. Splitter, whom the CFO had always considered to be his friend and whom he thought he could count on for support. Also as it turned out, Dr. Splitter was the only individual in the case who had kept good records over a long period of time concerning his consultations and staff problems. The upper level managers had failed to do so, particularly where it would have been helpful, such as documented performance appraisals or tracking complaints of other employees against the CFO.

Dr. Splitter appeared for the deposition but informed the attorneys that he could not be entirely objective in his testimony or provide expert witness testimony because he was a friend and racquetball partner of the ousted CFO. Although refusing to serve as an expert, he agreed to answer questions as a percipient (fact) witness. When it came time for cross examination he was asked about some incidents of sexual harassment that allegedly occurred, repeatedly, at work in his presence. Although this placed him in significant personal conflict, he was at least able to provide testimony about these incidents, which tended to mitigate the seriousness of the sexual harassment charges. However, he again offered a disclaimer to the court, that he may have lacked impartiality because he was a friend of the former CFO.

Dr. Splitter properly removed himself from the role of expert witness because his objectivity was impaired. He did his best to accurately provide the court with his accounts of questionable behavior by the CFO when specifically questioned in the role of percipient witness.

7.06 Compliance With Laws and Rules

In performing forensic roles, psychologists are reasonably familiar with the rules governing their roles. Psychologists are aware of the occasion-

ally competing demands placed upon them by these principles and the requirements of the court system, and attempt to resolve these conflicts by making known their commitment to this Ethics Code and taking steps to resolve the conflict in a responsible manner. (See also Standard 1.02, Relationship of Ethics and Law.)

Know what is required of you while performing forensic roles. Be aware of expectations and rules of the court system concerning subpoenas, serving as an expert or fact witness, unauthorized talking with plaintiffs or defendants, fees, confidentiality, release of raw data, and so on, even if you don't consider yourself to be a forensic psychologist. Abide by this Ethics Code when in doubt, and make known your ethical obligations if challenged.

Vignette: Dr. Sparsely received a *subpoena duces tecum* requiring her to produce all records of her patient and appear for a deposition. Her patient had been fired from his job as a supervisor in a construction company and was in litigation with his former employer concerning wrongful termination.

Because Dr. Sparsely had never been deposed before, she was unfamiliar with the rules concerning the payment of fees for appearing at a deposition. She was of the opinion, however, that she would be appearing as an expert witness and therefore should be paid her customary professional fee plus compensation for the time required to drive to and from the attorney's office. Shortly after receiving the subpoena she informed the attorney by letter of her expectations about being paid her professional fees and indicated her desire to receive a check in advance of the deposition date, or at least a letter of agreement that her fee would be paid. She stated that she would not appear for the deposition in person, although she would release the patient records if the fee were not paid.

Several days later while discussing matters with a colleague, she began to reconsider her actions. Her friend thought that her decision to refuse to appear for the subpoena was unwise, and he gave her some good advice. He suggested that, in general, when she received a subpoena she should (a) contact the patient directly to discuss the matter; (b) contact the patient's attorney, with the patient's permission, in order to review various options, if warranted; and (c) consult with the state or county psychological association for advice if needed, as an attorney or knowledgeable psychologist may be available. He also suggested that she review the forensic literature, including documents such as APA's (1991) "Specialty Guidelines for Forensic Psychologists." In addition, he gave Dr. Sparsely a copy of a recent journal article written by APA's Committee on Legal Issues entitled "Strategies for Private Practitioners Coping With Subpoenas or Compelled Testimony for Client Records and/or Test Data" (APA, 1996b).

Dr. Sparsely was pleased with the timely advice she received and promptly contacted an attorney, who was knowledgeable about mental health law. Much to her surprise, she learned that according to the court rules of her state she was obliged to appear for the deposition even if a fee agreement had not been reached in advance. The lawyer informed her that at this point, it was uncertain whether her formal role would be as an expert witness or as a percipient (fact) witness. As a percipient witness, she might only be expected to testify to the fact that she personally met with the plaintiff (her patient) on the dates indicated by her clinical and billing records. Or she might be asked to verify that her patient had in fact revealed certain information to her in the course of their consultations. In any case, she could not demand that her appearance for the deposition be contingent on a fee payment in advance, and her failure to show up could expose her to a possible contempt of court ruling, according to local law. As for her expected financial remuneration for her appearance— she may have to wait until she had provided her testimony or seek a court's ruling if there remained a dispute.

Because of Dr. Sparsely's lack of experience in the court system, she thought of several other questions to ask the lawyer and learned much that would be useful for her testimony. The lawyer was particularly useful in helping her to discriminate between information she learned from others (i.e., hearsay information) and her knowledge of fact that she herself witnessed. The rules of evidence governing her testimony would not allow her to introduce information learned from her client unless it was for the sole purpose of perhaps explaining her client's beliefs and his state of mind, rather than as evidence of actual fact. This was an important distinction because as a therapist, Dr. Sparsely was inclined to accept what her clients told her as accurate reports of other's behavior, believing what they said and accepting their characterizations of third parties as valid. As a result of this tendency, she had already formed opinions about her client's supervisor and other individuals in the company on the basis of her client's disclosures during therapy. Her tendency would have been to volunteer that she knew the supervisor to be a belligerent, crafty, abusive man and that her client had been unfairly treated by him for a period of over 5 years.

The lawyer firmly reminded Dr. Sparsely that she actually knew nothing about the supervisor aside from the subjective perceptions of her client. It would be essential for her to consistently indicate, if asked, that her client *alleged* that the supervisor was belligerent or abusive, not that he actually *was* this way. Because she had never met or observed him, she was not in the position of making statements about him based on her own perceptions, accurate or not. It was always important while testifying that she distinguish between what she was aware of by means of her own experience and what she had been told by another or read in a report. If she did not accurately make this distinction, she was at risk for investing the opinions of others with her own professional validation, when in fact, she had no valid ground for doing so.

This consultation with the attorney provided badly needed remedial knowledge about fundamental legal matters in providing testimony concerning her patient. Dr. Sparsely had the benefit of her attorney's wisdom concerning many aspects of interacting with the court system and continued her association with him when involved in future forensic matters. She also planned to take a forensic workshop at her earliest convenience in order to further supplement her knowledge.

8

Resolving Ethical Issues

8.01 Familiarity With Ethics Code

Psychologists have an obligation to be familiar with this Ethics Code, other applicable ethics codes, and their application to psychologists' work. Lack of awareness or misunderstanding of an ethical standard is not itself a defense to a charge of unethical conduct.

Know the requirements of this Ethics Code and review it periodically; ignorance of a rule is no defense before an ethics committee, state board of psychology, judge, or jury. Also know what other standards require as they apply to your work (e.g., supervisors of clinical social workers or psychiatrists should be familiar with their codes of ethics; researchers should observe relevant NIH standards for humans and animals; therapists or consultants using special techniques or working with special populations should observe relevant guidelines and standards).

Vignette: Dr. Hoonew had been providing marriage counseling for several months to Chip Fastbyte, a young man recovering from heroin addiction, and his wife Dawn, both of whom were computer software engineers. At the end of one session, Dr. Hoonew commented that he had become involved in a project that had nothing to do with therapy but could be "right up [their] alley." He told them that he was the CEO of a new company that was creating software for mental health care providers and researchers. It consisted of billing software, record keeping systems, psychological report writing applications, a variety of data storage formats, statistical analysis packages, and other useful software, all to be available on a single CD-ROM. The Fastbytes naturally took an interest in their therapist's other business venture and quickly offered to become involved by contributing their expertise. Dr. Hoonew was pleased with their interest and within a month had terminated the counseling relationship and hired the two to join his small staff. He thought that it was perfectly acceptable to employ the couple, as they had ceased being his clients, so no conflict of interest could exist. He hired them as full-time employees, including them in all planning meetings; offered them the full package of health and other benefits that all his employees enjoyed; and even invited them to his house for dinner to meet his wife and children.

Things went well for 2 months, until Chip "fell off the wagon" at a party with his old friends and eventually had a full relapse, reverting to his former level of heroin use. The couple's relationship began to deteriorate again, and soon old behavior patterns resurfaced, causing much distress. They clearly needed marriage counseling again, and Chip needed to stop using drugs, but they felt they could not turn to Dr. Hoonew because he was now their employer and had become a friend. He no longer could be objective as a therapist must be because the multiple professional and personal roles had become hopelessly entangled. It was necessary to start all over with a new therapist instead of being able to continue with someone who knew them well and could draw on the preexisting therapy relationship to address the current relapse.

Dr. Hoonew realized the hardship that he had imposed on this couple by employing them directly after ending their treatment. From the Fastbyte's perspective, however, the experience was actually quite different than that. They both felt that while marital therapy was still going on, Dr. Hoonew had encouraged them to consider working in his company by describing it to them and making subtle suggestions that their professional interests were indeed converging. Looking back at the sequence of events, all three individuals could see that marriage counseling had been truncated in the service of beginning a professional relationship, namely, employer–employee.

Although the Fastbytes did not formally bring a complaint, they discussed the matter with their new therapist. They decided that Standard 1.17, Multiple Relationships, was most relevant, particularly the phrase that psychologists are supposed to refrain "from entering into or *promising* another personal, scientific, professional, financial, or other relationship if it appears likely that such a relationship reasonably might impair the psychologist's objectivity or otherwise interfere with the psychologist's effectively performing his or her functions as a psychologist, or might harm or exploit the other party" (APA, 1992, p. 1601). They were resentful that they had to spend a significant amount of time, money, and energy with a new marital therapist and felt that they had been harmed by Dr. Hoonew's poor judgment in encouraging the possibility of a business relationship while they were still his clients.

In hindsight, while discussing the situation with the Fastbytes, Dr. Hoonew agreed that he had used poor judgment and that Standard 1.17 was indeed relevant. He claimed that he had been unaware of that particular rule or had not understood its implications. The standard concerning multiple relationships was stated quite differently in the 1989 edition of the Ethics Code, the one he was most familiar with, and he just had not taken the time to educate himself about all the changes in the revised version. He now understood the value of learning the ethics standards; that knowledge could help him avoid pitfalls and judgment errors in a variety of professional situations.

8.02 Confronting Ethical Issues

When a psychologist is uncertain whether a particular situation or course of action would violate this Ethics Code, the psychologist ordi-

narily consults with other psychologists knowledgeable about ethical issues, with state or national psychology ethics committees, or with other appropriate authorities in order to choose a proper response.

When in doubt about whether your situation or intended course of action might be unethical, ask! It's better to consult your state or county psychological association ethics committee, APA, an institutional review board, senior peers, those who teach ethics, or some other authority than to forge ahead when you are uncertain about the ethicality of some matter. Consulting another takes less time and energy than dealing with the results of a poor judgment call.

Vignette: Dr. Ona Webnow, a California psychologist, was considering the value of expanding her psychological services onto the Internet. She hired a webmaster and graphic designer to create an eye-catching web page for the Internet. It had many colors, moving figures, and psychological phrases aimed at indulging the curiosity of someone using the Internet who might be in psychological distress. Dr. Webnow offered on-line counseling, a referral service, business consulting, and peer consultation for mental health providers in both electronic mail and chat-room formats. Indeed, she was a jill-of-all-trades, or so she fancied herself.

Profit motive notwithstanding, she eventually did consider the ethical propriety of her proposed on-line work. She knew little about her legal or ethical obligation to provide informed consent before offering counseling to someone on-line. This, of course, had its own array of problems. For example, how could she ascertain whether the consumer was a minor or even know the consumer's gender, for that matter? She was aware that for some time Internet users had become sophisticated in donning on-line disguises and that the electronic medium could serve to facilitate deception in many ways. She wondered about the risks she might incur in providing on-line counseling to a minor who had represented him- or herself as an adult. She also wondered about the obligation to keep records and whether it also applied to counseling activities on the Internet. Because she also anticipated providing consultation to therapists on-line, she wondered if she would incur any legal liability or had any ethical obligations if the consultee turned out to be incompetent in treating their own patients?

Finally, she had some concern about confidentiality and the inherent problem of offering counseling or consulting in a medium that lent itself to instantaneous worldwide transmission, such as electronic chat rooms or electronic mail that could be easily forwarded by recipients to anyone of their choosing.

Dr. Webnow thought that her state board of psychology would be a good resource about the ethics of on-line psychological services. Indeed, the clerical person she spoke with raised her awareness about legal issues, such as possible problems in offering psychological services to a consumer living in a state where the psychologist held no license. Information concerning legal requirements offered by the board was helpful, but the individual she spoke with provided little guidance about the ethical matters mentioned above. Before long, however, Dr. Webnow's concerns about ethics became relegated to a lower level of importance as the increased press of daily business took over. Her enthusiasm about networking with colleagues and promoting her business was all consuming. Furthermore, she rationalized, she was on the "cutting edge" of new technology and could find few ethical standards that provided specific guidance about how to conduct business over the Internet. She viewed her work, therefore, as essentially exempt from the Ethics Code and decided to proceed on that basis.

Ultimately, her failure to attempt to interpret the existing code or to seek adequate guidance in these matters resulted in some serious errors in judgment. Furthermore, she lacked knowledge concerning the legal mandates about providing service over the Internet. She knew nothing of California's Telemedicine Act of 1996 (California Business & Professions Code, 1998), which required that she obtain informed consent in writing from a consumer prior to offering clinical services over the Internet in video format (which she was considering). She had never even considered informing potential clients about the benefits and risks of participating in on-line counseling or to obtain written consent from consumers participating in on-line counseling. She made no effort to verify the age of the consumers—whether they were a minor, if they were currently consulting with another therapist individually, and so on. She also failed to inform potential on-line consumers about the limits of her services. For example with individuals in crisis, as she did not intend to offer crisis intervention over the Internet. In addition, there was no mention in the introductory statements of her web page about confidentiality or the threats to confidentiality that were posed by the Internet. In short, Dr. Webnow seemed to have little awareness of some of the fundamental problems inherent in attempting to offer counseling over the Internet where one relies wholly on the printed word for obtaining and dispensing information and the significance of missing nonverbal cues, for both therapist and consumer. She was also unaware of the significant dearth of relevant research in this area and, more importantly, whether receiving counseling over the Internet was significantly different than reading a pop psychology book or had any long-term efficacy.

Dr. Webnow could easily have contacted APA or sought out individuals knowledgeable about ethics and experienced in using the Internet, as they were readily available. However, she felt that the onus was not on her to seek these answers, but rather that answers should be forthcoming in journals, newsletters, and other professional publications and that she bore little obligation to make an effort to educate herself.

She eventually had some disappointing experiences that taught her the consequences of inadequately addressing such fundamentally important standards as informed consent, privacy and confidentiality, and avoiding harm, to name a few. She finally acknowledged that no one could anticipate her professional actions in these uncharted waters, if she chose to navigate them, except herself. She also gained an appreciation for the potential for risk of harm to consumers and the responsibility she bore to consider all the relevant ethical issues. In time, guidelines, standards, rules, and additional legislation would be forthcoming. But until that happened, she realized that she should exercise caution and make the best use possible of existing ethical standards by extrapolating their application to psychological services offered over the Internet.

8.03 Conflicts Between Ethics and Organizational Demands

If the demands of an organization with which psychologists are affiliated conflict with this Ethics Code, psychologists clarify the nature of the conflict, make known their commitment to the Ethics Code, and to the extent feasible, seek to resolve the conflict in a way that permits the fullest adherence to the Ethics Code.

If you find a conflict between the policies of your workplace and the Ethics Code, clarify the nature of the conflict and let others know about your obligation to comply with this code. Then seek a resolution of the problem that permits maximal adherence to the Ethics Code.

Vignette: Dr. Ida Listig accepted her first postdoctoral position as a staff psychologist in a suburban private hospital that specialized in the treatment of chronic pain and chemical dependency. After working there for 1 month, she realized that some of the long-standing hospital policies in diagnosis and treatment were not necessarily in the patients' best interests, nor were they in conformance with the psychology Ethics Code. Staff frequently used diagnostic procedures that were unnecessary and costly for the patient and third-party payors. For example, every chronic pain patient was given a battery of neuropsychological tests as part of the initial evaluation, even though this was quite a departure from the usual and customary assessment procedures for chronic pain. Also testing and psychotherapy were routinely carried out by unqualified staff, such as registered nurses and unsupervised psychological assistants. Furthermore, most patients were routinely admitted to the hospital for "state of the art diagnostic procedures and observation," according to the brochure, regardless of the source of their pain, history of treatment, and equal outpatient treatment.

Chemical dependency patients were treated by an interdisciplinary team of therapists who often did not agree on treatment plans and were outright divided on such fundamental matters as abstinence, controlled drinking, and the benefits of the 12-step program. Also it was routine practice in the hospital to use "in-house tests," which were nothing more than photocopied versions of various copyrighted instruments of assessment. It had long been a policy of the staff to simply make photocopies of these copyrighted materials when supplies were exhausted rather than to order new copies from the publisher.

Many of these practices contributed to improving and maintaining the financial health of the institution and were well entrenched by the time Dr. Listig began working there. With some misgivings she approached Dr.

Sly Hardrock, chief of the psychology service, to discuss the reservations she had about carrying out duties that appeared to violate the Ethics Code. Specifically, she raised two major questions: (a) financial exploitation of patients (Standards 1.14, Avoiding Harm; 1.16, Misuse of Psychologists' Work; and 1.19a, Exploitative Relationships) and (b) staff incompetence (Standards 1.04, Boundaries of Competence; 1.22, Delegation to and Supervision of Subordinates; 2.02, Competence and Appropriate Use of Assessments and Interventions; 2.06, Unqualified Persons; and 4.02, Informed Consent to Therapy). She addressed several other areas of concern that seemed to be either unethical, illegal, or unprofessional.

Dr. Hardrock appeared disinterested in the ethical questions raised by his new employee. He had not been a member of any psychological association for many years, and thought that the APA Ethics Code therefore had no jurisdiction over him. As for his staff members who were active members of APA, they would have to make ethical compromises if they wanted to keep their very well-paying positions at the hospital. It was clear that Dr. Hardrock had no intention of changing hospital polices that had been in place for so long.

Reluctantly, Dr. Listig began her search for another position, although as it turned out she was not successful for nearly 1 year because there were few job openings in her geographical area. During that period, she did what she could to maximize her own compliance with the Ethics Code and to raise the ethical consciousness of other psychologists on the service about these important matters. In the last few months of her job at the hospital, she initiated a formal complaint against Dr. Hardrock with the state board of psychology. Although it was true that he was not a member of APA or the state psychological association, he held a psychology license and was therefore bound to comply with the state licensing laws that mandate compliance with the Ethics Code.[1]

8.04 Informal Resolution of Ethical Violations

When psychologists believe that there may have been an ethical violation by another psychologist, they attempt to resolve the issue by bringing it to the attention of that individual if an informal resolution appears appropriate and the intervention does not violate any confidentiality rights that may be involved.

If you think your colleague may have violated the Ethics Code and an informal approach seems best, discuss the matter directly with him or her rather than automatically contacting an ethics committee or state psychology board. In any case, do not simply turn a blind eye or a deaf ear. (Also always remember to respect the privacy of others, and bear in mind that a wronged party may not feel ready to pursue an ethics complaint until after some "recovery time" has passed, even though you might think that they should.)

---

[1]Note: Laws concerning compliance with the APA Ethics Code vary by state.

Vignette: Dr. Greaving was on the faculty of a small professional school of psychology and was well known for his enthusiastic teaching style and affable nature. At one point, however, his spirits had begun to sink, and it was clear that he was becoming increasingly depressed. A colleague, Dr. Sylvia Reacher, noticed that he was keeping rather unusual office hours, and several times each week was having dinner with a few select female graduate students. Although there was nothing specifically unethical about this practice, it raised a question in the colleague's mind, and she wondered whose needs were being met. It seemed to her that Dr. Greaving might be relying on the emotional support of his female students to lift his spirits during this time of emotional depression.

She also took note of the fact that one of his trainees, Inga, had begun seeing Dr. Greaving for supervision at 7:30 p.m. each Friday evening, when the building was virtually empty. Following supervision, the two of them would go out for dinner at a nearby restaurant. She waited, watchfully, to see if Inga would raise a question within the department or bring a complaint about her supervisor's changing relationship with her. This never happened, however, possibly because Inga ascribed a significant amount of social power to Dr. Greaving, and they were still in the early stages of a possible romantic relationship. The colleague also noted that on the mornings that they cotaught a seminar, she often smelled alcohol on his breath, noted that his words were slurred, and observed his usual eloquent style of presentation deteriorating.

One day Dr. Greaving confided in Sylvia that he was having difficulty sleeping and that he had been very dejected about his brother's recent positive HIV diagnosis. She listened empathetically to her friend and took the opportunity to mention that perhaps the stress of his brother's ill health was affecting his objectivity and competence at work. Pointedly, she raised the question of his late Friday night tête-à-têtes with his supervisee, Inga, and his possible overuse of alcohol.

Dr. Greaving resisted these ideas at first and denied that he had behaved in any way that was questionable or that he was drinking too much. The next day, however, he contacted Dr. Reacher and told her that he was relieved that someone had finally raised these questions with him. He told her that he actually had increased his daily alcohol consumption lately and was even drinking in the morning. He also acknowledged that he definitely did have amorous feelings for his supervisee that were leading him closer to a full romantic relationship with her, although there had been no sexual contact yet.

Slowly Dr. Greaving had become more impaired in his ability to provide competent and objective supervision to Inga and probably would not have taken any steps to remedy this situation until he had traveled farther down the road of an intimate relationship with her. Attempting to provide supervision while pursuing a romantic relationship was clearly at cross purposes but he had continued to engage in both these roles until Sylvia had called his attention to what was happening.

Because of the efforts of his friend, he began the process of his own rehabilitation by consulting with a therapist and began to consider attending 12-step meetings to explore his heavy reliance on alcohol. He understood that it would be best if Inga were to change supervisors and explained to her that he needed to withdraw from that role, given his current state of emotional stress. Dr. Reacher was pleased that her friend was responsive to her suggestions and obviously saw no immediate need to formalize a complaint to an ethics body. Dr. Greaving seemed well aware of his temporary incompetence and was taking appropriate steps to remedy it.

8.05 Reporting Ethical Violations

> *If an apparent ethical violation is not appropriate for informal resolution under Standard 8.04 or is not resolved properly in that fashion, psychologists take further action appropriate to the situation, unless such action conflicts with confidentiality rights in ways that cannot be resolved. Such action might include referral to state or national committees on professional ethics or to state licensing boards.*

If discussing your concerns with the psychologist in question is unproductive (e.g., you are "stonewalled" by the person), blow the whistle. This would apply to major transgressions, such as when a psychologist has sex with a patient, engages in fraudulent research, or repeatedly refuses to change after he or she has already been confronted about unethical conduct. Contact your state's or APA's ethics committee, call the state licensing board, or contact other authorities (hospital or university ethics committees, professional association ethics committees, or institutional review board, etc.).

Vignette: Dr. Heddy Bong was skilled in hypnosis and had been using it extensively in her practice with many patients. She was also a recovering cocaine abuser and had been drug free for almost 3 years. She attributed her success in stopping cocaine use to her unique application of hypnosis and thought that she had discovered a fool-proof cure for all chemical dependency. She was so pleased with her innovative techniques and convinced that they were far superior to all other programs, that she founded her own self-help movement called Alcoholic Hypnotics Anonymous (with the spirited acronym, AHA!).

She borrowed heavily from the 12-step programs' theory and format but added her own hypnotic training as a central feature, teaching hypnosis to all participants, and encouraging them to teach others. Her groups were open to all; she did not diagnose or discriminate, welcoming those who were depressed or had panic disorders right along side those who were actively suicidal, were paranoid, or had a dissociative or schizophrenic disorder. Hypnosis was for one and all who wanted to stop drinking, and "each one should teach one," as she believed that AHA! was the true cure for all and that conventional individual therapy was rapidly becoming an anachronism.

In fact, Dr. Bong was engaging in potentially dangerous activities. She was systematically assembling the very ingredients that could result in serious harm to individuals: a nonspecific treatment for chemically dependent people, some with dual diagnoses, and teaching a specialized technique (hypnosis) to those who were not qualified to use it with others.

Several colleagues approached her over a period of 6 months and questioned her professional activities, but she was unwilling to consider their objections to her professional conduct. She told them that she was not acting as a psychologist in the groups because as a recovering cocaine addict, she considered herself a "patient" too, and therefore the Ethics Code did not apply to her conduct. The fact that she used her doctoral title, promoted the groups with newspaper advertisements and on local radio and TV talk shows, and charged a fee for group attendance did not, in her mind, constitute rendering a psychological service.

Her concerned colleagues thought little would be gained by further attempts to point out the grave risk of her unprofessional conduct, and the high probability, ultimately, of harming others. They brought a formal complaint to the APA Ethics Committee, citing Standards 6.04, Limitation on Teaching; 1.04, Boundaries of Competence; 1.14, Avoiding Harm; and 1.06, Basis for Scientific and Professional Judgments. The ensuing investigation by the Ethics Committee revealed that several other standards also were pertinent. The colleagues were confident that they had done the right thing in reporting such egregious conduct to the Ethics Committee, especially in light of the fact that Dr. Bong had made vague references to suing them for slander if they continued to "harass" her.

8.06 Cooperating With Ethics Committees

> *Psychologists cooperate in ethics investigations, proceedings, and resulting requirements of the APA or any affiliated state psychological association to which they belong. In doing so, they make reasonable efforts to resolve any issues as to confidentiality. Failure to cooperate is itself an ethics violation.*

If an ethics committee comes knocking on your door, open it! Cooperate with the investigation (e.g., respond to letters, comply with mandated time frames and requests for information). You may defend yourself but do so within the context of the APA (1996a) or state Ethics Committee's formal Rules and Procedures. *Never* simply ignore a formal complaint; the consequences of such an action could be severe.

Vignette: Dr. Ari Gant was the human resources director of a large hospital system with many franchises in different cities. One day, Dr. Gant received a certified letter from his state psychological association notifying him that a formal complaint had been brought against him for his conduct as a psychologist. An African American man who had applied for work as an orderly was claiming racial discrimination in the hiring practices of the human resources department, seemingly a direct violation of Standard 1.10, Nondiscrimination. He was complaining about the department's policy of screening potential employees by using a structured interview and a 30-item multiple-choice test that attempted to assess candidates' professional judgment and interpersonal skills in a variety of typical hospital emergency and nonemergency situations.

Dr. Gant was a busy man; he was responsible directly or indirectly for the hiring, firing, and promotions of thousands of employees in eight different cities. He felt that he could not be bothered with an ethics complaint from APA, particularly when he felt that he had done nothing wrong.

He was given 60 days to respond to the charges in writing; specifically, he was to write his account of the complainant's assessment process at the hospital and show that it was not unfairly discriminatory. The complainant had signed a consent form allowing such disclosures and had also submitted his own written version of the purported discrimination to the APA Ethics Office. Because Dr. Gant considered an ethics complaint from APA to be less important than a civil lawsuit, he decided to disregard it and did not even inform the hospital attorneys or his own professional liability insurance carrier that a complaint had been filed against him. Being caught up in daily personnel crises, he refused to respond to additional attempts by the Ethics Committee to contact him and let the time slip by until long after the 60 days had passed.

He ultimately received a letter expelling him from APA for a period of 5 years for his failure to comply with an ethics investigation, which in itself was an ethics violation. Dr. Gant valued his membership in APA and was deeply distressed that such a severe sanction had been imposed for his failure to respond to the investigation.

8.07 Improper Complaints

Psychologists do not file or encourage the filing of ethics complaints that are frivolous and are intended to harm the respondent rather than to protect the public.

Never file a frivolous complaint, or one that is intended to harm or "punish" a colleague. The ultimate purpose of filing a complaint is to protect someone from harm, not to "get even" with another psychologist.

Vignette: Dr. Auslander had developed an innovative method of analyzing interpersonal communication and was beginning to promote it in a tentative way in his clinical and consulting work. It involved 5 minutes of careful tracking of an individual's breathing, head and upper body movements, voice volume, and other easily observed variables. Supposedly, by engaging in these observations at the outset of any conversation, an individual could gather enough information to respond in ways that would significantly improve the productivity of the interaction, particularly when there was conflict.

Although intrigued by his theories, some colleagues found Dr. Auslander's personal attributes and mannerisms to be offensive. He was an avowed atheist, gay, and perceived to be discourteous and occasionally rude to others. He also had a condescending manner that alienated some colleagues in professional and social settings.

One colleague in the department, Dr. Whimper, was particularly offended by Auslander's interpersonal style. After reaching his limit of tolerance following an unpleasant interchange one afternoon, he decided to "teach him a lesson" by bringing a formal ethics complaint. Because there was no way that he could formally complain about Auslander's rudeness—no ethical standard specifically addressed this—at least he could complain about what he considered to be his "shoddy research." He initiated a complaint to his state ethics committee, asserting that Dr. Auslander used and widely promoted invalidated techniques and made inaccurate statements, unsupported by any valid research.

When Dr. Auslander was contacted by the ethics committee, he was obliged to comply with its rules and procedures by responding to the charges within a specified time frame. This took a considerable amount of time and energy and was personally stressful. Dr. Auslander took his membership in the state association seriously and did not wish to jeopardize it, even though he thought that this was an unjustified complaint triggered by personal feelings instead of a true regard for ethics. Therefore he gave his full attention to the complaint process, responding to the charges within the specified time limits and providing answers to all questions, complete with documentation that was requested of him. The task was time consuming, taking nearly 9 months, and it was somewhat anxiety evoking to submit to the scrutiny of one's peers, even though he felt that he had committed no ethical infraction.

It was widely known that no matter how Dr. Auslander might have comported himself in nonprofessional settings, he was still a rigorous researcher who complied scrupulously with ethical standards when carrying out psychological work. For example, he was well aware that his theories concerning a method of interpersonal analysis were still in their early stages of development, and he had gone to great lengths to specifically avoid any statements that would mislead others into thinking otherwise. Whenever he made a formal presentation, he was careful to include a carefully worded disclaimer stating that his methods had little empirical validation for such variables as age, gender, ethnicity, physical impairment, and so on, and anyone attempting to use them should exercise caution until validating data from research studies began to accumulate.

In light of his well-deserved reputation for conducting research competently and exercising caution in his public statements about his methods he considered the complaint brought by Dr. Wimper to be an attempt to hurt him and his good name. After much deliberation he decided to raise the question that Dr. Whimper might have filed a capricious complaint against him and proceeded to contact the state ethics committee about a potential violation of Standard 8.07.

Appendix:
Rules and Procedures of
the APA Ethics Committee

Overview
Adoption and Application

In December 1995 the APA Board of Directors adopted these Rules and Procedures (1996b) to replace the earlier set (which was published in the December 1992 issue of the *American Psychologist, 47,* pp. 1612–1628). The Rules are available from the APA Ethics Office, 750 First Street, NE, Washington, DC 20002-4242.

Overview

This brief overview is intended only to help the reader to understand the structure of these Rules and Procedures (Rules). The overview is not binding on the Ethics Committee or participants in the ethics process and is not an independent source of authority.

These Rules are divided into five parts, which are further subdivided by sections and subsections. The table of contents lists the major section headings.

Parts I and II: General Provisions

Part I describes the objectives and authority of the Ethics Committee. Part II states the Committee's general operating rules. These address such areas as confidentiality and disclosures of information concerning ethics cases; maintenance and disposition of Ethics Committee records; the Committee's jurisdiction, including the time limits within which ethics complaints must be filed; requests to reopen a closed case; and descriptions of the various sanctions and directives that may be imposed.

Parts III–V: Processing and Review of Complaints and Other Matters by the Ethics Committee

Membership Matters

The Ethics Committee may review applications or reapplication for membership in APA and may review allegations that membership was obtained based upon false or fraudulent information. These procedures are described in Part III.

Investigations of Unethical Conduct

These Rules describe two types of investigations: show cause proceedings and reviews of alleged unethical conduct. The Committee may choose to deal with a matter according to either procedure and may convert an investigation from one type to another as appropriate. A show cause review is commenced based on an adverse action by another body; a review of alleged unethical conduct is initiated by a complainant or the Committee and charges violation of the Ethics Code.

Show Cause Proceedings

The show cause procedure, addressed in Part IV, can be used when another body—including criminal courts, licensing boards, and state psychological associations—has already taken specified serious adverse action against a member. For example, if a member has been convicted of a felony or equivalent criminal offense; has been expelled or suspended by a state psychological association; or has been decertified, unlicensed, or deregistered or had a certificate, license, or registration revoked or suspended by a state or local board, the Committee may notify the respondent that he or she has 60 days to explain why APA should not expel the respondent from membership on the basis of that prior action. The respondent may show that procedures used were not fair and may argue the merits of the previous action. The Committee recommends to the Board of Directors whether the respondent should be expelled or allowed to resign under stipulated conditions, reprimanded or censured, or cleared of the charges. Time limits for initiating show cause cases are stated in Part II, Section 5.3.4.

Complaints Alleging Violation of the Ethics Code

Investigations detailed in Part V include those brought by members and nonmembers of the Association and those initiated by the Ethics Committee (*sua sponte* complaints). Complaints must be submitted within specified time periods or allege serious misconduct for which a waiver of the time limit may be granted. (See Part II, Section 5.) Even with a waiver of the time limit, the Committee may not find violations for behavior that occurred 10 years or more before the complaint was filed.

Complaints are evaluated initially by the Ethics Office Director, or Investigators acting as the Director's designees, regarding jurisdictional issues such as whether the subject of the complaint, the respondent, is a member, whether the complaint form is correctly completed, and whether the time limits for filing have been met. Then the Chair of the Ethic Committee and Director of the Ethics Office or their designees determine whether there are grounds for action to be taken by the Committee (defined in Part V, Subsection 5.1). If necessary, the Chair and Director conduct a preliminary investigation (described in Part V, Subsection 5.3) to assist in making these threshold determinations. If the Committee has no jurisdiction or if cause for action does not exist, the complaint is dismissed. If the Committee has jurisdiction and cause for action exists, the Director will open a case, issue a specific charge letter, and conduct an investigation. The respondent is afforded an opportunity to comment on all evidence that will be considered by the Committee and upon which the Committee may rely in its review of the complaint. At the conclusion of the investigation, the case is referred to the Committee for review and resolution.

In resolving a case, the Committee may dismiss it; recommend that it be resolved with a reprimand or censure, with or without supplemental directives; recommend to the Board of Directors that the respondent be expelled from membership; or offer the member the option of resigning subject to stipulated conditions and subject to approval by the Board of Directors.

If the Committee recommends any action other than dismissal or stipulated resignation, the respondent has a right to an independent case review and evaluation or, in the case of a recommendation of expulsion, a formal hearing or an independent adjudication. In an independent adjudication following a recommendation of censure or reprimand, the respondent provides a rationale for nonacceptance of the Committee's recommendation, and a three-member panel, selected by the respondent from six members of the Board of Directors' standing Hearing Panel, provides the final adjudication based on the written record. The Director implements the final adjudication, whether based on the panel's decision or the respondent's acceptance of the Committee's recommendation.

A formal hearing is an in-person proceeding before a formal hearing committee, which makes an independent recommendation to the Board of Directors. The respondent may elect to have an independent adjudication instead of a formal hearing. The Board reviews the recommendation of the hearing committee, independent adjudication panel, or, if no hearing was requested, the Ethics Committee, and must adopt that recommendation unless specified defects require the matter to be remanded for further actions.

Adoption and Application

The revised Rules and Procedures of the Ethics Committee of the American Psychological Association, which are set forth below, were approved by the APA Board of Directors on December 9, 1995, with an effective date of June 1, 1996. The Rules will be applied from that date forward to all complaints and cases pending on the effective date, except, as provided in Part II, Subsection 1.2 of the 1992 Rules, "no amendment shall adversely affect the rights of a member of the Association whose conduct is being investigated by the Ethics Committee or against whom the Ethics Committee has filed formal charges" as of the effective date. In the event that application of the revised Rules and Procedures would adversely affect such rights, the pertinent provisions of the Rules and Procedures in effect at the time the member came under the scrutiny of the Ethics Committee will be applied. Failure by the Committee or APA to follow these Rules and Procedures shall be cause to set aside action taken under these Rules only in the event such failure has resulted in genuine prejudice to the respondent.

Part I. Objectives and Authority of the Committee

1. Objectives

The fundamental objectives of the Ethics Committee (hereinafter the Committee) shall be to maintain ethical conduct by psychologists at the highest professional level, to educate psychologists concerning ethical standards, to endeavor to protect the public against harmful conduct by psychologists, and to aid the Association in achieving its objectives as reflected in its Bylaws.[1]

2. Authority

The Committee is authorized to

2.1 Formulate rules or principles of ethics for adoption by the Association;

2.2 Investigate allegations of unethical conduct of members (to include fellows) and associates (hereinafter members) and, in certain instances, student affiliates and applicants for membership;

2.3 Resolve allegations of unethical conduct and/or recommend such action as is necessary to achieve the objectives of the Association;

2.4 Report on types of complaints investigated with special description of difficult cases;

2.5 Adopt rules and procedures governing the conduct of all the matters within its jurisdiction;

2.6 Take such other actions as are consistent with the Bylaws of the Association, the Association Rules, the Association's Ethics Code, and these Rules and Procedures, and as are necessary and appropriate to achieving the objectives of the Committee;

2.7 Delegate appropriate tasks to subcommittees, ad hoc committees, and task forces of the Ethics Committee; to Committee Associates; or to employees or agents of the Association, as necessary or appropriate. All of these individuals and groups shall in any such event be fully bound by these Rules and Procedures.

Part II. General Operating Rules

1. General Provisions

1.1 APA Documents.[2] The Committee shall base its actions on applicable governmental laws and regulations, the Bylaws of the Association, the Association Rules, the Association's Ethics Code, and these Rules and Procedures.

1.2 Applicable Ethics Code. Conduct is subject to the Ethics Code in

---

[1]The Ethics Committee seeks to protect the public by deterring unethical conduct by psychologists, by taking appropriate action when an ethical violation has been proved according to these Rules and Procedures, and by setting standards to aid psychologists in understanding their ethical obligations. Of course, in no circumstances can or does the Committee or the Association guarantee that unethical behavior will not occur or that members of the public will never be harmed by the actions of individual psychologists.

[2]For a copy of the relevant sections of the current Bylaws and Association Rules, contact the APA Ethics Office.

effect at the time the conduct occurred. If a course of conduct continued over a period of time during which more than one Ethics Code was in effect, each Ethics Code will be applicable to conduct that occurred during the time period it was in effect.

1.3 Rules and Procedures. The Committee may adopt rules and procedures governing the conduct of all matters within its jurisdiction and may amend such rules from time to time upon a two-thirds vote of the Committee members, provided that no amendment shall adversely affect the rights of a member of the Association whose conduct is being investigated by the Ethics Committee or against whom the Ethics Committee has recommended expulsion, stipulated resignation, voiding membership, censure, or reprimand at the time of amendment. Changes to the Rules and Procedures must be ratified by the Board of Directors acting for the Council of Representatives.

1.4 Compliance With Time Requirements. The APA and the respondent shall use their best efforts to adhere strictly to the time requirements specified in these Rules and Procedures. Failure to do so will not prohibit final resolution unless such failure was unduly prejudicial. Upon request, the Director may extend time limits stated in these Rules for submitting statements or responses if there is good cause to do so. In all cases in which a time limit for submitting a response is stated in these Rules and Procedures, the period specified is the number of days allowed for receipt of the response by the Ethics Office.

1.5 Computation of Time. In computing any period of time stated by these Rules, the day of the act, event, or default from which the designated period of time begins to run shall not be included. The last day of the period shall be included unless it is a Saturday, a Sunday, or a legal holiday, in which event the period runs until the end of the next business day.

2. Meetings and Officers

2.1 Frequency and Quorum. The Committee shall meet at reasonable intervals as needed. A quorum at such meetings shall consist of the majority of the elected members of the Committee.

2.2 Selection of Officers. The Chair and Vice Chair shall be elected annually at a duly constituted meeting.

2.3 Authority. The Vice Chair shall have the authority to perform all the duties of the Chair when the latter is unavailable or unable to perform them and shall perform such other tasks as are delegated by the Chair or by these Rules.

2.4 Majority Rule. Except as otherwise noted in these Rules and Procedures, all decisions shall be by majority vote of those elected members present or, in the case of a vote by mail, a majority of those elected members qualified to vote.

2.5 Designation of Responsibilities. The Chief Executive Officer of the Association shall designate a staff member to serve as Director of the

Ethics Office. Whenever they appear in these Rules, "Chair," "Vice Chair," "Director," and "President" shall mean these individuals or their designees.

2.6 Attendance. Attendance at the Ethics Committee's deliberation of cases is restricted to elected members of the Committee, Committee Associates, the Director of the Ethics Office, the Ethics Office staff, members of the Board of Directors, Legal Counsel of the Association, and other duly appointed persons authorized by the Committee to assist it in carrying out its functions, except when the Committee, by two-thirds vote, authorizes the presence of other persons.

3. Confidentiality and Notifications

3.1 Requirement of Confidentiality. All information concerning complaints against members shall be confidential, except that the Director may disclose such information when compelled by a valid subpoena, in response to a request from a state or local board or similar entity,[3] when otherwise required by law, or as otherwise provided in these Rules and Procedures. Such information may also be released when the Chair and the Director agree that release of that information is necessary to protect the interests of (a) the complainant or respondent; (b) other investigative or adjudicative bodies; (c) the Association; or (d) members of the public, and release will not unduly interfere with the Association's interest in respecting the legitimate confidentiality interests of participants in the ethics process and its interest in safeguarding the confidentiality of internal peer review deliberation.

3.2 Access by Staff, Legal Counsel, and Other Duly Appointed Persons. Information may be shared with Legal Counsel of the Association, with the Chief Executive Officer of the Association, with staff of the Association's Central Office designated by the Chief Executive Officer to assist the Committee with its work, and with other duly appointed persons authorized by the Committee to assist it in carrying out its functions. Subject to the confidentiality provisions in these Rules, these persons are authorized to use this information for the purposes set out in these Rules regardless of whether the person providing the information has executed a release.

3.3 Notification in Connection With Investigation or Final Disposition of Investigation. Where these Rules provide for notification of final disposition of a matter, this notification shall include the ethical stan-

---

[3]For purposes of these Rules and Procedures, a reference to state or local boards or similar entities shall include state, local, or provincial licensing boards (whether located in the United States or Canada); state, local, or provincial boards of examiners or education in those cases where the pertinent licensing or certification is secured from such entities; or in states or provinces with no licensing authority, nonstatutory boards established for similar purposes (such as registering bodies).

dard(s)[4] that were judged to have been violated and, if violation is found, the standards not violated, and the sanction (including a statement that directives were given), if any. In show cause proceedings under Part IV, this notification shall describe the type of underlying action (e.g., loss of license) without reference to the underlying behavior. In matters in which membership is voided under Part III, Subsection 3.3, the notification shall indicate that membership was voided because it was obtained on the basis of false or fraudulent information. In any of these matters, the rationale may also be included (a) if the notification is required by these Rules, at the discretion of the Board or Committee; (b) if the notification is not required, at the discretion of the entity or person (i.e., the Board, the Committee, or the Director) authorizing the notification; or (c) as set forth in a stipulation.

3.3.1 Respondent. The Director shall inform the respondent of the final disposition in a matter. This notification shall include the rationale for the Association's actions. As used in these Rules and Procedures, the term *respondent* includes any member, student affiliate, or membership applicant who is under the scrutiny of the Ethics Committee.

3.3.2 Complainant. The Director shall inform the complainant of the final disposition in a matter. The Director may also at any time, as a matter of discretion, provide such information as is necessary to notify the complainant of the status of a case.

3.3.3 Membership. The Director shall report annually to the membership the names of members who have lost membership due to unethical behavior and the ethical standard(s) violated or the type of underlying action for a show cause case or that membership was voided because it was obtained on the basis of false or fraudulent information. No report to membership shall be made for stipulated resignations in which such a report was not stipulated.

3.3.4 Council of Representatives. The Director shall report annually and in confidence to the Council the names of members who have been allowed to resign under stipulated conditions.

3.3.5 Other Entities. When the Board of Directors, the Committee, or the Director (for stipulated resignations as provided in Part IV, Subsection 12.1.2) determines that further notification is necessary for the protection of the Association or the public or to maintain the standards of the Association, the Director shall communicate the final disposition to those groups and/or individuals so identified. Such notification may be made to (a) affiliated state and regional associations,[5] (b) the American Board of Professional Psychology, (c) state or local boards or similar entities, (d) the Association of State and Provincial Psychology Boards, (e) the Council for

---

[4]In this document *ethical standard(s)* refers to the ethical standard(s) in the Ethical Principles of Psychologists and Code of Conduct, the ethical principle(s) in the Ethical Principles of Psychologists, or the enforceable provisions of any subsequent ethics code.

[5]For purposes of these Rules and Procedures, a state association shall include territorial, local, or county psychological associations, and in cases of Canadian members of the Association, provincial psychological associations.

the National Register of Health Service Providers in Psychology, and/or (f) other appropriate parties.

3.3.6 Other Parties Informed of the Complaint. The Director may inform such other parties as have been informed of any matter reviewed under these Rules of the final disposition of that matter. Parties with knowledge of a matter may have been informed by the Committee, the Director, the respondent, or the complainant.

3.3.7 Notification in Cases That Have Been Converted. In any cases that have been converted under Part II, Subsections 7.3 or 7.4, the complainant and other persons informed of the complaint shall be notified of final disposition, including the fact that there has been a stipulated resignation, as set forth in Part IV, Subsections 12.1.2 and 12.2.1 and Part V, Subsection 7.6.5.

3.3.8 Disclosure of Fact of Investigation. The Director may disclose to any of the entities enumerated in Subsection 3.3.5 (a)–(f) of this part the fact that an individual is under ethical investigation in cases deemed to be serious threats to the public welfare (as determined by a two-thirds vote of the Committee), but only when to do so before final adjudication appears necessary to protect the public.

3.3.9 Notification of Additional Parties at the Request of Respondent. The Director may notify such additional parties of the final disposition as are requested by the respondent.

3.3.10 Notification of Loss of Membership Upon Written Request. The Director shall inform any person who submits a written inquiry concerning a psychologist that a former member has lost membership due to unethical behavior or that an individual's membership was voided because it was obtained on the basis of false or fraudulent information. The notification will not include actions that were already decided or were under the scrutiny of the Committee prior to June 1, 1996, or stipulated resignations unless so stipulated.

3.4 Initiation of Legal Action Constitutes Waiver. Initiation of a legal action against the Association or any of its agents, officers, directors, employees, or volunteers concerning any matters considered or actions taken by the Ethics Committee or Director shall constitute a waiver by the person initiating such action of any interest in confidentiality recognized in these Rules or other organic documents of the Association with respect to the subject matter of the legal action.

3.5 Communication for Investigation or Other Functions. Nothing in this section shall prevent the Director from communicating any information (including information from the respondent, complainant, or a witness) to the respondent, complainant, witnesses, or other sources of information to the extent necessary to facilitate the performance of any functions set forth in these Rules and Procedures.

4. Records

4.1 Confidentiality of Ethics Files. Files of the Committee related to investigation and adjudication of cases shall be confidential, within the limitations of Section 3 of this part, and shall be maintained consistent with these Rules and Procedures.

4.2 Investigation Files. Investigation records containing personally identifiable information shall be maintained for at least five years after a matter is closed.

4.3 Files Involving Loss of Membership. In cases in which members have lost membership, records shall be maintained indefinitely, except as provided in Subsection 4.4 of this part.

4.4 Readmission or Death of a Member. Records concerning members whom the Association has readmitted to membership or determined to be deceased shall be maintained for at least five years after that determination was made.

4.5 Records for Educative Purposes. Nothing in these Rules and Procedures shall preclude the Committee from maintaining records in a secure place for archival or record keeping purposes, or from using or publishing information concerning ethics matters for educative purposes without identifying individuals involved.

5. Jurisdiction

5.1 Persons. The Committee has jurisdiction over individual members (to include fellows), associate members, and applicants for membership in the American Psychological Association. The Committee shall also have jurisdiction over student affiliates, but only to the extent that the conduct at issue is not under the direct supervision of the student's educational program or of a training site that is officially approved by the program as part of the student's supervised training.[6]

5.2 Subject Matter. The Committee has jurisdiction to achieve its objectives and perform those functions for which it is authorized in these Rules and Procedures and other organic documents of the Association.

5.3 Time Limits for Complaints and Show Cause Notices

5.3.1 Complaints by Members. Except as provided in Subsections 5.3.5 and 5.3.6 of this part, the Committee may consider complaints brought by members of the Association against other members only if the complaint is received less than three years after the alleged conduct either occurred or was discovered by the complainant.

5.3.2 Complaints by Nonmembers and Student Affiliates. Except as provided in Subsections 5.3.5 and 5.3.6 of this part, the Committee may consider complaints brought by nonmembers and student affiliates only if the complaint is received less than five years after the alleged conduct either occurred or was discovered by the complainant.

---

[6]Whether an individual is a member of the Association is determined according to the Bylaws, Association Rules, and other pertinent organic documents of the Association. Under the current rules, nonpayment of dues results in discontinuation of membership only after two consecutive calendar years during which dues to the Association have remained unpaid. For a copy of the relevant sections of the current Bylaws and Association Rules, contact the APA Ethics Office. For purposes of these Rules and Procedures, high school and foreign affiliates are not members of the Association.

5.3.3 Sua Sponte Complaints. Except as provided in Subsection 7.4 of this part, the Committee may initiate a *sua sponte* complaint under Part V of these Rules and Procedures only if it does so, or has provided the notice specified in Subsection 5.6.2 of this part, less than 1 year after it discovered the alleged unethical conduct and less than 10 years after the alleged conduct occurred, except that whether or not such periods have expired, the Committee may initiate a *sua sponte* complaint less than 1 year after it discovered that any of the following actions had become final and less than 10 years after the following alleged conduct occurred: (a) a felony conviction, (b) a finding of malpractice by a duly authorized tribunal, (c) expulsion or suspension from a state association for unethical conduct, or (d) revocation, suspension, or surrender of a license or certificate, or deregistration for ethical violations by a state or local board or similar entity, or while ethical proceedings before such board were pending.

5.3.4 Show Cause Notices. The Committee may issue a show cause notice under Part IV of these Rules and Procedures only if it does so, or has provided the notice specified in Subsection 5.6.2 of this part, less than 1 year after the date it discovered that the applicable predicate for use of show cause procedures (i.e., an event described in Part IV, Section 1) had become final and less than 10 years after the alleged conduct occurred, except this latter time limit shall be 20 years in any matter involving an offense against a minor.

5.3.5 Exceptions to Time Limits for Complaints by Members and Nonmembers

5.3.5.1 Threshold Criteria. Any complaint not received within the time limits set forth in this section shall not be considered unless, with respect to complaints subject to Subsections 5.3.1 and 5.3.2 of this part, the Chair and Director (with the vote of the Vice Chair if agreement is not reached by the Chair and Director) determine that each of the following criteria is met:

5.3.5.1.1 The behavior alleged involved one of the following: sexual misconduct; felony conviction; insurance fraud; plagiarism; noncooperation; blatant, intentional misrepresentation; or other behavior likely to cause substantial harm;

5.3.5.1.2 The complaint was received less than 10 years after the alleged conduct occurred.

5.3.5.2 Determination to Supersede Applicable Time Limit. Where the Chair and Director have determined (with the vote of the Vice Chair if agreement is not reached by the Chair and Director) that the threshold criteria in Subsection 5.3.5.1 are met, the applicable limit shall be superseded.

5.3.6 Conduct Outside the Time Limits. The Committee may consider evidence of conduct outside these time limits in connection with the commencement, investigation, review, or disposition of a matter involving conduct that is within the applicable time limits. However, the Committee may impose sanctions only for conduct that occurred within the time limits. In order for a sanction to be imposed for conduct occurring outside the time limits, the Chair and Director must decide to supersede the time limits applicable to that conduct as stated in Subsection 5.3.5 of this part.

5.3.7 Reopened Investigations. In a matter reopened under Part II, Section 6, the investigation shall be considered within the time limits as long as the complaint in the original matter was received, or the original investigation was initiated, in a timely manner or a decision was made to supersede the time limit under Part II, Subsection 5.3.5. The Committee may not proceed with such an investigation, however, if the new evidence is received more than 10 years after the date the alleged unethical behavior occurred (except that this time limit shall be 20 years in any case that was initiated as or converted to a show cause case and involves an offense against a minor).

5.4 Resignation Barred. Except as provided in Subsection 11.4 of this part of these Rules, no one under the scrutiny of the Committee will be allowed to resign from the Association either by letter of resignation, by nonpayment of dues, or otherwise.

5.5 Concurrent Litigation. Civil or criminal litigation involving members shall not bar action by the Committee; the Committee may proceed or may stay the ethics process during the course of litigation. Delay in conducting the investigation by the Committee during the pendency of civil or criminal proceedings shall not constitute waiver of jurisdiction.

5.6 Other Concurrent Disciplinary Proceedings

5.6.1 Concurrent Jurisdiction. Disciplinary proceedings or action by another body or tribunal shall not bar action by the Committee; the Committee may proceed or may stay the ethics process during the course of such proceedings. Delay in conducting the investigation by the Committee during the pendency of such proceedings shall not constitute a waiver of jurisdiction. Where the Committee learns that disciplinary action by another authorized tribunal has been stayed, such stay shall neither require nor preclude action by the Committee. When another body or tribunal has investigated the same allegations and found no merit to the allegations, the Ethics Committee may, in its discretion, decide not to open a matter or, if a matter has already been opened, the Ethics Committee may close the matter.

5.6.2 Nonfinal Disciplinary Action by Another Body. The Chair, Vice Chair, and Director may decide not to open a *sua sponte* or show cause case when a state or local board or similar entity has taken disciplinary action against an Association member if the action is either not final or the member has not completed all directives, probation, or other requirements and if the behavior at issue is not likely to result in expulsion from the Association. If this decision is made, the member will be notified that the matter is under the scrutiny of the Committee, that the member will be monitored until completion of actions required by the state or local board or similar entity, that failure to complete the action may result in further action by the Committee, and that completion of such requirements may result in the Committee taking no further action.

5.7 Referral and Retention of Jurisdiction. The Committee may at any time refer a matter to another recognized tribunal for appropriate action. If a case is referred to another tribunal, the Committee may retain jurisdiction and consider the matter independently under these Rules and Procedures.

6. *Reopening a Closed Case*

If significant new evidence of unethical conduct comes to the attention of the Committee after a matter has been closed, the investigation may be reopened and acted upon under regular procedures. If, in the judgment of the Director, such information is furnished, the new evidence shall be submitted to the Committee, which may reopen the investigation if it agrees that the criteria listed below are satisfied. To be considered under this rule, new evidence must meet each of the following criteria:

6.1 The evidence was brought to the attention of the Committee after the investigation was closed;

6.2 The evidence could not with reasonable diligence have been brought to the attention of the Committee before the investigation was closed;

6.3 The evidence was provided to the Committee in a timely manner following its discovery;

6.4 The evidence would probably produce a different result.

7. *Choice and Conversion of Procedures*

7.1 Choice of Procedures. Where a case might be adjudicated according to the show cause procedures in Part IV of these Rules and Procedures, the Chair and the Director shall determine whether to proceed under Part IV or Part V of these Rules and Procedures.

7.2 Conversion of Show Cause Action to *Sua Sponte* Action. The Chair and the Director may convert a proceeding begun by show cause procedures under Part IV to a *sua sponte* action under Part V. In the event of such conversion, the complaint shall be deemed filed in a timely manner if the show cause proceeding was initiated in a timely fashion.

7.3 Conversion to Show Cause Action. Where the predicates for use of show cause procedures stated in Part IV, Section 1 are present, the Chair and the Director may convert a proceeding begun as a *sua sponte*, member, or nonmember complaint under Part V to a show cause proceeding under Part IV if the predicates are based on some or all of the same underlying conduct as was the basis for the original proceeding. In such event, the show cause proceeding shall be deemed initiated in a timely manner as long as the original proceeding was commenced within the time limits applicable to that proceeding or a decision was made to supersede the time limit under Part II, Subsection 5.3.5.

7.4 Conversion of Action Initiated by a Complainant to a *Sua Sponte* Action. The Chair and the Director may convert a proceeding commenced following a complaint submitted by a member or nonmember (including a proceeding in which the complaint is withdrawn) into a *sua sponte* action under Part V, Subsection 2.2. The action will be deemed filed in a timely manner as long as the member or nonmember complaint was received within the time limits applicable to the initial complaint or a decision was made to supersede the time limit in Part II, Subsection 5.3.5.

8. Correspondence and Documentation

8.1 Use of Correspondence. The Committee shall conduct as much of its business as is practical through correspondence, including telecopied information.

8.2 Personal Response. Although the respondent has the right to consult with an attorney concerning all phases of the ethics process, the respondent must respond to charges and recommendations of the Ethics Committee personally and not through legal counsel or another third party. If the respondent shows good cause as to why he or she cannot respond personally, the Director may waive this requirement.

8.3 Transcription of Audiotapes, Videotapes, and Similar Data Compilations. It shall be the responsibility of the individual or entity submitting to the Committee an audiotape, videotape, or similar data compilation to provide an accurate transcription of the information it contains. The Director may reject any audiotape, videotape, or similar data compilation provided unaccompanied by a transcription as required in this subsection unless and until such transcription is provided.

8.4 Service of Documents. For purposes of notice, service shall be made by delivery to the respondent or the respondent's attorney or by mail or common carrier to the respondent or the respondent's attorney at the respondent's or attorney's last known address. Delivery within this rule means handing the correspondence to the respondent or the attorney or leaving it at the respondent's office or place of abode or the attorney's office with a receptionist, secretary, clerk, or other person in charge thereof, or, if there is no one in charge, leaving it in a mailbox or a conspicuous place at that address. Service by mail is complete upon mailing. Where, after good faith efforts, the Committee has been unable to locate the respondent, it may give notice by publishing in a newspaper of general circulation in the respondent's last known place of domicile a notice to contact the Ethics Office concerning an important matter.

8.5 Material From the Public Domain. The Committee may consult authoritative resources from the public domain (e.g., the Directory of the American Psychological Association and the National Register of Health Service Providers in Psychology) without providing this material to the respondent.

9. Failure to Cooperate With Ethics Process

Members are required to cooperate fully and in a timely fashion with the ethics process. Failure to cooperate shall not prevent continuation of any proceedings and itself constitutes a violation of the Ethics Code that may warrant being expelled from the Association.

10. Board of Directors' Standing Hearing Panel

The President of the Association shall appoint members of the Standing Hearing Panel. Standing Hearing Panel members shall serve a three-year renewable term. The Standing Hearing Panel shall consist of at least 30 members at least 5 of whom shall be public members, and the remainder shall be members of the Association in good standing and shall not include any present members of the Ethics Committee.

11. Available Sanctions

On the basis of circumstances that aggravate or mitigate the culpability of the member, including prior sanctions, directives, or educative letters from the Association or state or local boards or similar entities, a sanction more or less severe, respectively, than would be warranted on the basis of the factors set forth below, may be appropriate.

11.1 Reprimand. Reprimand is the appropriate sanction if there has been an ethics violation but the violation was not of a kind likely to cause harm to another person or to cause substantial harm to the profession and was not otherwise of sufficient gravity as to warrant a more severe sanction.

11.2 Censure. Censure is the appropriate sanction if there has been an ethics violation and the violation was of a kind likely to cause harm to another person, but the violation was not of a kind likely to cause substantial harm to another person or to the profession and was not otherwise of sufficient gravity as to warrant a more severe sanction.

11.3 Expulsion. Expulsion from membership is the appropriate sanction if there has been an ethics violation and the violation was of a kind likely to cause substantial harm to another person or the profession or was otherwise of sufficient gravity as to warrant such action.

11.4 Stipulated Resignation. Stipulated resignation may be offered by the Committee as follows:

11.4.1 At the time of the respondent's initial response to the show cause notice, contingent upon execution of an acceptable affidavit admitting responsibility for the violations charged, under Part IV, Subsection 12.1;

11.4.2 Following a Committee finding that the respondent has committed a violation of the Ethics Code or failed to show good cause why he or she should not be expelled, contingent on execution of an acceptable affidavit and approval by the Board of Directors, under Part IV, Subsection 12.2, or Part V, Subsection 7.6.

12. Available Directives

12.1 Cease and Desist Order. Such a directive requires the respondent to cease and desist specified unethical behavior(s).

12.2 Other Corrective Actions. The Committee may require such other corrective actions as may be necessary to remedy a violation, protect the interests of the Association, or protect the public. Such a directive may not include a requirement that the respondent make a monetary payment to the Association or persons injured by the conduct.

12.3 Supervision Requirement. Such a directive requires that the respondent engage in supervision.

12.4 Education, Training, or Tutorial Requirement. Such a directive requires that the respondent engage in education, training, or a tutorial.

12.5 Evaluation and/or Treatment Requirement. Such a directive requires that the respondent be evaluated to determine the possible need for treatment and/or, if dysfunction has been established, obtain treatment appropriate to that dysfunction.

12.6 Probation. Such a directive requires monitoring of the respondent by the Committee to ensure compliance with the Ethics Committee's mandated directives during the period of those directives.

13. Matters Requiring the Concurrence of the Chair of the Committee and Director of the Ethics Office

Whenever matters entrusted by these Rules and Procedures to the Chair and Director require the concurrence of those officers before certain action may be taken, either officer in the event of disagreement may refer the matter to the Vice Chair, who together with the Chair and Director, shall make a final determination by majority vote.

Part III. Membership

1. Applications

1.1 Specific Jurisdiction. The Committee has the authority to investigate the preadmission scientific and professional ethics and conduct of all applicants for membership or student affiliation in the Association and to make recommendations as to whether an individual shall become a member or student affiliate. In addition, the Committee has the authority to consider all applications submitted by individuals who were previously denied admission as a result of unethical behavior and to make recommendations as to whether such an individual shall become a member or student affiliate. The Membership Committee shall transmit all applications on which there is an indication of possible preadmission unethical conduct and all applications from individuals who were previously denied admission as a result of unethical behavior or as a result of a recommendation by the Ethics Committee to the Director of the Ethics Office.

1.2 Procedures for Review. The Director shall transmit to the Committee a copy of the membership application and any other materials pertinent to the case. The Director shall take such steps, including contacting the applicant or other sources of information, as are necessary and appropriate to making a fair determination. Upon review, the Committee may recommend to the Membership Committee that the application be granted or to the Board of Directors that the application be denied. If a recommendation is made to deny the application, the applicant shall be informed of the basis for that recommendation and shall have 30 days to submit a written response for consideration by the Board of Directors.

2. Applications for Readmission

2.1 Specific Jurisdiction. The Ethics Committee has the authority to review and make recommendations concerning all applications for readmission by persons who have lost membership as a result of unethical behavior or whose membership was voided because it was obtained on the basis of false or fraudulent information. The Membership Committee shall transmit all such applications for readmission to the Director of the Ethics Office.

2.2 Elapsed Time for Review. Applications for readmission by members who have lost membership due to unethical behavior (including submission of false or fraudulent information in a membership application) shall be considered by the Committee only after five years have elapsed from the date of that action. Applications for readmission by members who have been permitted to resign shall be considered only after the stipulated period or, where no period has been stipulated, three years have elapsed.

2.3 Procedures for Review. The Director shall transmit to the Committee a summary of the application for readmission and the record of the previous case against the former member. In all cases, the ex-member must show that he or she is technically or ethically qualified and has satisfied any conditions upon readmission established by the Board. The Committee shall make one of the following recommendations to the Membership Committee and, as it deems appropriate, shall provide the rationale therefor.

2.3.1 Readmit. Recommend that the former member be readmitted;

2.3.2 Deny Readmission. Recommend that readmission be denied;

2.3.3 Defer Readmission. Recommend that the application for readmission be deferred until certain conditions have been met;

2.3.4 Investigate Further. Charge the Director to investigate issues specified by the Committee and to place the matter before the Committee at a future date.

3. Allegations That Membership Was Obtained Under False or Fraudulent Pretenses

3.1 Specific Jurisdiction. The Committee has the authority to investigate allegations that membership was obtained on the basis of false or fraudulent information and to take appropriate action. The Membership Committee shall transmit all such allegations to the Director of the Ethics Office.

3.2 Procedures for Review. The respondent will be given notice of the allegations that membership was obtained on the basis of false or fraudulent information, a copy of any evidence relating to these allegations that is submitted to the Committee, and an opportunity to respond in writing. The Director may take any other steps, such as contacting other sources of information, that are considered necessary and appropriate to making a fair determination in the circumstances of the case. The Director shall transmit to the Committee a copy of the membership application and any other materials pertinent to the case.

3.3 Committee's Recommendation. Upon completion of this review, the Committee may recommend to the Board of Directors that it void the election to membership in the Association of any person who obtained membership on the basis of false or fraudulent information.

3.4 Procedures Subsequent to Committee's Recommendation to Void Membership. If the respondent does not accept the Committee's recommendation, the respondent shall, within 30 days of receipt of the recommendation, either submit a written response to the Board of Directors, request a formal hearing in writing, or request an independent adjudication in writing and provide a written rationale for nonacceptance. The respondent's failure to respond within 30 days after notification shall be deemed acceptance of the Committee's recommendation and a waiver of the right to a formal hearing or an independent adjudication. If a written response is submitted, the Ethics Committee shall have 30 days to reply in a written statement to the Board. If a formal hearing is requested, it shall be conducted according to the procedures explained in Part V, Subsections 10.2 through 10.3.4 of these Rules and Procedures. If an independent adjudication is requested, it shall be conducted according to the procedures explained in Part V, Subsections 9.2.2 through 9.2.7 and Subsections 10.3 through 10.3.4.

3.5 Action by the Board of Directors. Within 180 days after receiving the record, the Committee's recommendation, any written response and statement described in Subsection 3.4, above, or any recommendation from a Hearing Committee or Independent Adjudication Panel, the Board of Directors shall vote whether to void the respondent's membership or not.

Part IV. Show Cause Procedures Based Upon Actions by Other Recognized Tribunals

1. Predicates for Use of Show Cause Procedures

1.1 Felony or Equivalent Offense. If a member has been convicted of a felony (including any felony as defined by state/provincial law and any other criminal offense with a possible term of incarceration exceeding one year) and such conviction is not under appeal, the show cause process may be used, if determined by the Chair and the Director to be appropriate.

1.2 Expulsion, Suspension, Unlicensure, Decertification, or Other Actions. If one of the following actions has been taken and is not under appeal, the show cause process may be used, if determined by the Chair and the Director to be appropriate: (a) a member has been expelled or suspended from an affiliated state or regional psychological association; (b) a member has been denied a license, certificate, or registration, has been unlicensed, decertified, or deregistered, has had a license, certificate, or registration revoked or suspended by a state or local board or similar entity, or has voluntarily surrendered a license or certificate of registration as a result of pending allegations. The show cause procedures may also be used if a state or local board or similar entity has taken any of the actions specified in (a) or (b) above and has then in any way stayed or postponed that action.

2. Notice by the Committee and Response by Respondent

The respondent shall be notified by the Director that he or she has been barred from resigning membership in the Association (subject only to the terms of Section 12 of this part) and, on the basis of Part IV of these Rules and Procedures, will be afforded 60 days in which to show good cause as to why he or she should not be expelled from membership in the Association.

3. Showing by Respondent That Prior Proceeding Lacked Due Process

In addition to a response to the substance of the charges under Section 2 of this part, the respondent may seek within the 60-day period to show that the other recognized tribunal did not follow fair procedure. If the Committee finds merit to this contention, it may exercise its discretion under Part II, Subsection 7.2 of these Rules and convert the matter to a *sua sponte* action under Part V, or it may dismiss the complaint.

4. Investigation

The Committee may conduct a further investigation, including seeking additional information from the respondent or others or requesting that the respondent appear in person. Any evidence not obtained directly from the respondent and relied upon by the Committee in connection with its review and recommendation shall first have been provided to the respondent, who shall have been afforded not less than 15 days to respond thereto in writing.

5. Failure to Respond

If the 60-day period expires without receipt of a response, the respondent shall be notified that unless a response is received within 30 days, the

Committee members may review the matter and vote by mail. If no response is received, the Committee may vote by mail to take one of the actions specified in Subsection 6 of this part.

6. Review and Recommendation by the Committee Following a Response

Upon receipt of the respondent's response and upon conclusion of any necessary further investigation, or the expiration of 60 days without response, the case shall be reviewed by the Ethics Committee. Members of the Ethics Committee and Ethics Committee Associates may be assigned to review and summarize the case. Members and Associates may also be assigned to participate on a panel to review the case and make a preliminary recommendation prior to review by the full Ethics Committee. Ethics Committee Associates may also attend and participate in the full Committee meetings, but shall not vote on the full Committee's disposition of a case. When review of a case has been completed, the Committee shall vote to take one of the following actions:

6.1 Remand

6.2 Dismiss the Matter

6.3 Recommend One of the Following Actions to the Board of Directors:

6.3.1 Reprimand or Censure, With or Without Directives. The Committee may recommend that the respondent be reprimanded or censured, with or without one or more directives.

6.3.2 Expulsion. The Committee may recommend that the respondent be expelled from the Association; or, the Committee may recommend the sanction of stipulated resignation, under the procedure in Subsection 12.2 of this part.

7. Notification of Respondent

The Director shall notify the respondent of the Committee's recommendation and shall provide the respondent the opportunity to file a written request with the Board of Directors.

8. Respondent's Response to Recommendation

Within 15 days of receipt of notification of the Committee's recommendation, the respondent may file a written response with the Board of Directors. The response should be mailed to the Ethics Office.

9. Committee's Statement

The Ethics Committee shall have 15 days from the time it receives the respondent's written response, or from the time such response was due, to file a written statement, if any. A copy will be provided to the respondent.

10. Respondent's Final Response

Within 15 days of receipt of the Ethics Committee's statement, if any, the respondent may submit to the Director a written response to that statement.

11. Review by the Board of Directors

Within 180 days after receiving the record, the Committee's recommendation, any written response by the respondent, any written statement by the Committee, and any final response from the respondent, the Board of Directors shall vote whether to accept from the Committee's recommended sanction, to issue a different sanction, or to dismiss the case. The Board may select a sanction more or less severe than that recommended by the Committee, or it may remand the matter to the Ethics Committee for further consideration.

12. Stipulated Resignation

12.1 Stipulated Resignation With Admission of Violation in Respondent's Initial Response to the Show Cause Notice

12.1.1 Respondent's Offer of Stipulated Resignation With Admission of Violation. In his or her initial response to the Committee's notice to show cause under Section 2 of this part, the respondent may offer to resign membership in the Association with admission of violation. Such an offer must include a statement of intent to execute an affidavit acceptable to the Committee (a) admitting the violation underlying the criminal conviction, expulsion, unlicensure, decertification, or deregistration, and (b) resigning membership in the Association.

12.1.2 Director's Response and Proposed Affidavit of Stipulated Resignation. When the respondent makes such an offer, the Director will forward to the respondent a proposed affidavit of stipulated resignation. Such stipulations shall include the extent to which the stipulated resignation and its basis shall be disclosed and a minimum period of time, after resignation, during which the resigned member shall be ineligible to reapply for membership.

12.1.3 Acceptance by Respondent. Within 30 days of receipt, the respondent may resign membership in the Association by signing and having notarized the proposed affidavit and returning it to the Committee. Resignation shall be effective upon the Committee's timely receipt of the signed notarized affidavit.

12.1.4 Rejection by Respondent. If the member fails to sign, have notarized, and return an acceptable affidavit within 30 days or formally notifies the Committee of rejection of the proposed affidavit, the offer of stipulated resignation shall be deemed rejected. The respondent shall be afforded an additional 30 days within which to supplement his or her response to the Committee's show cause notice. The matter shall then be resolved according to the applicable procedures in this part. All materials submitted by the respondent shall be part of the file to be considered by the Committee and/or the Board of Directors in connection with the case.

12.1.5 Availability of Stipulated Resignation With Admission of Violation. Stipulated resignation with admission of violation is available only at the time and in the manner set forth in this section. Unless stipulated resignation with admission of violation is accomplished at the time in the manner stated in this section, respondents may not resign while under scrutiny of the Ethics Committee except as stated in Subsection 12.2 of this part.

12.2 Stipulated Resignation After Review and Recommendation by the Committee. In lieu of the recommendations set forth in Section 6 of this part, with the agreement of the respondent, the Committee may recommend that the respondent be permitted to resign from the Association under stipulations stated by the Committee, according to the following procedure:

12.2.1 Offer of Stipulated Resignation by Committee. When the Committee finds that another body has taken one of the actions specified in Part IV, Section 1 against a member, the Committee may offer, contingent upon approval by the Board of Directors, the respondent the opportunity to resign from the Association under mutually agreed upon stipulations. Such stipulations shall include the extent to which the stipulated resignation and its basis shall be disclosed and a minimum period of time, after resignation, during which the resigned member shall be ineligible to reapply for membership. The Committee may, in its discretion, also vote to recommend to the Board and inform the respondent of an alternative sanction chosen from among Subsections 11.1–11.3 of Part II of these Rules in the event the respondent does not accept the offer of stipulated resignation.

12.2.2 Notification of Respondent. In such cases, the respondent shall be notified, in writing, of the Committee's offer of stipulated resignation and that he or she may accept the Committee's offer within 30 days of receipt. The respondent shall also be notified of any alternative recommended sanction.

12.2.3 Acceptance by Respondent. Within 30 days, the respondent may accept the offer of stipulated resignation by signing a notarized affidavit of resignation acceptable to both the respondent and the Committee and forward the signed notarized affidavit to the Committee. Such resignation shall become effective only with the approval of the Board, as set forth in this section.

12.2.4 Transmittal to Board of Directors. If the respondent accepts the stipulated resignation, the Committee shall submit a copy of the affidavit of resignation, with the record in the matter and the rationale for recommending stipulated resignation on the terms set forth in the affidavit, to the Board of Directors.

12.2.5 Action by Board of Directors. Within 180 days, the Board of Directors shall take one of the following actions:

12.2.5.1 Acceptance of Stipulated Resignation. The Board of Directors shall accept the respondent's resignation on the terms stated in the affidavit of resignation, unless it is persuaded that to do so would not be in the best interest of the Association and/or of the public. If the resignation is accepted by the Board, the Director shall so notify the respondent.

12.2.5.2 Reprimand or Censure. The Board may reject the stipulated resignation and impose a lesser sanction (reprimand or censure with or without directives). If the Board selects this option, the respondent shall be so notified and shall have 30 days to submit a written request seeking reconsideration of the Board's decision. If no such request is submitted, the Board's decision shall become final. If a request for reconsideration is submitted, the Board shall choose from the options set forth in Subsection 12.2.5 (including adherence to its prior decision).

12.2.5.3 Remand to the Committee. The Board may choose to reject the affidavit of resignation and remand the matter to the Committee for further consideration. If the Board selects this alternative, the Director shall so notify the respondent and the Committee shall then reconsider the matter.

12.2.6 Rejection of Stipulated Resignation by Respondent. If the respondent fails within 30 days to accept the recommended resolution, or formally notifies the Committee of rejection of the offer of stipulated resignation within the 30-day period, the offer of stipulated resignation shall be deemed rejected. The Committee shall reconsider the matter or, if an alternative recommended sanction has previously been identified by the Committee, such alternative recommended sanction shall automatically become the recommended sanction. The Director shall notify the respondent of the recommendation and of his or her opportunity to file written responses with the Board of Directors, as stated in Section 8 of this part. Sections 8–11 of this part shall also apply.

Part V. Complaints Alleging Violation of the Ethics Code

1. Initiation of Actions

Ethics proceedings against a member are initiated by the filing of a complaint or, in the case of a *sua sponte* action, by the issuance of a letter notifying the respondent that a *sua sponte* action has been commenced.

2. Complaints

2.1 Complaints Submitted by Members or Nonmembers. Complaints may be submitted by members or nonmembers of the Association.

2.2 *Sua Sponte* Action. When a member appears to have violated the Association's Ethics Code, the Committee may proceed on its own initiative. The Committee may, at any time, exercise its discretion to discontinue a *sua sponte* action. If the Committee does so, the respondent shall be so notified.

2.3 *Sua Sponte* Action Based Upon a Member's Filing of a Capricious or Malicious Complaint. To prevent abuse of the ethics process, the Committee is empowered to bring charges itself against a complainant if the initial complaint is judged by two thirds of Committee members voting to be (a) frivolous and (b) intended to harm the respondent rather than to protect the public. The filing of such a complaint constitutes a violation of the Ethics Code.

2.4 Countercomplaints. The Committee will not consider a complaint from a respondent member against a complainant member during the course of its investigation and resolution of the initial complaint. Rather, the Committee shall study all sides of the matter leading to the first complaint and consider countercharges only after the initial complaint is finally resolved. The Committee may waive this procedure by a vote of at least two thirds of the voting Committee members and consider both complaints simultaneously.

2.5 Anonymous Complaints. The Committee shall not act upon anonymous complaints. If material in the public domain is provided anonymously, the Committee may choose to consider such material in connection with a *sua sponte* matter or other complaint or may initiate a *sua sponte* action but only if the respondent has been provided with a copy of the material and afforded an opportunity to respond to the material.

2.6 Complaints Against Nonmembers. If the complaint does not involve an individual within the jurisdiction of the Committee, the Director shall inform the complainant and may suggest that the complainant contact another agency or association that may have jurisdiction.

2.7 Consecutive Complaints. When a complaint is lodged against a member with respect to whom a case involving similar alleged behavior was previously closed, materials in the prior case may be considered in connection with the new case and may be considered as evidence as long as the Ethics Committee and/or the Board of Directors is informed of the final disposition of the original case.

2.8 Simultaneous Complaints. When more than one complaint is simultaneously pending against the same member, the Committee may choose to combine the cases or to keep them separate. In the event the cases are combined, the Committee shall take reasonable steps to ensure that the legitimate confidentiality interests of any complainant, witness, or respondent are not compromised by combination.

3. Procedures for Filing Complaints

A complaint by a member or nonmember shall be comprised of

3.1 A completed APA Ethics Complaint Form;

3.2 Such releases as are required by the Committee;

3.3 A waiver by the complainant of any right to subpoena from APA or its agents for the purposes of private civil litigation any documents or information concerning the case.[7]

3.4 For purposes of determining time limits, a complaint shall be considered filed with APA as soon as a completed complaint form has been received by the Ethics Office. A deficiency or omission in the preparation of the complaint form may, at the discretion of the Director, be disregarded for purposes of determining compliance with time limits.

4. Preliminary Evaluation of Complaints by the Director

The Director shall review each complaint to determine if jurisdictional criteria are met and if it can be determined whether cause for action exists.

4.1 Lack of Jurisdiction. If jurisdictional criteria are not satisfied, the matter shall be closed and the complainant so notified.

4.2 Information Insufficient to Determine Jurisdiction.

4.2.1 Request for Supplementation of Complaint. If the information is not sufficient to determine whether jurisdictional criteria are met, the Director shall so inform the complainant, who will be given 30 days from receipt of the request to supplement the complaint.

4.2.2 Consequences of Failure to Supplement Complaint. If no response is received from the complainant within 30 days from receipt of the request, the matter may be closed. If at a later date the complainant shows good cause for delay and demonstrates that jurisdictional criteria can be met, the supplemented complaint shall be considered.

4.3 Process With Respect to Superseding Applicable Time Limit

4.3.1 Consideration by Chair and Director. If a complaint otherwise within the jurisdiction of the Ethics Committee appears to have been filed outside the applicable time limit, the Chair and the Director will determine whether the criteria set forth in Part II, Subsection 5.3.5 appear to be satisfied. If they agree that the criteria do not appear to be satisfied, the matter will be closed, unless there are other allegations that are filed in a timely manner, in which case processing of the timely allegations continues under Section 5, below. If they agree that the criteria appear to be satisfied, the Director will contact the respondent according to the procedure in Subsection 4.3.2, below. If they are not in agreement on whether or not those criteria appear to be satisfied, the Vice Chair shall review the matter and cast the deciding vote.

4.3.2 Response by Respondent Where Criteria Appear To Be Satisfied. If a determination is made according to Subsection 4.3.1 above that the criteria of Part II, Subsection 5.3.5 appear to be satisfied, the Director shall notify the respondent and provide the respondent with a copy of the complaint and any other materials the Director deems appropriate. The

---

[7]This waiver is required to help assure participants in the APA ethics process, including complainants, that the process will not be inappropriately used to gain an advantage in other litigation.

respondent shall have 30 days from receipt of these materials to address whether the criteria of Part II, Subsection 5.3.5 are met.

4.3.3 Determination by Chair and Director. If the respondent does not provide a response under Subsection 4.3.2, above, the decision made under Subsection 4.3.1, above, shall become final. In any case in which the respondent provides a response, the Chair and the Director shall consider whether the criteria set forth in Part II, Subsection 5.3.5 are satisfied, based upon any materials provided by the complainant and respondent, and any other information available to the Chair and the Director. If they agree that the criteria are not satisfied, the matter will be closed, unless there are other allegations that are filed in a timely manner, in which case processing of the timely allegations continues under Section 5, below. If they agree that the criteria are satisfied, processing continues under Section 5, below. If they are not in agreement on whether or not those criteria are satisfied, the Vice Chair shall review the matter and cast the deciding vote.

5. Evaluation of Complaints by Chair and Director

All complaints not closed by the Director under Section 4 of this part shall be reviewed by the Chair and the Director to determine whether cause for action by the Ethics Committee exists.

5.1 Cause for Action Defined. Cause for action shall exist when the respondent's alleged actions and/or omissions, if proved, would in the judgment of the decision maker constitute a breach of ethics. For purposes of determining whether cause for action exists, incredible, speculative, and/or internally inconsistent allegations may be disregarded.

5.2 Information Insufficient to Determine Cause for Action

5.2.1 Request for Supplementation of Complaint. If the information is not sufficient to determine whether a case should be opened, the Director may so inform the complainant, who will be given 30 days from receipt of the request to supplement the complaint. The Chair and Director may additionally, or in the alternative, commence a preliminary investigation under Subsection 5.3 of this part.

5.2.2 Consequences of Failure to Supplement Complaint. If no response is received from the complainant within 30 days, the matter may be closed. If at a later date the complainant shows good cause for delay and responds to the request for supplementation, the supplemented complaint shall be considered.

5.3 Preliminary Investigation Due to Insufficient Information. If the Chair and Director agree that they lack sufficient information to determine whether a case should be opened, in either a case initiated by a complainant or in a *sua sponte* action, a preliminary investigation may be initiated.

5.3.1 Notification to Respondent. If a preliminary investigation is opened, the Director shall so inform the respondent in writing. The Director will include a copy of all evidence in the file; a copy of the APA Ethics Code; the Committee's Rules and Procedures; and a statement that information submitted by the respondent shall become a part of the record and can be used if further proceedings ensue.

5.3.2 Time for Respondent Response. The respondent shall have 30 days after receipt of the notification of a preliminary investigation to file an initial response.

5.3.3 Information From Other Sources. Additional information may be requested from the complainant, respondent, or any other appropriate source. The Committee will not rely upon information submitted by such sources unless it has been shared with the respondent and the respondent has been afforded an opportunity to respond thereto.

5.3.4 Action if There Continues to Be Insufficient Information. At the conclusion of the preliminary investigation, if the Director and Chair determine that they still lack evidence sufficient to determine whether cause for action exists, the matter shall be closed.

5.4 Determination of Cause for Action. If the Chair and Director agree that cause for action exists, they shall consider whether to open a formal case under Subsection 5.5, below. If the Chair and Director agree that cause for action does not exist, the matter shall be closed. If the Chair and Director disagree on whether or not there is cause for action by the Committee, the matter shall be reviewed by the Vice Chair, who will cast the deciding vote.

5.5 Decision to Open a Case. In any case in which the determination has been made that cause for action exists, the Chair and Director shall consider whether (a) there is a reasonable basis to believe the alleged violation cannot be proved by a preponderance of the evidence and (b) the allegations would constitute only minor or technical violations that would not warrant further action, have already been adequately addressed in another forum, or are likely to be corrected. If they agree that one or more of the conditions are met, the matter shall be closed. Otherwise, the matter shall be opened as a case.

5.6 Educative Letter. If a matter is closed under Sections 4 or 5 of this part, the Chair and Director may, if appropriate, send an educative letter to the respondent.

5.7 Reconsideration of Decision to Open. A matter not opened under either Subsection 5.4 or 5.5, above, may be reconsidered by the Committee only if it does so in accordance with Part II, Section 6.

5.8 Supplementary or Alternative Action. The Chair and Director may recommend that the complainant refer the complaint to an appropriate state psychological association, state board, regulatory agency, subsidiary body of the Association, or other appropriate entity, or they may make such referral on their own initiative. Such referral does not constitute a waiver of jurisdiction over the complaint provided that the Committee opens a formal case within 24 months from the date of referral.

6. Case Investigation

6.1 Issuance of Charge Letter and Response From Respondent

6.1.1 Charge Letter. If a case is opened, the Director shall so inform the respondent in a charge letter. The charge letter shall contain a concise description of the alleged behaviors at issue and identify the specific section(s) of the Ethics Code that the respondent is alleged to have violated. The Director shall enclose a copy of any completed Ethics Complaint Form and any materials submitted to date by the complainant or on the complainant's behalf that will be included in the record before the Committee; a copy of the APA Ethics Code and the Committee's Rules and Procedures; and a statement that information submitted by the respondent shall become a part of the record, and can be used if further proceedings ensue.

6.1.2 Significance of Charge Letter. A charge letter does not constitute or represent a finding that any unethical behavior has taken place, or that any allegations of the complaint are or are not likely to be found to be true.

6.1.3 Issuance of New Charge Letter to Conform to Evidence Discovered During Investigation. At any time prior to final resolution by the Committee, in order to make the charges conform to the evidence developed during the investigation, the Director and Chair may determine that a new charge letter should be issued setting forth ethical standard(s) and/ or describing alleged behaviors different from or in addition to those contained in the initial charge letter. In a *sua sponte* case, the date of issuance shall, for purposes of applicable time limits, be deemed to relate back to the date of the initial letter notifying the respondent that a *sua sponte* action has been initiated. The new charge letter shall in all other respects be treated exactly as an initial charge letter issued according to Subsection 6.1.1 of this part.

6.1.4 Time for Respondent's Response. The respondent shall have 30 days after receipt of the charge letter to file an initial response. Any request to extend the time for responding to the charge letter must be made in writing, within the 30 days, and must show good cause for an extension.

6.1.5 Personal Appearance. The Chair and Director may request the respondent to appear personally before the Committee. The respondent has no right to such an appearance.

6.2 Information From Other Sources. Additional information may be requested from the complainant, respondent, or any other appropriate source.

6.3 Referral to Committee. When, in the sole judgment of the Chair and Director, the investigation is complete, the case will be referred to the Committee for review and resolution. The Director shall notify the complainant and respondent that the matter has been referred to the Committee.

6.4 Documentation Subsequent to Investigation and Prior to Resolution by the Committee. Within 30 days after receipt of notification that the case is being referred to the Ethics Committee for review and resolution, the complainant and respondent may submit any additional information or documentation. Any materials submitted in a timely manner by the complainant or on the complainant's or respondent's behalf will be forwarded to the respondent. Within 15 days from receipt of those materials, the respondent may submit any additional information or documentation. All such materials submitted within these time limitations shall be included in the file to be reviewed by the Ethics Committee. Materials submitted outside of the time limit will not be included in the file materials relative to the ethics case and will not be reviewed by the Ethics Committee.

In the sole discretion of the Director, where good cause for noncompliance with these time limits is shown by the complainant or the respondent, the resolution of the case may be postponed until the next scheduled meeting of the Ethics Committee, and the information or documentation provided outside of the time limit may be included in the file materials to be reviewed by the Committee at that later time. In the sole discretion of the Director, in the event the respondent fails to comply with these time limits, the information or documentation provided outside of the time limits may be included in the file materials to be reviewed by the Committee and the matter maintained for resolution by the Committee as originally scheduled.

7. Review and Resolution by the Committee

The Ethics Committee may assign a member of the Committee or an Ethics Committee Associate to serve as a case monitor. The monitor may provide assistance to assure that an adequate record is prepared for Ethics Committee review and in such other respects as necessary to further the objectives of these Rules and Procedures.

Upon conclusion of the investigation, the case shall be reviewed by the Ethics Committee. Members of the Ethics Committee and Ethics Committee Associates may be assigned to review and summarize the case. Members and Associates may also be assigned to participate on a panel to review and make a preliminary recommendation prior to review by the full Ethics Committee. Ethics Committee Associates may also attend and participate in the full Ethics Committee meetings, but shall not vote on the full Committee's disposition of a case. When review of a case has been completed, the Ethics Committee shall vote to take one of the following actions described below: remand, dismiss the charges, recommend reprimand or censure, recommend expulsion, or recommend stipulated resignation. In addition to any of these actions, the Committee may vote to issue an educative letter. The Committee may choose to dismiss some charges but find violation and take disciplinary action on the basis of other charges in the charge letter. The respondent shall then be notified of the Committee's action, the ethical standard(s) involved, if any, the rationale for the Committee's decision, any sanction, and any directives.

7.1 Remand. The Committee may remand the matter to the Director for continued investigation or issuance of a new charge letter according to Subsection 6.1.3 of this part.

7.2 Dismiss the Charges

7.2.1 No Violation. The Committee may dismiss a charge if it finds the respondent has not violated the ethical standard as charged.

7.2.2 Violation Would Not Warrant Further Action. The Committee may dismiss the complaint if it concludes that any violation it might find (a) would constitute only a minor or technical violation that would not warrant further action, (b) has already been adequately addressed in another forum, or (c) is likely to be corrected.

7.2.3 Insufficient Evidence. The Committee may dismiss a charge if it finds insufficient evidence to support a finding of an ethics violation.

7.3 Educative Letter. Where the Committee deems it appropriate, the Committee may issue an educative letter, to be shared only with the respondent, concerning the behaviors charged or other matters. An educative letter may be issued whether the Committee dismisses the charges or recommends finding violations.

7.4 Recommend Reprimand or Censure. If the Committee find that the respondent has violated the Ethics Code, but decides that the nature of the respondent's behavior is such that the matter would be most appropriately resolved without recommending loss of membership, the Committee will recommend reprimand or censure of the respondent, with or without one or more available directives. See Part II, Subsections 11.1, 11.2, and Section 12.

7.5 Recommend Expulsion. The Committee may recommend expulsion if it concludes that there has been an ethics violation, that it was a kind likely to cause substantial harm to another person or the profession, or that it was otherwise of such gravity as to warrant this action.

7.6 Recommend Stipulated Resignation. In lieu of the other resolutions set forth in this section, with the agreement of the respondent, the Committee may recommend to the Board that the respondent be permitted to resign under stipulations set forth by the Committee, according to the following procedure:

7.6.1 Offer of Stipulated Resignation by the Committee. When the Committee finds that the respondent has committed a violation of the Ethics Code, the Committee may offer to enter into an agreement with the respondent, contingent upon approval by the Board of Directors, that the respondent shall resign from the Association under mutually agreed upon stipulations. Such stipulations shall include the extent to which the stipulated resignation and underlying ethics violation shall be disclosed and a minimum period of time after resignation during which the respondent shall be ineligible to reapply for membership. The Committee may also vote to recommend and inform the member of an alternative sanction chosen from among Subsections 11.1–11.3 of Part II of these Rules in the event the member does not accept the offer of stipulated resignation.

7.6.2 Notification of Respondent. In such cases, the respondent shall be notified, in writing, of the Committee's recommended sanction of stipulated resignation and that he or she may accept the Committee's recommended sanction within 30 days of receipt. The respondent shall also be notified of any alternative recommended sanction.

7.6.3 Acceptance by Respondent. Within 30 days, the respondent may accept the recommended sanction of stipulated resignation by executing a notarized affidavit of resignation acceptable both to the respondent and the Committee and forwarding the executed notarized affidavit to the Committee. Such resignation shall become effective only with the approval of the Board, as set forth in Subsection 7.6.5 of this part.

7.6.4 Transmittal to Board of Directors. If the respondent accepts the recommended sanction of stipulated resignation, the Committee shall submit a copy of the affidavit of resignation, with the record in the matter and the rationale for recommending stipulated resignation on the terms stated in the affidavit, to the Board of Directors.

7.6.5 Action by Board of Directors. Within 180 days, the Board of Directors shall accept the respondent's resignation on the terms stated in the affidavit of resignation, unless it is persuaded that to do so would not be in the best interest of the Association and/or of the public. If the resignation is accepted by the Board, the Director shall notify the complainant and respondent of the final disposition of the case.

7.6.6 Rejection of Stipulated Resignation by Respondent. If the respondent fails to accept the determination within 30 days, or formally notifies the Committee of rejection of the offer of stipulated resignation within the 30-day period, the offer of stipulated resignation shall be deemed rejected. The Committee shall reconsider the matter or, if an alternative recommended sanction has previously been identified by the Committee, such alternative recommended resolution shall automatically become the recommended sanction according to Subsection 7.4 or 7.5 of this part.

7.6.7 Rejection of Stipulated Resignation by Board. If the Board rejects this affidavit of resignation under Subsection 7.6.5 of this part, the Committee shall so notify the respondent and reconsider the matter.

8. Procedures Subsequent to Dismissal by Committee

The Committee may reconsider a case dismissed under Subsection 7.2 of this part only if it does so in accordance with Part II, Section 6.

9. Procedures Subsequent to Committee Recommendation of Reprimand or Censure

If the Committee proceeds under Subsection 7.4 of this part, the following procedures shall govern:

9.1 Acceptance of Reprimand or Censure. If the respondent accepts the Committee's recommended sanction and directives, if any, the right of independent adjudication shall be waived, any directives will be implemented by the Director, and the case will remain open until the directives are met. The respondent's failure to respond within 30 days of notification shall be deemed acceptance of the Committee's recommended sanction and directives.

**9.2 Independent Adjudication After Recommended Sanction of Rep-

rimand or Censure. The method of adjudication for a recommended sanction of reprimand or censure is an independent adjudication based on the written record by a three-person Independent Adjudication Panel.

9.2.1 Request for Independent Adjudication and Rationale for Nonacceptance. The respondent may exercise his or her right to independent adjudication by furnishing the Committee, within 30 days after notification of the Committee's recommendation, a written request for independent adjudication and rationale for nonacceptance of the recommendation.

9.2.2 Statement by Committee. Within 30 days of receipt of the respondent's rationale for nonacceptance, the Committee may prepare a statement and provide a copy to the respondent. No statement by the Committee is required.

9.2.3 Respondent's Final Response. Within 15 days of receipt of the Ethics Committee's statement, if any, the respondent may submit to the Director a written response to that statement.

9.2.4 Selection of Independent Adjudication Panel

9.2.4.1 Provision of Standing Hearing Panel List. Within 60 days of receipt of the request for an independent adjudication, the Director shall provide the respondent with the names and curricula vitae of six members of the Board of Directors' Standing Hearing Panel, of whom at least one shall be a public member. The proposed panel members need not include any member having a particular speciality or representing a particular geographic location. The Director shall make inquiry and ensure that proposed panel members do not have a conflict of interest as defined by applicable law and appear otherwise able to apply fairly the APA Ethics Code based solely on the record in the particular case.

9.2.4.2 Designation of Panel Members. Within 15 days after receipt of the six-member list, the respondent shall select three of the six to constitute the Independent Adjudication Panel. The Panel shall include not fewer than two members of the Association. Whenever feasible, the respondent's selection will be honored. If at any time prior to the conclusion of the adjudication, any panelist cannot serve on the Independent Adjudication Panel for any reason, the respondent shall be notified promptly and afforded the opportunity within 10 days of receipt of notification to replace that individual from among a list of not fewer than four members of the Board of Directors' Standing Hearing Panel. In the event the respondent fails to notify the Director of his or her initial or replacement selections in a timely fashion, the right to do so is waived, and the President of the Association shall select the member(s), whose name(s) shall then be made known to the respondent.

9.2.4.3 Designation of Chair of Independent Adjudication Panel. The President shall designate one of the three Panel members to serve as Chair. The Chair of the Panel shall ensure that the Panel fulfills its obligations according to these Rules and Procedures.

9.2.5 Provision of Case File to Independent Adjudication Panel. Within 15 days of selection of the Independent Adjudication Panel, receipt of the Committee's statement according to Subsection 9.2.2 of this part, if any; receipt of the respondent's final response according to Subsection 9.2.3 of this part, if any; or if no statement or response is received, the expiration of the time period for such statement or response, whichever occurs latest, the Director will provide the case file to the members of the Independent Adjudication Panel. The case file shall include the complaint and all correspondence and evidence submitted to the Ethics Committee, the respondent's rationale for nonacceptance of the Committee's recommendation, the Committee's statement, if any, and the respondent's final response, if any.

   9.2.6 Consideration and Vote by Independent Adjudication Panel. Within 60 days of receipt of the case file, the members of the Panel shall confer with each other and, solely on the basis of the documentation provided and deliberations among themselves, shall vote to take one of the following actions:

   9.2.6.1 Adopt the Committee's Recommended Sanction and Directives
   9.2.6.2 Adopt a Lesser Sanction and/or Less Burdensome Directives
   9.2.6.3 Dismiss the Case

   9.2.7 Decision of Independent Adjudication Panel. Decisions of the Independent Adjudication Panel will be made by majority vote, and at least two reviewers must agree to written findings, a sanction, if any, and a directive or directives, if any. The Committee bears the burden to prove the charges by a preponderance of the evidence. The panelists' votes and the majority's written decision must be submitted to the Ethics Office within the 60-day period set forth in Subsection 9.2.6 of this part. If no two panelists can agree as to the appropriate outcome or a written decision, the case will be referred back to the Committee for further action.

   9.2.8 Finality of Decision by Independent Adjudication Panel. The decision of the Independent Adjudication Panel is unappealable. The decision is binding on the Committee and the respondent except that subsequent to the Panel's decision, the Committee may determine that directives are impractical or unduly burdensome and may choose to reduce or dismiss directives required in the Panel's decision. A decision by the Panel either to impose a sanction and/or directive(s) or to dismiss the case will be implemented by the Director as the final adjudication, unless modified by the Committee.

   9.2.9 Notification. The Director shall inform the respondent and complainant, if any, of the final disposition. The respondent shall be provided a copy of the majority's written decision.

10. Procedures Subsequent to Committee Recommendation of Expulsion

If the Committee proceeds under Subsection 7.5 of this part, the following procedures shall govern:

   10.1 Acceptance of Recommendation of Expulsion. If the respondent accepts the Committee's recommendation to the Board of Directors that he or she be expelled from membership, the right to a formal hearing shall be waived, and the Committee shall proceed with its recommendation to the Board of Directors according to Subsection 10.3.5 and other subsections of this part. In such event, the recommendation of the Ethics Committee shall be treated as the equivalent of the recommendation of a Formal Hearing Committee that the respondent be expelled from membership. The respondent's failure to respond within 30 days after notification shall be deemed acceptance of the Committee's recommendation.

10.2 Formal Hearing After Recommendation of Expulsion. The method of adjudication for a recommended sanction of expulsion issued under Subsection 7.5 of this part is a formal hearing before a three-member Hearing Committee. Upon request, the respondent will be provided with a copy of the APA Ethics Office's "Guidelines for Formal Hearings." These guidelines are for guidance and information purposes only and are not binding on the APA, the Ethics Committee, or hearing participants. The proceedings are governed solely by the Rules and Procedures of the Ethics Committee and the Ethical Principles of Psychologists and Code of Conduct. Alternatively, a respondent may request an independent adjudication to be provided according to the procedures described in Subsections 9.2.2 through 9.2.7 of this part of these Rules in place of the Subsections 10.2.2 through 10.2.6. The Independent Adjudication Panel will make a recommendation that will be subject to review by the Board of Directors as described in Subsection 10.3.

10.2.1 Request for Formal Hearing. The respondent may exercise his or her right to a formal hearing by requesting a hearing in writing within 30 days of notification of the Committee's recommendation. Alternatively, the respondent may request an independent adjudication by furnishing the Committee a written request for independent adjudication and a written rationale for nonacceptance of the Committee's recommendation within 30 days after notification of the Committee's recommendation.

10.2.2 Formal Hearing Date and Hearing Committee

10.2.2.1 Establishment of Hearing Date and Provision of Standing Hearing Panel List. Within 60 days after the receipt of the respondent's request for a formal hearing, the Director shall establish the date of the hearing and provide the respondent with the date and the names and curricula vitae of six members of the Board of Directors' Standing Hearing Panel. The six identified members of the Board of Directors' Standing Hearing Panel shall include at least one public member. The proposed panel members need not include any member having a particular specialty or representing a particular geographic location. The Director shall make inquiry and ensure that proposed panel members do not have a conflict of interest as defined by applicable law and appear otherwise to apply fairly the Ethics Code based solely on the record in the particular case.

10.2.2.2 Designation of Hearing Committee Members. The Hearing Committee shall consist of three individuals, selected from among the six individuals from the Board of Directors' Standing Hearing Panel identified according to Subsection 10.2.2.1 of this part. The Hearing Committee shall include not fewer than two members of the Association. Within 15 days after the receipt of the names and curricula vitae, the respondent shall notify the Director of his or her selections for the Hearing Committee.

Whenever feasible, the respondent's selections will be honored. In the event an individual selected by the respondent cannot serve on the Hearing Committee for any reason, the respondent shall be notified and afforded the opportunity within 10 days of receipt of notification to replace that individual from among a list of not fewer than four members of the Board of Directors' Standing Hearing Panel. If the respondent fails to notify the Director of his or her initial or replacement selections in a timely fashion, the right to do so is waived and the President shall select the Hearing Committee member(s), whose name(s) shall then be made known to the respondent.

10.2.2.3 *Voir Dire* of Designated Hearing Committee Members. At the time the respondent selects the three designated Hearing Committee members, the respondent may submit in writing, to the Director, a request to question designated Hearing Committee members with respect to potential conflict of interest. If the President has chosen the three Hearing Committee members, the respondent shall have 15 days after receipt of their names to submit such a request. Upon receipt of such written request, the Director shall convene by telephone conference call, or otherwise, a formal opportunity for such questioning by the respondent or the respondent's attorney. Legal Counsel for the Association shall preside at such *voir dire*, shall be the sole judge of the propriety and pertinency of questions posed, and shall be the sole judge with respect to the fitness of designated Hearing Committee members to serve. Failure by the respondent to submit a timely request shall constitute a waiver of the privilege to conduct *voir dire*.

10.2.2.4 Designation of Chair of Hearing Committee. The President shall designate one of the three Hearing Committee members to serve as Chair. The Chair of the Hearing Committee and Legal Counsel for the Association shall assure proper observance of these Rules and Procedures at the formal hearing.

10.2.3 Documents and Witnesses

10.2.3.1 Committee. At least 30 days prior to the scheduled date of the formal hearing, the Ethics Committee shall provide the respondent and the Hearing Committee with copies of all documents and other evidence, and the names of all witnesses that may be offered by the Committee in its case in chief.

10.2.3.2 Respondent. At least 15 days prior to the scheduled date of the formal hearing, the respondent shall provide the Ethics Committee and the Hearing Committee with copies of all documents and other evidence, and the names of all witnesses that may be offered by the respondent.

10.2.3.3 Rebuttal Documents and Witnesses. At least 5 days prior to the scheduled date of the formal hearing, the Committee shall provide the respondent and the Hearing Committee with copies of all documents and other evidence, and the names of all witnesses that may be offered in rebuttal.

10.2.3.4 Audiotapes, Videotapes, and Similar Data Compilations. Audiotapes, videotapes, and similar data compilations are admissible at the formal hearing, provided usable copies of such items, together with a transcription thereof, are provided in a timely fashion according to the provisions of this section.

10.2.3.5 Failure to Provide Documents, Other Evidence, and Names of Witnesses in a Timely Fashion in Advance of the Formal Hearing. Failure to provide copies of a document or other evidence or the name of a witness in a timely fashion and consistent with this section and these Rules and Procedures is grounds for excluding such document, other evidence, or witness from evidence at the formal hearing, unless good cause for the omission and a lack of prejudice to the other side can be shown.

10.2.4 Formal Hearing Procedures

10.2.4.1 Presiding Officers

10.2.4.1.1 The Chair of the Hearing Committee shall preside at the hearing. The General Counsel of the Association shall designate Legal Counsel to assist the Hearing Committee.

10.2.4.1.2 Legal Counsel for the Hearing Committee shall be present to advise on matters of procedure and admission of evidence and shall represent neither the Ethics Committee nor the respondent at the formal hearing.

10.2.4.2 Legal Representation of the Respondent and Committee

10.2.4.2.1 Respondent. The respondent may choose, at the respondent's own expense, to be represented by a licensed attorney.

10.2.4.2.2 Committee. The General Counsel of the Association may designate Legal Counsel to advise the Ethics Committee. The Chair of the Ethics Committee, the Chair's designee, or Legal Counsel to the Committee presents the Committee's case.

10.2.4.3 Rules of Evidence. Formal rules of evidence shall not apply. All evidence that is relevant and reliable, as determined for the Hearing Committee by Legal Counsel for the Hearing Committee, shall be admissible.

10.2.4.4 Rights of the Respondent and the Committee. Consistent with these Rules and Procedures, the respondent and the Committee shall have the right to present witnesses, documents, and other evidence, to cross-examine witnesses, and to object to the introduction of evidence.

10.2.4.5 Burden of Proof. The Ethics Committee shall bear the burden to prove the charge by a preponderance of the evidence.

10.2.5 Decision of the Hearing Committee. The decision shall be by a simple majority vote. Within 30 days of the conclusion of the hearing, the Hearing Committee shall submit in writing to the Board of Directors, through the Director, its decision and the rationale for that decision. The Hearing Committee may decide to

10.2.5.1 Adopt the Committee's Recommendation to the Board of Directors

10.2.5.2 Recommend to the Board of Directors a Lesser Sanction With or Without Directives

10.2.5.3 Dismiss the Charges

10.2.6 Notice to the Respondent and the Ethics Committee. Within 15 days of receipt of the Hearing Committee's decision, a copy of the decision and the rationale for the decision shall be provided to the respondent and the Ethics Committee. If the Hearing Committee determines that the charges must be dismissed, the Ethics Committee will implement this as the final adjudication.

10.3 Proceedings Before the Board of Directors

10.3.1 Referral to Board of Directors. If the Hearing Committee or Independent Adjudication Panel recommends that the respondent be expelled from membership or otherwise disciplined, the matter will be referred to the Board of Directors. The Director shall provide the materials of record to the Board, including a copy of the Hearing Committee's or Independent Adjudication Panel's decision; the respondent's timely response, if any, under Subsection 10.3.2 of this part; the Ethics Committee's timely statement, if any, under Subsection 10.3.3 of this part; the respondent's timely final response, if any, under Subsection 10.3.4 of this part; and the record.

10.3.2 Respondent's Response. Within 30 days of receipt of the Hearing Committee's or Independent Adjudication Panel's decision, the respondent may file a written response with the Board of Directors, through the Ethics Office. A copy of the respondent's written response shall be retained by the Chair of the Ethics Committee.

10.3.3 Ethics Committee's Statement. Within 15 days of receipt of the respondent's response or the date such response was due, the Ethics Committee may prepare a written statement and provide a copy to the respondent.

10.3.4 Respondent's Final Response. Within 15 days of receipt of the Ethics Committee's statement, if any, the respondent may file with the Board of Directors, through the Director, a written request to the Ethics Committee's statement. A copy of this response shall be retained by the Chair of the Ethics Committee.

10.3.5 Action by the Board of Directors. Within 180 days of receipt of the recommendation of the Hearing Committee or Independent Adjudication Panel (or of the Ethics Committee if no subsequent adjudication was held), together with any timely responses thereto and the record, the Board of Directors will consider these materials and will take action as follows.

10.3.5.1 Adopt. The Board of Directors shall adopt the recommendation, unless by majority vote it finds grounds for nonacceptance, as set forth in Subsection 10.3.5.2.

10.3.5.2 Not Adopt After Determining Grounds for Nonacceptance. Only the following shall constitute grounds for nonacceptance of the recommendation by the Board:

10.3.5.2.1 Incorrect Application of Ethical Standard(s). The Ethics Code of the Association was incorrectly applied.

10.3.5.2.2 Erroneous Findings of Fact. The findings of fact were clearly erroneous.

10.3.5.2.3 Procedural Errors. The procedures used were in serious and substantial violation of the Bylaws of the Association and/or these Rules and Procedures.

10.3.5.2.4 Excessive Sanction or Directives. The disciplinary sanction or directives recommended are grossly excessive in light of all the circumstances.

10.3.5.3 Consequences of Nonacceptance. If the Board of Directors finds grounds for nonacceptance, it shall refer the case back to the Ethics Committee. In its discretion, the Ethics Committee may return the matter for reconsideration before a newly constituted Hearing Committee or Independent Adjudication Panel or may continue investigation and/or readjudicate the matter at the Committee level.

10.4 Notification. If the Board of Directors does not adopt the recommendation, it shall notify the Ethics Committee in writing why the decision was not accepted, citing the applicable ground(s) for nonacceptance under Subsection 10.3.5.2 of this part.

10.5 Reconsideration. If a reconsideration is instituted, the procedures of relevant subsections of this part shall apply. Unless any of the following is offered by the respondent, none shall be part of the record before the second Hearing Committee or Independent Adjudication Panel: the original Hearing Committee's or Independent Adjudication Panel's report; the respondent's written responses or Ethics Committee's written statements made under Subsections 10.3.2, 10.3.3, and 10.3.4 of this part; and the Board of Directors' rationale for nonacceptance of the original Hearing Committee's or Independent Adjudication Panel's recommendation. If the respondent offers any portion of any of the foregoing documents as evidence in the reconsideration, the Committee may introduce any portion of any or all of them.

References

American Psychological Association. (1981). Ethical principles of psychologists. *American Psychologist, 36,* 633–638.

American Psychological Association. (1985). *Standards for educational and psychological testing.* Washington, DC: Author.

American Psychological Association. (1991). Specialty guidelines for forensic psychologists. *Law and Human Behavior, 15,* 655–665.

American Psychological Association. (1992). Ethical principles of psychologists and code of conduct. *American Psychologist, 47,* 1597–1611.

American Psychological Association. (1993a). *Guidelines for ethical conduct in the care and use of animals.* Washington, DC: Author.

American Psychological Association. (1993b). *Guidelines for providers of psychological services to ethnic, linguistic, and culturally diverse populations. American Psychologist, 48,* 45–46.

American Psychological Association. (1993c). Record-keeping guidelines. *American Psychologist, 48,* 984–986.

American Psychological Association. (1994a). Guidelines for child custody evaluations in divorce proceedings. *American Psychologist, 49,* 677–680.

American Psychological Association. (1994b). *Publication manual of the American Psychological Association* (4th ed.). Washington, DC: Author.

American Psychological Association. (1996a). Rules and procedures. *American Psychologist, 51,* 529–548.

American Psychological Association. (1996b). Strategies for private practitioners coping with subpoenas or compelled testimony for client records and/or test data. *Professional Psychology: Research and Practice, 23,* 245–251.

American Veterinary Medical Association. (1986). Report of the AVMA Panel on Euthanasia. *Journal of the American Veterinary Medical Association, 188*(3), 252–268.

Bernstein, E. M., & Putnam, F. W. (1986). Development, reliability, and validity of a dissociation scale. *Journal of Nervous and Mental Disease, 174,* 727–735.

California Business & Professions Code, § 2290.5 (1996). In G. Alexander & A. Scheflin (Eds.), *Law and mental disorder* (p. 94). Durham, NC: Carolina Academic Press (1998).

Canter, M. B., Bennett, B. E., Jones, S. E., & Nagy, T. F. (1994). *Ethics for psychologists: A commentary on the APA Ethics Code.* Washington, DC: American Psychological Association.

Institute of Laboratory Animal Resources, Commission on Life Sciences (National Research Council). (1996). *Guide for the care and use of laboratory animals.* Washington, DC: Author.

Iversen, I. H., & Lattal, K. A. (Eds.). (1991). *Experimental analysis of behavior.* Amsterdam, The Netherlands: Elsevier Science.

National Commission for the Protection of Human Subjects of Biomedical and Behavioral Research. (1979). *The Belmont report: Ethical principles and guidelines for the protection of human subjects of research* (HHS Pub. No. 8887–809). Washington, DC: U.S. Government Printing Office.

Shor, R. E., & Orne, E. C. (1962). *The Harvard Group Scale of Hypnotic Susceptibility, Form A.* Palo Alto, CA: Consulting Psychologists Press.

Spiegel, H., & Spiegel, D. (1978). *Trance and treatment: Clinical use of hypnosis.* New York: International Universities Press.

Tellegen, A., & Atkinson, G. (1974). Openness to absorbing and self-altering experiences ("absorption"), a trait related to hypnotic susceptibility. *Journal of Abnormal Psychology, 83,* 268–277.

Title 45 C.F.R., Pt. 46. (1991). Protection of Human Subjects, National Institutes of Health, Office for the Protection of Research Ethics.

Title 9 C.F.R., Chap. 1, Subchap. A: Animal Welfare, Pt. 1–3 (1992). U.S. Department of Agriculture.

Trials of war criminals before the Nuremberg Military Tribunals under Control Council Law. (1949). *2*(10), 181–182. Washington, DC: U.S. Government Printing Office.

Weitzenhoffer, A. M., & Hilgard, E. R. (1962). *Stanford Hypnotic Susceptibility Scale, Forms A & B.* Palo Alto, CA: Consulting Psychologists Press.

World Medical Association. (1991). Declaration of Helsinki. *Law, Medicine and Health Care, 19*(3–4), 264–265. (Original work published 1989, as amended by the 41st World Medical Assembly, Hong Kong)

Index

About the Author

Thomas F. Nagy received his PhD from the University of Illinois at Champaign-Urbana in 1972. He is currently in independent practice in Palo Alto (CA), is an assistant clinical professor in the Department of Psychiatry and Behavioral Sciences at the Stanford University School of Medicine, and is on the staff of Stanford's Complementary Medicine Clinic. For the past 2 decades, Dr. Nagy's professional activities have focused on ethics and ethical issues for psychologists. He has served as chair of the Illinois Psychological Association Ethics Committee (1982–1986), member of the APA Ethics Committee (1985–1987), chair of the APA Ethics Committee Task Force (1986–1989), member of the subcommittee that revised the Ethical Principles of Psychologists (1989–1992), and member of the California Psychological Association Ethics Committee (1988–1993).

Dr. Nagy provides psychological services and ethical consultation to psychologists, attorneys, educators, and consumers. He is a fellow of APA's Division 42 (Independent Practice) and of the Society for Clinical and Experimental Hypnosis. He is also the recipient of the Illinois Psychological Association's Special Award for Outstanding Contribution to the Profession of Psychology (1986) and the Santa Clara County (CA) Award for Significant Contributions to the Field of Psychology by a Psychologist (1999). He has been interviewed on radio and TV and in the print media on the subject of ethics in the practice of psychology.

Dr. Nagy has written on ethical issues related to professional competence, managed health care, and psychology over the Internet and is a coauthor of *Ethics for Psychologists: A Commentary on the APA Ethics Code* (APA, 1994).